MW01116445

Spanish Short Stories

*Level Up Your Vocabulary and Cultural
Awareness from Beginner to Intermediate
and Have Fun Along the Way*

Free Bonuses from Cecilia Melero

Hi Spanish Learners!

My name is Cecilia Melero, and first off, I want to THANK YOU for reading my book.

Now you have a chance to join my exclusive Spanish language learning email list so you can get the ebooks below for free as well as the potential to get more Spanish books for free! Simply click the link below to join.

P.S. Remember that it's 100% free to join the list.

Access your free bonuses here:
https://livetolearn.lpages.co/spanish-short-stories-paperback/

Table of Contents

Part 1: Spanish Short Stories for Beginners

Grow Your Vocabulary and Cultural Awareness While Having Fun

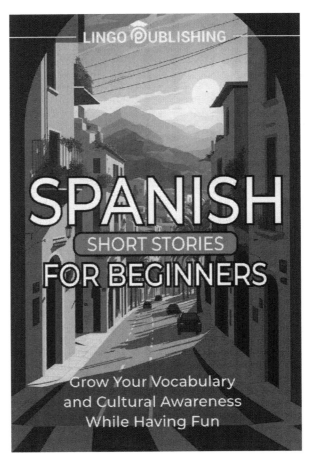

Introduction

Hi! Do you want to learn Spanish in an easy and educational way? Do you know a few Spanish words but can't use them in a conversation? Then you're in the right place! This is a book of short stories in Spanish where you can learn the language through reading comprehension and see how Spanish works in daily conversations.

Each chapter will have a structure specifically designed to assimilate the language easily. First, we will introduce you to a brief story in Spanish, followed by a vocabulary list. Then, you will find a summary of the story in Spanish, which will help you solve the exercises: a series of questions in Spanish, followed by a few comprehension questions in English. If you still have doubts after this, you will find a summary of the story in English to ensure that you've understood everything. Lastly, you will see a brief section with interesting facts about Spanish culture. At the end of the book, you will find the answers to all the questions and every story's translation.

In the first two chapters, you will find useful phrases to start and end a conversation and to meet someone. You will learn how to ask someone's name and find out about their interests, studies, and where they live. And, of course, you will also learn how to answer these questions.

In the third chapter, we will talk about jobs: what some of the most common jobs are, what people do in them, and how to talk about work (what we like and dislike about it), among many other things. In the fourth chapter, we will be dealing with objects: here, we will see a lot of specific vocabulary, colors, materials, and shapes.

In chapter 5, we will go shopping. We will see what questions to ask when buying something and how to ask about sizes, colors, and prices. And in chapter 6, we will learn to ask for directions (and understand the answers!) We will see how to ask for directions to a place, for the means of transportation, and much more.

In chapter 7, we will talk about something we all love: food. We will learn how to order food in a restaurant and what dishes we can have. Then, we will see a little more about Spanish gastronomy. In chapter 8, we will get into the world of universities, study, subjects, majors, and all things and actions related to education.

In chapter 9, we will learn to deal with things that can happen to any traveler: getting lost in a city, missing a train, or losing our luggage. What should we do? How should we ask the questions to solve the problem? Then, in chapter 10, we will talk about the human body, the parts that can hurt, how to consult a doctor and how the public health system works in Spain. In chapter 11, we will learn a bit of vocabulary about parties: how to congratulate someone, how to make a toast, and some vocabulary about family.

Finally, in the last two chapters, we will learn to talk about plans. First, in chapter 12, we will describe a daily routine and what we've done during the day. Then, in chapter 13, we will talk about the future: the plans we have, our dreams, and our goals.

And with that, we will reach the end! You will be surprised by the amount of vocabulary you will learn just by reading and understanding these stories in Spanish. Let's get started!

Chapter 1: ¡Hola! – Greetings

Story in Spanish: El cumpleaños

Lucía está **emocionada** Hoy es el cumpleaños de Javier, su hijo, que vive en Sevilla. Está sentada delante del **ordenador**, a punto de comprar unos **billetes de avión** para ir a visitarlo. Pero quiere confirmar con él las **fechas**. Sabe que trabaja mucho y no quiere molestarlo. Cuando lo llama, la conversación no sale muy bien.

- ¡**Hola** Javi!

- **Buenos días**, mamá.

- ¡Feliz cumpleaños! ¿**Cómo estás**?

- **Bien**, pero **estoy ocupado** ahora, mamá. ¿Podemos hablar más tarde?

- Sí, claro. **Hasta luego.**

- **Adiós.**

Lucía corta, esperando volver hablar con su hijo por la tarde y así confirmar su **viaje**. Después de trabajar, lo llama de nuevo.

- **Buenas tardes**, Javi, ¿puedes hablar ahora?

- ¿**Qué tal**, mamá? **Más o menos.**

- Es que pensaba darte una sorpresa e ir a visitarte, pero quería hablar contigo antes de comprar los billetes para saber en qué fechas te parece mejor.

- No puedo hablar ahora, mamá. Luego te llamo. **Hasta mañana.**

Javier cuelga sin esperar una respuesta. Lucía se preocupa. ¿Es que su hijo no la quiere ya? Ni siquiera le ha dicho "qué alegría mamá, te llamo mañana, **que duermas bien, te quiero, un beso...**". ¡Nada de eso!

Lucía llama de nuevo, pero el móvil de Javier está **apagado**, así que le **deja un mensaje**.

- **Buenas noches**, Javi, lamento no encontrarte. **Qué lindo día** te ha tocado por tu cumpleaños, ¿no? Aquí en Madrid ha habido un sol espectacular. Bueno, Javi, se nota que estás ocupado. No te preocupes: cancelaré el viaje a Sevilla. Llámame cuando puedas. **Hablamos mañana.** ¡Chao!

Lucía prepara la cena, pensando en Javier y en lo raro que está. Es por eso que quiere ir a visitarlo: para ver cómo está, dónde vive, qué come... Mientras piensa en eso, suena el timbre de su casa.

- **¿Quién es?**

- Buenas noches. Tengo una entrega para la señora Lucía Suárez.

- ¿De parte de quién?

- No sé, pero viene desde Sevilla.

Lucía corre a abrir la puerta, emocionada. Y cuando la abre se **choca**, cara a cara, con su hijo.

- ¡Hola, mamá! ¡Sorpresa!

Vocabulary List

Español	Inglés
emocionado, emocionada	thrilled
el ordenador	computer
el billete de avión	plane ticket
la fecha	date
Hola	Hello
Buenos días	Good morning

¿Cómo estás?	How are you?
Bien	Fine
Estar ocupado/a	To be busy
Hasta luego	So long
Adiós	Goodbye
el viaje	trip
Buenas tardes	Good afternoon
¿Puedes hablar ahora?	Can you talk now?
¿Qué tal?	What's up?
Más o menos	Kind of
Hasta mañana	See you tomorrow
Que duermas bien	Sleep tight
Te quiero	I love you
Un beso	a kiss
apagar	to turn off
dejar un mensaje	to leave a message
Buenas noches	Good evening

Qué lindo día	What a nice day
Hablamos mañana	Talk to you tomorrow
Chao	Bye
¿Quién es?	Who is it?
chocar	to crash

Summary of the Story in Spanish

Lucía está un poco ansiosa porque es el cumpleaños de su hijo Javier, que vive en Sevilla. Está esperando hablar con él para comprar unos boletos para ir a visitarlo. Lo llama por la mañana, pero Javier está ocupado y no puede hablar. Cuando lo llama a la tarde le cuenta que quiere ir a visitarlo, pero Javier también está ocupado en ese momento. A la noche vuelve a intentarlo, pero el móvil de Javier está apagado. Lucía decide cancelar el viaje. Más tarde, llaman al timbre de su casa. Cree que alguien le trae un paquete desde Sevilla, pero en realidad es Javier, que le ha dado una sorpresa y ha ido a visitarla.

Exercises

1. Une cada saludo con su traducción en inglés.

    a. Buenas tardes   Good morning

    b. Buenos días   Good evening

    c. Buenas noches   Good afternoon

2. Elige del cuento cuatro maneras distintas de decir *bye*.

3. ¿Cuál de estas oraciones está escrita correctamente?

    a. Cuál lindo día.

    b. Lindo qué día.

    c. Qué lindo día.

4. Completa el siguiente diálogo usando las siguientes palabras: *buenas tardes, bien, hasta luego, hola, ¿cómo estás?, ocupada, adiós.*

    A: Mari, ¡_____!

    B: _____ _____, Pedro.

    A: ¿____ ____?

B: Estoy _____. ¿Y tú?

A: Ahora un poco _____. Después hablamos. ¡_____!

B: _____ _____.

5. ¿Cómo saluda Lucía a Javier cada vez que lo llama? ¿Son siempre las mismas palabras?

Comprehension Questions

1. Where does Lucía's son live?
2. How does Lucía want to surprise her son?
3. Why can't Lucía talk to Javier?
4. Why is Lucía worried?
5. Who rings Lucía's doorbell?

Summary of the Story in English

Lucía wants to talk with her son, Javier, who lives in Seville. Today it's his birthday, and Lucía wants to visit him. When she calls him in the morning, Javier tells her that he is busy and cannot talk. In the afternoon, Lucía tries again, and she tells him that she wants to buy a plane ticket to go visit him, but Javier tells her again that he is busy. Then, in the evening, she calls him again, but Javier's phone is off, so Lucía leaves a voice message, telling him not to worry and that she won't be visiting him. Later, she receives a package, and when she goes to pick it up... it's Javier, who wanted to surprise her!

Did you know...

Chances are you know the basic forms of greeting and saying "farewell" in Spanish: *hola* ("hello") and *adiós* ("goodbye"). But they aren't the only ones!

There are many ways to greet a person in Spanish. Depending on the moment of the day, we can say *buenos días* ("good morning"), *buenas tardes* ("good afternoon"), or *buenas noches* ("good evening"). Besides, you can say phrases such as *¿qué tal?* ("how are you?") or *¿cómo va todo?* ("how's everything going?"). To say goodbye to someone, you can use phrases such as *hasta luego* ("see you later"), *nos vemos* ("see you"), *que te vaya bien* ("good luck") or simply *chao* ("bye").

In addition to these phrases – which are common to all Spanish-speaking countries – each country has specific ways of greeting and saying "farewell" to someone. For example, in Colombia, it is common to ask *¿qué hubo?* ("how's it going?"). In Mexico, it's common to say *¿qué onda?* ("what's up?"). In Argentina, you may hear *¿cómo va?* ("how are you?") or ¿*qué hacés?* ("what's up?"). In this last country, people use *voseo;* that is, they use *vos* instead of *tú* and verbs in the second-person singular are conjugated in a different way.

Chapter 2: ¿Cómo te llamas? – Introducing Yourself

Story in Spanish: La entrevista

El **entrevistador** abre la puerta. Deja salir al candidato anterior, un **muchacho** alto con la barba **corta**. Se dan la mano **con firmeza**. Después el muchacho sale de la **sala de espera**, y el entrevistador saluda a Carmen.

– **Pasa** – dice el entrevistador.

Carmen entra a la oficina. Es **amplia** y luminosa. Se sienta en una silla de madera no demasiado cómoda. El entrevistador da la vuelta al **escritorio** hasta ubicarse frente a ella.

– Mi nombre es Javier Alonso – dice el entrevistador, mientras extiende su mano. Carmen la toma y le da un **apretón**. Tú eres Carmen Pérez Hernández, ¿no es así?

– Fernández – responde Carmen, tímidamente.

– ¿Cómo? – pregunta Javier.

– Mi **apellido** es Fernández – dice Carmen. Soy Carmen Pérez Fernández.

– Oh, lo siento – contesta Javier. Debo haber leído mal tu currículum.

Javier **revisa** los papeles sobre su escritorio. Finalmente, pone el currículum de Carmen justo sobre el **teclado** de su computadora.

– Aquí está – dice Javier. Pérez Fernández, claro. ¿Te importa si completamos algunos datos? Tu currículum es muy bueno, pero necesitamos más información.

- No hay problema - contesta Carmen.

- ¿Cuántos años tienes? - pregunta Javier.

- Treinta y dos - responde Carmen.

- Muy bien - dice Javier. ¿Dónde vives?

- En Alcorcón - contesta Carmen.

- Excelente, o sea que estás a solo unos minutos en **coche** - dice Javier. Continuemos con lo demás. Aquí dice que estudiaste en la Politécnica de Madrid.

- Sí, me gradué de Ingeniería Informática hace cinco años - responde Carmen. Después hice un máster de negocios en la Complutense.

- De acuerdo, con eso terminamos la parte de educación - dice Javier. Háblame de tu experiencia laboral.

- Mi primer trabajo fue en Telefonía Móvil, cuando aún estudiaba. Programadora junior - contesta Carmen. Allí estuve tres años. Después pasé cinco años en un pequeño estudio de videojuegos, San Isidro. En ese lugar tenía que hacer un poco de todo, tareas de programación, pero también gerenciales. Por eso hice el máster.

- ¿Y después? - pregunta Javier.

- Me fui al Banco Industrial - responde Carmen. Hasta hace un par de **meses**.

- ¿Y por qué estás interesada en trabajar aquí en Data S. A.? - pregunta Javier.

- Creo que es una gran oportunidad para mí - responde Carmen. Estoy en un momento de mi carrera en el que estoy buscando mayores responsabilidades. Quiero hacer crecer un proyecto y **sentirlo** propio. Y creo que puedo hacer eso en Data S. A.

- Excelente. Bueno, ya casi terminamos - dice Javier. Solo falta que me hables un poco de ti. ¿Tienes algún pasatiempo, algún interés que te gustaría **compartir**?

- Me gusta mucho **escalar** - contesta Carmen. En general voy a una **palestra** en Leganés. Pero cada dos semanas, más o menos, **cojo** el coche y voy a Sierra de los Gredos. Prefiero hacerlo en la naturaleza.

- Siempre quise hacer escalada - responde Javier. Nunca lo hice, no sé por qué.

- Bueno, si sigues interesado, en Leganés hay una pared excelente -

dice Carmen. Se llama Vértigo.

- ¡Lo tendré en cuenta! - contesta Javier. Muchas gracias por tu tiempo, Carmen. Te llamaremos dentro de la próxima **semana** para informarte de nuestra decisión.

- Gracias a ti, Javier - responde Carmen.

Vocabulary List

Español	Inglés
el entrevistador	interviewer
el muchacho	young man
corto/a	short
con firmeza	firmly
la sala de espera	waiting room
pasar	to come in
amplio/a	spacious
el escritorio	desk
el apretón (de manos)	handshake
el apellido	last name
revisar	to go through
el teclado	keyboard
el coche	car

el mes	month
sentir	to feel
compartir	to share
escalar	climbing
la palestra	climbing wall
coger	to take
la semana	week

Summary of the Story in Spanish

Carmen Pérez Fernández asiste a una entrevista de trabajo en una empresa de informática. Su entrevistador, Javier Alonso, la hace pasar a la oficina. Después de confundirse con su apellido, Javier le pregunta por su edad, su lugar de residencia, sus estudios, su experiencia laboral y sus intereses. Carmen le cuenta dónde obtuvo su título de grado y su máster, y describe su paso por una empresa telefónica, un estudio de videojuegos y un banco. Finalmente, discuten su interés por su principal pasatiempo: la escalada.

Exercises

1. Elige la oración gramaticalmente correcta.
    a. Carmen buscan trabajo.
    b. Javier es entrevistador en una empresa.
    c. Carmen es treinta y dos años.
    d. Javier está impresionada.

2. Completa este diálogo con las siguientes palabras: *se llama, nombre, responde, apellido.*
   A: ¿Cuál es tu _____? – pregunta Javier.
   B: Pérez Fernández – _____ Carmen.
   A: ¿Sabes una cosa? – dice Javier. Mi madre _____ Carmen.
   B: Es un _____ muy común – contesta Carmen.

3. Elige la palabra que corresponda.
    a. Carmen (tiene/tienen) treinta y dos años.
    b. Hernández no (es/está) el apellido correcto.
    c. La oficina es (amplio/amplia).
    d. Carmen quiere (el/la) trabajo.
4. ¿Cuál de las siguientes oraciones es incorrecta?
    a. ¿Cómo te llamas?
    b. ¿Cuál es tu nombre?
    c. Tu nombre, por favor.
    d. Nombre, te llamas.
5. ¿Dónde vive Carmen?
    a. En Leganés.
    b. En Alcorcón.
    c. En Madrid.
    d. En Sierra de los Gredos.

Comprehension Questions

1. What's Javier's office like?
2. Where did Carmen study?
3. What was Carmen's last job?
4. Has Javier ever climbed?
5. What's the name of the climbing wall in Leganés?

Summary of the Story in English

Carmen Pérez Fernández attends a job interview at an IT company. Her interviewer, Javier Alonso, brings her into the office. After being confused with her last name, Javier asks her about her age, her place of residence, her studies, her work experience, and her interests. Carmen tells him where she got her undergraduate and master's degrees, and she describes her time at a phone company, a video game studio, and a bank. Finally, they discuss her main hobby: climbing.

Did you know...

In Spain, the most common male names are Antonio, José, and Manuel. The most common female names are María, Carmen, and Laura. In Spanish, many feminine names are nouns or adjectives; that is, words that appear in the dictionary, like Celeste ("light blue"), Soledad ("loneliness"), Esperanza ("hope"), Luz ("light") or Luna ("moon").

It is common to name children after someone, whether it is a relative (grandparent or parent) or a famous person the parents look up to. In this way, it isn't rare to find a man called Manuel whose son is also called Manuel, though they both get different nicknames (Manolo and Manolito, for example).

Many people have compound names, which means that their name is made out of two elements. In general, the first element is María, Ana, Juan, or José. Some common compound names in Spanish are José María, Juan Manuel, or José Luis (masculine names) and María José, Ana Paula, or María Laura (feminine names).

We shouldn't confuse compound names with a *segundo nombre*. A *segundo nombre* is an extra name that people give their children after the first name. For example, if someone is called Pedro Luis Suárez, "Luis" is his *segundo nombre*.

The most common last names in Spain are García, Rodríguez, Fernández, and López. It's common for people to have two last names: the first one would belong to the paternal family, and the second to the maternal family. For this reason, in Spain, it's common to find people sharing the first and second last name, like Juan García García or Francisca Rodríguez Rodríguez. In general, in Spain women keep their last name when they get married.

Chapter 3: Mi trabajo – My Job

Story in Spanish: Trabajos y profesiones

1 - Francisco, el profesor

Francisco es **maestro** de Historia en un instituto del centro de Madrid. Le encanta transmitir su conocimiento a los alumnos. Sus clases suelen ser muy interesantes, y Francisco abre el debate para que todos los estudiantes digan lo que piensan.

2 - Roberto, el conductor de autobús

Roberto **se dedica a** conducir un autobús en Granada. La parte que más le gusta de su trabajo es hablar con los turistas y recomendarles sitios de interés, como el castillo de la Alhambra o las sierras. Lo que menos le gusta de ser **conductor** es cuando le toca el **turno nocturno**: a Roberto le encanta llegar temprano a casa para estar con sus gatos.

3 - Mónica, la empresaria

Mónica es una exitosa **empresaria**: es la gerente de marketing de la revista de moda más vendida en todo Barcelona. El momento favorito de Mónica es cuando cierra un trato con un **cliente**. A pesar de su ajetreada vida, Mónica también disfruta de las cosas simples, como un paseo en el parque o una buena charla con sus amigas.

4 - Pedro, el panadero

Pedro abre su **panadería** todas las mañanas a las siete en punto. Algunos dicen que los suyos son los mejores pasteles de todo Murcia. Cuando hay pocos clientes, Pedro aprovecha para organizar la **mercadería**, limpiar la **tienda** o contactar a sus proveedores. Es un trabajo solitario, pero por suerte se lleva muy bien con Fernanda, la dueña de la

librería que hay en la acera de enfrente.

5 - Marta, la médica

Marta es una joven médica **pediatra** que trabaja en un hospital de Valencia. Ella *ama* su trabajo: curar a los niños es lo que más feliz le hace en el mundo. Lo malo de su trabajo es cuando le toca hacer **guardias** muy largas y debe dejar a su hija pequeña al cuidado de una **canguro**.

6 - Fernando, el camarero

Fernando es **camarero** en un bar con vistas al mar que hay en Palma de Mallorca. Generalmente atiende las mesas, aunque a veces le toca estar detrás de la barra. Al principio no era muy buen **coctelero**, pero ahora es experto: ¡hace los mejores tragos de las islas Baleares!

Example Dialogue

Martín: ¡Hola! Lamento molestarte, pero ¿podrías decirme la contraseña de la wifi de este café?

Paula: Por supuesto. La contraseña es el nombre de este café; o sea, "Flamenco". Y no me molestas para nada. De hecho, quizá hablar con alguien me ayude a recuperar la inspiración.

Martín: ¿Inspiración? Déjame adivinar: ¿eres escritora?

Paula: No exactamente. Soy periodista. Trabajo en un periódico en línea.

Martín: Eso suena muy interesante. Seguramente tendrás que hacer un montón de entrevistas, investigaciones y reportajes.

Paula: Sí, es parte de mi trabajo. ¡Y me encanta! Es solo que ahora estoy algo bloqueada. Me han pedido que escriba una columna para la sección de cultura, pero no se me ocurre nada... En fin, ¿tú a qué te dedicas?

Martín: Yo soy artista. Estudié Bellas Artes en la universidad y me dediqué durante años a la pintura clásica. Sin embargo, actualmente me enfoco más en el collage digital. Descubrí que es una de las ramas del arte que más me entusiasman. Este fin de semana expondré algunas de mis obras aquí en Madrid.

Paula: Oye... creo que tengo el artículo perfecto para la columna de cultura. ¿Te importaría concederme una entrevista?

Vocabulary List

Español	Inglés
el maestro, la maestra	teacher
dedicarse a	to do for a living
el conductor, la conductora	driver
el turno nocturno	night shift
el empresario, la empresaria	businessman, businesswoman
el cliente, la clienta	client
la panadería	bakery
la mercadería	merchandise
la tienda	store
la librería	bookstore
el pediatra, la pediatra	pediatrician
la guardia	on call
el canguro, la canguro	babysitter
el camarero, la camarera	waiter, waitress
el coctelero, la coctelera	bartender

Summary of the Story in Spanish

Te hemos presentado a seis personas diferentes con trabajos distintos. Primero, tenemos a Francisco, un profesor de Historia. Luego está Roberto, un conductor de autobuses en Granada. Mónica, por su parte, es una exitosa empresaria, mientras que Pedro se dedica a vender pasteles en Murcia. Para finalizar, hemos hablado de Marta, una médica pediatra, y de Fernando, un camarero y coctelero en un bar con vistas al mar.

Después de presentarte a estas seis personas, te hemos propuesto un diálogo entre una periodista y un artista plástico. Aunque estas dos personas no se conocen, ¡pronto descubren que tienen un montón de cosas de las que hablar!

Exercises

1. Completa los espacios.
   a. Mónica es _____.
   b. Marta deja a su hija al cuidado de una _____.
   c. Al principio, Fernando no era muy buen _____.
   d. Paula, la _____, hace muchos reportajes.

2. Decide dónde se desarrolla cada una de las actividades.
   a. Panadero   Autobús
   b. Chófer   Bar
   c. Gerenta de marketing   Panadería
   d. Camarero   Revista de modas

3. Elige cuál de las siguientes frases está escrita de manera correcta.
   a. Norma se dedica para cantar en bares del centro de la ciudad.
   b. Norma se dedica a cantar en bares de la central de la ciudad.
   c. Norma se dedica a cantar en bares del centro de la ciudad.
   d. Norma se dedica a cantaba en bares del centro de la ciudad.

4. Completa los espacios. Utiliza las siguientes palabras: *bufete - abogado - juez - derecho - facultad.*
   Mi hijo está estudiando _____ porque quiere convertirse en un gran _____. Toma clases en la _____ de leyes. Su sueño es trabajar en un _____. Quién sabe: ¡quizá algún día

llegue a ser _____!

5. Elige la palabra correcta en cada una de las frases.

    a. Lucía (trabaja/trabajo) en una empresa de cosméticos.

    b. Marcelo se (dedicó/dedica) a reparar muebles.

    c. Marisa está (empleada/emplea) en un restaurante.

    d. Tomás es (periodismo/periodista).

Comprehension Questions

1. What's the best part of Roberto's job?
2. What does Mónica enjoy besides work?
3. Where is Pedro's bakery?
4. Where does Marta work?
5. What is Paula's job?

Summary of the Story in English

We've introduced you to six different people with different jobs. First, we have Francisco, a History teacher. Then there's Roberto, a bus driver in Granada. Mónica, for her part, is a successful businesswoman, while Pedro sells cakes in Murcia for a living. To finish, we have Marta, a pediatrician, and Fernando, a waiter and bartender in a bar with views of the sea.

After introducing you to these six people, we've proposed a dialogue between a journalist and a visual artist. Even though these two people don't know each other, they soon discover that they have many things to talk about!

Did you know...

Spanish people have a deeply-rooted work culture. The office hours are usually from 09 h to 17 h (In Spain, the 24-hour clock is used, which means that 17 h is 5 p.m.). They do a mid-morning pause to have a snack, and at around 14 h, they have a lunch break. In Madrid, there are many office buildings, most of them downtown.

Besides office jobs, in Spain, there are many jobs related to gastronomy, tourism, hospitality, and commerce. According to statistics, it's the country with the largest amount of bars and restaurants in the world: one for every 175 inhabitants. Therefore, there are many waiters, bartenders, and cooks. In this type of work, shifts usually last four, six, or eight hours, and they can be in the morning, in the afternoon, or at night. In general, people who work in the culinary sector have flexible work hours and arrange their shifts week by week.

Besides the jobs common in every country, there are many traditionally Spanish jobs. In one of the stories in this book (chapter 9), we introduce you to Manolo, a lighthouse keeper. Unfortunately, this job will soon disappear due to the incorporation of complex computer systems. When a lighthouse keeper retires, he isn't replaced by someone else, but his job starts being performed by a computer.

Another traditional Spanish job is that of a knife sharpener, a traveling salesperson known for visiting people door to door with a small harmonica. This salesperson works in quiet neighborhoods of small towns (chances are you won't find them walking around the center of Madrid at rush hour). They also exist in other Latin American countries that had a great influx of Spanish immigration, like Argentina and Uruguay.

Chapter 4: Esto es... – Daily Objects

Story in Spanish: Recuerdos

El doctor termina de examinar a Rafael y dice:

– Puede volver a su casa hoy. Pero tengan en cuenta que todo será más difícil. No recuerda nada previo al accidente.

Rafael escucha las palabras, pero no llega a comprenderlas. Está desorientado. Sabe que está con su esposa y sus padres, pero no los reconoce.

– ¿Vamos, cariño? – dice Ana, su esposa.

Rafael se da cuenta de que están todos muy entusiasmados. Los ha escuchado comentar que tienen la esperanza de que, una vez que Rafael vea sus cosas, comience a recordar. Llegan a una casa sencilla, con **paredes de piedra** y grandes **ventanales**.

Es una casa pequeña. En el comedor hay un **sillón** de color **verde**, gastado por los años. La televisión está apoyada sobre una **mesa** vieja, de **mármol**. Rafael se queda un rato mirándola.

– ¿La recuerdas? – le pregunta su madre. Es la mesa que estaba en la casa de tus abuelos.

Rafael **asiente**. No quiere decepcionar a su madre, pero lo cierto era que estaba mirando una hormiga que caminaba por encima de la mesa.

Recorre el lugar con la mirada. Sobre una biblioteca hay, además de **libros**, varias **fotografías**. En la mayoría de las fotos aparece él junto a

Ana, sus padres u otras personas que no conoce.

Sus padres van a la cocina a preparar café, y Ana lo acompaña a su habitación. Empiezan a sacar las cosas de la **maleta**.

– ¿Cuánto tiempo he estado en el hospital? – pregunta Rafael.

– Tres semanas, cariño – responde Ana mientras saca de la maleta dos jerseys, un ordenador, un **móvil**, el **cargador** del móvil, un **cepillo de dientes** y una **manta**. ¿Quieres comer algo? ¿Beber algo?

– Un vaso de agua estaría bien – dice Rafael.

– Claro. Voy a buscarlo – responde Ana, y se marcha del dormitorio.

Rafael se queda solo en una habitación desconocida. Las **sábanas** de la **cama** son **suaves** y las **almohadas** se ven cómodas.

Enfrente suyo hay un **armario de madera**. De pronto, siente una certeza: si abre ese armario encontrará, en el último **cajón**, una vieja **caja de cartón**. Emocionado, corre hacia el armario, abre el último cajón y allí está. La abre sin saber qué hay dentro. Decepcionado, descubre que es un **costurero**: hay **agujas**, **hilo**, **alfileres** y **botones**. Nada de eso despierta ningún recuerdo. Cuando la está por guardar, un botón **blanco** llama su atención y lo coge, aunque no sabe por qué.

Baja a encontrarse con su familia, jugueteando con el botón. Ana lo ve y comienza a llorar.

– ¿Recuerdas ese botón, Rafa?

Rafael la mira, y ve una imagen muy clara en su cabeza: están en ese mismo comedor, Rafael tiene un **anillo** en la mano y se agacha, pero cuando lo hace, un botón de su **camisa** sale disparado y golpea a Ana en la nariz. Ambos comienzan a reír y Ana exclama:

– ¡Está bien, me casaré contigo, pero no me golpees!

Entonces Rafael llora también: está empezando a recordar.

Vocabulary List

Español	Inglés
la pared de piedra	stone wall
el ventanal	window
el sillón	armchair

verde	green
la mesa	table
el mármol	marble
asentir	to nod
el libro	book
la fotografía	photograph
la maleta	suitcase
el móvil	mobile phone
el cargador	charger
el cepillo de dientes	toothbrush
la manta	blanket
la sábana	sheet
la cama	bed
suave	soft
la almohada	pillow
el armario	wardrobe
de madera	wooden

el cajón	drawer
la caja de cartón	cardboard box
el costurero	sewing box
la aguja	needle
el hilo	thread
el alfiler	pin
el botón	button
blanco	white
el anillo	ring
la camisa	shirt

Summary of the Story in Spanish

Rafael está en el hospital, ha tenido un accidente y ha perdido la memoria. El médico le dice que puede ir a su casa, pero le advierte a su familia que será difícil, ya que todavía no recuerda nada. Cuando llega a su casa, Rafael comienza a recorrerla y a observar todos los objetos para intentar recordar algo, pero no lo logra. Cuando se sienta solo en su habitación, recuerda una caja de cartón guardada en el armario. La caja es en verdad un costurero y Rafael se decepciona, pero luego encuentra un botón que llama su atención. Cuando su esposa le pregunta por el botón, Rafael recuerda que es el botón que se salió de su camisa el día que le propuso matrimonio y ambos se emocionan.

Exercises

1. Completa estas oraciones, usando las siguientes palabras: *cajón, cama, blanco, costurero, libros, botón, fotografías.*

   a. Rafael se sienta en su _____.

   b. En la biblioteca hay _____ y _____.

   c. En el último _____ Rafael encuentra un _____.

   d. Rafael coge un _____ color _____.

2. Selecciona la forma correcta.

   a. Pared con piedra.

   b. Pared de piedra.

   c. Pared a piedra.

3. Selecciona los objetos que puedes encontrar en un costurero.

   a. sillón

   b. agujas

   c. mesa

   d. sábanas

   e. hilo

   f. cargador

4. Conecta las siguientes palabras con su traducción en inglés.

   a. Cepillo de dientes   Ring

   b. Mármol   Suitcase

   c. Anillo   Toothbrush

   d. Maleta   Marble

5. Selecciona la palabra correcta para estas oraciones.

   a. Había un sillón (verde/verdes).

   b. El botón era (blanco/blanca).

   c. Encontró muchas (fotografía/fotografías) suyas.

   d. La mesa era (vieja/viejo).

Comprehension Questions

1. What happened to Rafael after the accident?

2. Why was Rafael staring at the marble table?

3. Who is Ana?

4. Why does Rafael open the last drawer of the wardrobe?

5. What does Rafael remember, thanks to the white button?

Summary of the Story in English

Rafael is in the hospital; he's had an accident, and he's lost his memory. The doctor says he can go home but warns his family that it will be difficult since he still doesn't remember anything. When he arrives home, Rafael begins to walk around and observe all the objects to try to remember something, but he's not successful. When he sits alone in his bedroom, he remembers a cardboard box stored in the closet. The box is a sewing box, and Rafael is disappointed, but then he sees a button that sparks his attention. When his wife asks him about the button, Rafael remembers that it's the button that came out of his shirt the day he proposed, and they both get emotional.

Did you know...

Aside from the objects, colors, and materials we saw in the story, there are other, more specifically, Spanish objects that we can find in Spain. You're surely thinking about fans and castanets and, even though there is a lot of that, those are not the only things.

For example, in Spain, if you talk about a *bota*, we can be talking about a piece of footwear (a boot) or a container to drink from. These containers are made of leather and fur and have a shape similar to that of a leg of ham. They are pretty big and have a string to wear as a bag.

The *alpargatas* ("espadrilles") are another typical element you can find in Spain. Even though they are used in many Latin American countries, some people claim that they are of Spanish origin. It's a type of cool and simple footwear that is usually made of canvas, and its sole is made of jute or rubber. They used to be of one color throughout, but nowadays, there are stores that have many models to choose from.

When you visit Spain, you should go to a bar to eat *tapas*, or, as they say, *ir de tapeo*. *Tapas* are small dishes, so you will have to order several of them to amount to a full meal. They may come in small pots or on top of toasts. The most common *tapas* are made of Iberian ham, shrimp, tomatoes with olive oil, and other pickled vegetables. One thing's for certain: you should pair your *tapas* with a *caña de cerveza*. The *caña* is the unit of measure used for beer.

Chapter 5: ¿Cuánto cuesta eso? – Shopping

Story in Spanish: La boda

Paulina y su madre, Gloria, caminan por una **acera** de Madrid. De pronto, se detienen frente a un **escaparate**. Es una tienda dedicada a los **vestidos de novia**. Paulina saca su móvil y confirma que llegaron a la dirección correcta. Entonces entran. Las recibe Adriana, una de las vendedoras.

– Buenos días, mi nombre es Adriana – dice. ¿Puedo ayudarlas?

– Sí, muchas gracias – responde Gloria . Mira, mi hija se casará en unos meses, y estamos buscando un vestido sencillo. Será una **fiesta** íntima.

– Nada demasiado recargado, **por favor** – dice Paulina . No es mi estilo.

– De acuerdo – contesta Adriana . Estoy segura de que encontraremos algo. Acompañadme, por favor.

Adriana guía a Gloria y a Paulina hasta el fondo de la tienda. Allí tienen tres **percheros** con distintos modelos de vestidos. Adriana toma uno y se lo muestra a Paulina.

– ¿Algo como esto? – pregunta Adriana.

– Sí, aunque.... Bueno, no exactamente – responde Paulina. Se mira frente al **espejo** con el vestido sobre el torso.

– Es bellísimo – dice Gloria.

- No estoy diciendo que sea feo - contesta Paulina. Solo que no es para mí. ¿Qué otras opciones tienes?

- Si quieres, puedes **probarte** uno de estos - dice Adriana mientras toma otro vestido. Son de nuestra nueva colección. Es modesto, pero elegante. Si fuera negro, podrías usarlo en una gala.

Paulina toma el vestido y lo mira detenidamente. Una sombra cruza por sus ojos, y luego se dirige a su madre.

- ¿La nueva colección? - pregunta Paulina. No creo que...

- Anda, pruébatelo - responde Gloria. Aunque sea para ver cómo te queda.

- Supongo que no hará **daño** - dice Paulina. Adriana, ¿tienes **talla** 40?

- Seguro - responde Adriana. Toma, este te servirá.

Paulina entra al **probador** con el vestido, y pasa allí unos minutos. Cuando sale, tiene una expresión sorprendida, casi **atónita**.

- Es... - dice Paulina. No consigue terminar la **oración**.

- Es muy **bonito** - completa Gloria. Déjame ver la **espalda**... Sí, es realmente muy bonito.

- Es perfecto - contesta Paulina.

- ¿Cuánto **cuesta**? - pregunta Gloria.

- Bueno, como les dije, es un modelo de nuestra última colección - responde Adriana. Eso significa que el **precio** es... no es **barato**.

- Podemos seguir mirando - dice Paulina.

- No, Pauli, el vestido es perfecto - contesta Gloria. No nos **rindamos** tan fácil. ¿De cuánto estamos hablando?

- Dos mil trescientos euros - dice Adriana. Intenta suavizar la noticia con una sonrisa, pero no lo consigue.

Gloria lanza un **suspiro**. Paulina deja el vestido inmediatamente sobre uno de los percheros. Teme romperlo por accidente.

- Supongo que podemos **estirarnos**... - dice Gloria después de unos segundos.

- Mamá, no - responde Paulina. Es muy **caro**. Está muy por encima de nuestro **presupuesto**.

- Ya sé, Pauli - dice Gloria. Pero tú te **casarás** una sola vez en la vida. Bueno, una vez por lo menos. Pero no sabremos si habrá otra.

Paulina sonríe un poco. Su madre nunca entendió qué le veía a Arturo. No le cae mal, solo le parece un poco **soso**. Pero está más que dispuesta a respetar la decisión de su hija.

- Disculpen la interrupción - dice Adriana de pronto. Yo... Bueno, tengo una **oferta** que hacerles.

- ¿Cómo? - pregunta Paulina.

- Ocurre que las vendedoras tenemos un **descuento**, ya saben - dice Adriana. Un descuento para empleados. Bastante grande. Como del treinta por ciento, creo. Lo podemos usar una sola vez al año, y yo cumplo un año aquí en dos semanas, así que...

- ¿Lo harías por mí? - dice Paulina, súbitamente emocionada.

Adriana **se encoge de hombros**.

- Dijiste que era el vestido perfecto - contesta.

- ¡Gracias! - dice Paulina mientras **abraza** a Adriana. ¡Muchísimas gracias!

- De nada, un placer - dice Adriana, levemente incómoda. Pero tengo una condición.

En ese momento, Paulina suelta a Adriana y toma distancia. De pronto, siente la sombra de la duda otra vez.

- ¡Tienen que invitarme a la **boda**! - dice Adriana finalmente.

- ¡Pues claro que sí! - responde Paulina. Anótate la fecha ya mismo, por favor.

Vocabulary List

Español	Inglés
la acera	sidewalk
el escaparate	shop window
el vestido de novia	wedding dress
la fiesta	party
por favor	please

el perchero	rack
el espejo	mirror
probar	to try
la talla	size
el daño	harm
el probador	fitting room
atónito, atónita	stunned
la oración	sentence
bonito, bonita	cute
la espalda	back
costar	to cost
el precio	price
barato, barata	cheap
rendirse	to give up
el suspiro	sigh
estirarse	to stretch
caro, cara	expensive

el presupuesto	budget
casarse	to get married
soso, sosa	bland
la oferta	offer
el descuento	discount
encogerse de hombros	to shrug
abrazar	to hug
la boda	wedding

Summary of the Story in Spanish

Paulina se casará con Arturo en unos meses. Por eso está buscando vestidos de novia con su madre, Gloria. Entonces entran a una tienda, donde las recibe Adriana, una vendedora. Allí, Paulina mira varios vestidos sin que nada la convenza. Finalmente, encuentra uno que le gusta. El problema es que es demasiado caro. Cuando Paulina y Gloria están a punto de darse por vencidas, Adriana les ofrece usar su descuento de empleada. De esa forma, podrán llevarse el vestido pagando un treinta por ciento menos. Paulina le agradece con un abrazo. Entonces Adriana pone una condición. ¡Quiere ser invitada a la boda!

Exercises

1. Elige cuál de las siguientes oraciones es incorrecta.

    a. Adriana trabaja como vendedora.

    b. Gloria es la madre de Paulina.

    c. Paulina casará pronto.

    d. La tienda tiene muchos vestidos.

2. Completa el diálogo con estas palabras: *cuestan, espejo, probármelos, talla, baratos, probador, gracias.*
   - ¿Cuánto _____ estos zapatos? - pregunta Paulina.
   - ¿Los blancos? - responde Adriana. Cincuenta euros.
   - ¡Son muy _____! - contesta Paulina. ¿Puedo _____, por favor?
   - No hay problema - dice Adriana. ¿Qué _____ eres?
   - Ocho - contesta Paulina.
   - Aquí tienes - responde Adriana. ¿Quieres pasar al _____?
   - No, _____ - contesta Paulina. Puedo ponérmelos aquí mismo, frente al _____.

3. Elige la oración escrita de manera correcta.
   a. El descuento es mucho bueno.
   b. El presupuesto es ajustada.
   c. La oferta es tentadora.
   d. La precia es elevada.

4. Elige la palabra correcta en cada caso.
   a. Paulina se casará (con/a) Arturo.
   b. Adriana (trabaja/trabajo) en una tienda de ropa.
   c. Gloria (es/está) emocionada por la boda.
   d. El vestido es (nuevo/nueva).

5. ¿Hace cuánto trabaja Adriana en la tienda?
   a. Diez años.
   b. Casi dos años.
   c. Menos de un año.
   d. Seis meses.

Comprehension Questions

1. What are Paulina and Gloria looking for?
2. Why is the dress that Paulina likes more expensive?
3. What does Gloria think of her future son-in-law?
4. What does Adriana offer them?
5. What is Adriana's condition?

Summary of the Story in English

Paulina will marry Arturo in a few months. That's why she's looking for wedding dresses with her mother, Gloria. They go to a store where Adriana, a salesperson, welcomes them. There, Paulina looks at a few dresses, but nothing convinces her. Finally, she finds one that she likes. The problem is that it's too expensive. When Paulina and Gloria are about to give up, Adriana offers to use her employee discount. In this way, they will be able to get the dress paying thirty percent less. Paulina thanks her with a hug. Then, Adriana sets a condition. She wants to be invited to the wedding!

Did you know...

Spain is a country with vibrant commerce. Great cities, like Madrid, Barcelona, or Seville, are filled with independent designers' clothes stores and also luxury brands' exclusive shops. In Madrid, the Malasaña or Chueca districts are ideal for finding urban clothes, while Salamanca is the preferred district for buying jewelry and dresses.

In Spain, it's very usual to go shopping at apartment stores: buildings of several stories where you can find anything from food to electronic appliances, clothes, and makeup, all from different brands. Minimarkets are also common; they are called *tiendas de ultramarinos* and are stores distributed throughout big cities that sell many goods and remain open until very late at night.

Lastly, nothing is more charming than the *mercadillos*. In these places, you can find artisanal food and beverages, as well as antiquities, clothes, and very curious objects. Some of the most famous *mercadillos* are El Rastro, in Madrid, and La Boquería, in Barcelona, but each town or city in Spain has its own. In Latin America, the most famous ones are in San Telmo, in Buenos Aires (Argentina), San Juan, in Mexico City (Mexico), and Paloquemao, in Bogota (Colombia).

Chapter 6: ¿Dónde está…? – Going to Places

Story in Spanish: El turista

Sebastián camina por el Barrio Gótico, desorientado y cansado. El bolso le pesa y hace mucho calor. Ha pasado varios días en Barcelona, pero aún no se ha familiarizado con el casco antiguo. Parece un laberinto: está lleno de callecitas, callejones y callejuelas.

«Quien diseñó la ciudad seguramente se divirtió pensando en la cantidad de turistas que se iban a perder», piensa Sebastián con una sonrisa, y deja el bolso en el suelo para tomar aire durante un momento.

Entonces, un hombre vestido con un traje pasa caminando cerca. «Tiene que ser un residente», piensa Sebastián. «¿Qué turista va de traje por la calle?».

- **Disculpe**, señor - dice Sebastián. **Necesito llegar al aeropuerto. ¿Podría indicarme cómo ir?**

- Por supuesto – contesta el hombre. Necesita tomar un metro y un autobús. Siga caminando por esta calle y verá la **estación de metro** de la línea 3. Tome el metro y baje en la Plaza España. Allí encontrará la **parada del autobús** que va al **aeropuerto**.

- Muchas gracias. - Sebastián sigue caminando en la dirección que le ha dado el hombre.

Llega al metro sin problemas, se baja en la Plaza España y luego **toma el autobús**. Afortunadamente, el viaje es rápido. Es domingo por la mañana y hay muy poco tránsito en Barcelona.

Al llegar a su **destino**, se encuentra con otro problema. ¡El aeropuerto es demasiado grande! Mira su reloj: son las ocho de la mañana y su vuelo sale a las nueve en punto. Todavía necesita registrarse y despachar su equipaje. Y, además, se está muriendo de hambre porque no desayunó nada.

Sebastián se acerca al mostrador de información. Del otro lado hay una mujer.

– Buenos días, señora – le dice. Necesito registrarme y despachar mi equipaje. **¿Dónde están** los mostradores?

– ¿**Hacia dónde se dirige**, señor?

– Voy a Madrid con la aerolínea Nubes Esponjosas.

– Tiene que subir dos pisos. Puede usar la escalera mecánica.

– ¿Y **dónde queda** la escalera mecánica?

– A unos doscientos metros en línea recta. También puede utilizar el ascensor, que **se encuentra** al final de ese pasillo.

– Muchas gracias. ¡Ah! Y otra cosa... ¿**Puede decirme dónde hay una** cafetería?

– Claro. Hay un patio de comidas en el tercer piso del aeropuerto. De todas formas, ¡le aconsejo que se dé prisa, o perderá el vuelo!

Sebastián le agradece a la mujer y sale corriendo en dirección a la escalera mecánica. ¡Ya habrá tiempo de desayunar unos churros con chocolate en Madrid!

Vocabulary List

Español	Inglés
Disculpe	Excuse me
Necesito llegar a...	I need to get to the...
¿Podría indicarme cómo ir?	Can you tell me how to get there?
la estación de metro	subway station
la parada del autobús	bus stop

el aeropuerto	airport
tomar el autobús	to take the bus
el destino	destination
¿Dónde está...?	Where is...?
¿Hacia dónde se dirige?	Where are you flying?
¿Dónde queda...?	Where is...?
Se encuentra	Is located in
¿Puede decirme dónde hay...?	Can you tell me where there's...?

Summary of the Story in Spanish

Sebastián es un turista perdido por las calles de Barcelona. Necesita llegar al aeropuerto porque a las nueve de la mañana tiene su vuelo de regreso a Madrid. Un hombre le dice cómo llegar al aeropuerto: debe tomar un metro y luego un autobús.

Sebastián llega sin problemas, aunque se da cuenta de que no es tan fácil encontrar el mostrador de su aerolínea. Le pregunta a una mujer que trabaja en el aeropuerto dónde puede hacer el registro y despachar su equipaje. Ella le da las indicaciones, y le advierte que tiene un margen de tiempo muy ajustado. Por eso, Sebastián debe renunciar a su desayuno.

Exercises

1. Completa los espacios en blanco con las siguientes palabras: *líneas, red, transporte, trenes, metro, estaciones.* El _____ es uno de los medios de _____ más veloces. El de Madrid fue inaugurado en 1919 y tiene 12 _____ y 276 _____. En algunas estaciones de la _____ del metro de Madrid se puede realizar trasbordo con _____ y con autobuses.

2. Une cada verbo con el artículo o la preposición y con el sustantivo correspondientes. El objetivo es formar una frase. Por ejemplo:

viajar en avión.

viajar	un	indicación
pedir	en	avión
tomar	al	aeropuerto
llegar	una	autobús

3. ¿Cuál de las siguientes preguntas no funciona para pedir indicaciones a la Sagrada Familia de Barcelona?

    a. ¿Podría indicarme dónde está la Sagrada Familia?

    b. Busco la Sagrada Familia, ¿me diría cómo llego allí?

    c. Quisiera saber cuándo se construyó la Sagrada Familia.

    d. ¿Me diría qué autobús me deja cerca de la Sagrada Familia?

4. En el siguiente diálogo, completa los espacios en blanco con la palabra correcta.

A: ¿Me diría cómo _____ (llego/tengo) al centro de la ciudad?

B: Sí, puede ir _____ (a pie/de pie) o tomarse un medio de _____ (transportación/transporte). ¿Qué prefiere?

A: Lo segundo, por favor.

B: Vale. Puede _____ (tomar/agarrar) el autobús número 35. La _____ (parada/pared) está en esa esquina.

A: De acuerdo, ¡muchas gracias!

5. Elige cuál es la frase correcta.

    a. ¿En dónde parada tengo que bajarme?

    b. ¿En qué parada tengo que bajarme?

    c. ¿Qué parada tengo que bajarme?

    d. ¿Qué parada tengo que bajar?

Comprehension Questions

1. Why does Sebastián get lost in Barcelona?

2. How many means of transportation does Sebastián need to use to get to the airport?

3. Why isn't there much traffic?

4. At what time does his flight leave?

5. Where is the food court?

Summary of the Story in English

Sebastián is a tourist lost in the streets of Barcelona. He needs to get to the airport because he has a flight back to Madrid at nine a.m. A man tells him how to get to the airport: he has to take the subway and then a bus.

Sebastián arrives without a problem, although he realizes it's not so easy to find his airline's counter. He asks a woman who works at the airport where he can check in and drop his bags off. She gives him directions and warns him that he has a very tight time frame. That's why Sebastián gives up his breakfast.

Did you know...

Barcelona is the second largest city in Spain, after Madrid. It is the capital of the autonomous community of Catalonia and is situated on the shores of the Mediterranean Sea, but it is surrounded by mountains. One of the most important mountains is Montjuic, which has an amazing palace at the top. From the summit of Montjuic, you can see a great part of the city.

In medieval times, Barcelona turned into one of the most important political and social centers in all of Europe. Quarters like the Gothic or the Raval, in Old Town, are home to hundred-year-old buildings with great architectural, cultural, and historic value.

Barcelona is a very touristic and animated city filled with bars. In almost every corner of the city, you can find a gastronomic venue with tables on the streets (known as *terrazas*) where you can drink a beer or eat some *tapas*.

Lastly, the Catalan capital is a cosmopolitan city with a great cultural and social offerings. Great artists have developed their work there, like Joan Miró and Pablo Picasso (who each have their own museum), not to speak of the famous Antoni Gaudí, who designed many buildings that embellish the city. Among the most important works by this architect, there is the Sagrada Familia or the beautiful Park Güell.

Chapter 7: ¿Qué comemos? - Eating in a restaurant

Story in Spanish: La amiga

Lisa llega primero al restaurante. Se sienta en una mesa junto a la ventana; al cabo de 5 minutos, llega Gloria. Lisa y Gloria eran amigas cuando eran pequeñas, pero luego han dejado de verse. Esta es la primera vez que quedan para comer en 10 años. Tienen mucho de qué hablar.

– ¿Quieres mirar el menú? – pregunta Lisa a Gloria – la **especialidad** de este lugar son las pastas, me parece que no tienen otros **platos**.

– No, está bien, ya sé qué quiero – responde Gloria, mientras llama al camarero con un gesto. – Bueno, ¡cuéntame de ti!

Antes de que Lisa pueda responder, llega el camarero.

– Quisiera **pedir** un plato de **ravioles** con **salsa fileto**, por favor – pide Lisa.

– Quiero un **pescado** a la **parrilla** – dice Gloria.

– No servimos pescado, señora – le dice el camarero.

– Vale, pero yo debo comer pescado, así que vas y preguntas si me hacen uno de esos o qué – responde Gloria mientras le hace un gesto al camarero con la mano para que se vaya. – Bueno, Lisa, cariño, ¿cómo estás?

Lisa está un poco espantada con la actitud de su amiga, pero no quiere armar una escena así que sigue charlando.

- Bueno, yo estoy trabajando en una librería y...

- ¡Ah! - la interrumpe Gloria - me encantan las librerías. Siempre que voy intento no llevarme todo, ¡pero es muy difícil! ¿Sabes que mi padre trabajó una vez en una librería? ¿La tuya tiene alguna especialidad? La de mi padre era sobre todo de libros de cocina y viajes, ¿cómo se llaman esos? Vale, no sé, pero son lugares muy mágicos, ¿a que sí?

Mientras Gloria habla, llega el camarero y le dice que, efectivamente, no sirven pescado allí. Que puede pedir algo que esté en el menú. Gloria, sin mirar la carta, le pide una **porción** de paella.

- No servimos paella, señora. Servimos pastas y algunas **carnes**, pero no tenemos nada de pescado.

Gloria hace un gesto de desagrado.

- Vale, no me traigas nada, compartiré lo que ha pedido ella.

Lisa está tan espantada con la actitud de su amiga que no se anima a decirle nada. Ella se **muere de hambre**, pero no quiere contradecirla, quiere que este **almuerzo** termine cuanto antes. Gloria sigue hablando y hablando hasta que llega la comida. Lisa intenta **pinchar** un ravioli, pero Gloria toma el plato, prueba uno y llama al camarero:

- ¡Esto está **frío**! Me lo calientas, ahora.

Lisa está colorada, no puede creer los malos modos de su amiga. Intenta decir algo, pero Gloria ya está hablando de nuevo:

- Yo intenté trabajar, ¿sabes? Pero no era lo mío, era muy difícil para mí cumplir un horario, que me digan lo que tengo que hacer... ya sabes, soy una mujer muy libre.

El camarero vuelve con el plato de ravioles **humeantes**. Eso está muy **caliente**. Lisa no puede ni acercarse uno a la boca y Gloria tampoco. Igualmente, llama al camarero nuevamente.

- Esto no tiene **sal**, está **asqueroso**. Mi amiga y yo nos vamos de aquí, por el pésimo servicio. ¡Gracias por nada! - grita Gloria, mientras se levanta. - ¿Vamos?

Lisa está mirando la escena, alucinada.

- No, Gloria, gracias, yo me quedaré aquí a comer los ravioles... Pero hasta luego, amiga, ¡que te vaya muy bien!

Cuando Gloria se va ofendida, Lisa mira al camarero:

- ¡Te pido disculpas por el comportamiento de mi amiga! ¿Podrías traerme la **cuenta**, por favor? Te dejaré una buena **propina**, puedes estar seguro.

Vocabulary List

Español	Inglés
la especialidad	specialty
el plato	dish
pedir	to order
los ravioles	ravioli
la salsa fileto	filetto sauce
el pescado	fish
la parrilla	grill
la porción	serving, piece
la carne	beef
morir de hambre	to be starving
el almuerzo	lunch
pinchar	to prick (as in pinprick)
frío, fría	cold
humeante	steaming
caliente	hot
la sal	salt
asqueroso, asquerosa	disgusting

la cuenta	check
la propina	tip

Summary of the Story in Spanish

Lisa y Gloria son amigas de la infancia, pero no se ven hace muchos años. Quedan para almorzar en un restaurante. Lisa pide ravioles y Gloria, sin mirar el menú, pide un plato de pescado. El camarero le dice que no sirven pescado. Gloria insiste y luego pide paella, que tampoco tienen. Finalmente, decide compartir lo que había pedido Lisa. Mientras tanto, habla sin parar y no deja que Lisa cuente nada de su vida. Cuando llega el plato de pasta, lo devuelve de mal modo, primero diciendo que el plato estaba frío y luego que no tenía sal. Finalmente, Gloria se va, ofendida, pero Lisa se queda en el restaurante, comiendo su comida y disculpándose con el camarero.

Exercises

1. Completa el siguiente párrafo con las palabras correctas.

   Quisiera _____ (pedir/pinchar) un _____ (parrilla/pescado), por favor. Si es posible, lo quisiera sin _____ (sal/caliente).

2. Selecciona la frase correcta.

   a. ¿Podrías ordenarme la cuenta, por favor?

   b. ¿Podrías traerme la cuenta, por favor?

   c. ¿La cuenta podrías traerme, por favor?

   d. ¿La cuenta podrías ordenarme, por favor?

3. Conecta cada palabra con su traducción

   a. Carne   fish

   b. Almuerzo   tip

   c. Pescado   beef

   d. Propina   lunch

4. ¿Cuál de las siguientes frases está escrita incorrectamente?

   a. Quisiera ver el menú

   b. Pediré los ravioles

   c. Propina te dejaré

   d. Este plato está frío

5. Completa este párrafo con las siguientes palabras: *pescado, cuenta, asqueroso, especialidad, pastas.*

Voy a pedir la _____ del restaurante, me han dicho que sus _____ son muy sabrosas. Pero no debes pedir el _____, es _____. Se lo diré cuando traiga la _____.

Comprehension Questions

1. What does Gloria want to eat?
2. Where does Lisa work?
3. What is the restaurant's specialty?
4. What's the problem with the ravioli, according to Gloria?
5. What does Lisa promise the waiter?

Summary of the Story in English

Lisa and Gloria are childhood friends, but they haven't seen each other in years. They get together for lunch at a restaurant. Lisa orders ravioli, and Gloria, without looking at the menu, orders fish. The waiter tells her they don't serve fish. Gloria insists and then asks for paella, which they don't serve either. Finally, she decides to share what Lisa has ordered. In the meantime, she talks nonstop and doesn't let Lisa say anything about her life. When the pasta dish arrives, she returns it rudely, saying first that the dish was cold and then that it had no salt. Finally, Gloria leaves, offended, but Lisa stays at the restaurant, eating her food and apologizing to the waiter.

Did you know...

If you visit Spain, one thing's for sure: you'll eat very well! Gastronomy is a very important part of Spanish culture, and there are many traditional dishes that you need to try, starting with the *paella* (though you should know where to order it, so as not to be like Gloria...). *Paella* is a rice-based dish with saffron and seafood, typical in all of Spain.

You should also try the Spanish potato *tortilla*, another classic. The *tortilla* is made with potatoes and eggs, and from then on, you can add different things: onion, *chorizo*, bacon, or ham... in a nutshell, almost anything goes well in a *tortilla*.

Another traditional dish of Spanish cuisine is the *gazpacho*, a cold soup with tomatoes, onion, garlic, cucumber, and olive oil. This soup is very refreshing for hot summer days. Generally, it's eaten with pieces of toasted bread.

In winter, you should definitely try the *cocido madrileño*. This dish has two parts: first, to warm up, you're served a *cocido* soup, which is the broth where the ingredients of the dish were cooked. Then, separately, those ingredients are served: meat, chicken, cold meat, chickpeas, and vegetables.

Lastly, you can't leave Spain without first trying the famous Iberian ham, olive oil, and olives that are produced in the country. They're delicious!

Chapter 8: Tengo que estudiar - Studying and going to school

Story in Spanish: Una elección difícil

Martín está sentado en su habitación, rodeado de **folletos** de distintas **universidades**. Su madre le ha dicho que no puede salir hasta que no tome una decisión. Todos sus compañeros de la escuela ya han decidido qué **carrera** van a **estudiar**, pero él todavía no lo sabe.

A Martín no le gusta estudiar. En el verano trabajó en el café de su tío como barista y quiere dedicarse a eso. Le gusta hacer dibujos en la espuma del café, atender a los clientes y hablar con ellos. No quiere tener que preparar **exámenes**. No le gusta **leer** ni hacer trabajos para la escuela. Pero su familia le ha dicho que tiene que estudiar una carrera, que es una obligación.

Sus amigos tampoco lo ayudan, están muy seguros de sus carreras y quieren convencerlo, pero ninguna le gusta.

- Debes estudiar **Economía** como yo - le repite su amigo Pedro. Así algún día podremos ser presidentes.

- No, ¡debes estudiar **Arquitectura**! Haremos edificios hermosos, museos, catedrales... - intenta convencerlo su amiga Paula.

- Martín, no los escuches, ven a estudiar **Arte** conmigo. Aprenderemos un poco de todo, luego podrás hacer lo que más te guste. - Su amigo Joaquín es el más parecido a él, pero la carrera de Arte tampoco le llama la atención.

Su hermana está estudiando **Ingeniería**, así que esa carrera ya está descartada. No quiere hacer lo mismo que ella.

Debe decidirlo ahora: los exámenes para entrar a la universidad son el mes que viene y tiene que empezar a prepararse. Sus **asignaturas** favoritas en la escuela son la **Educación Plástica**, la **Historia** y la **Educación Física**. Odia las **Matemáticas**, la **Física** y la **Biología**.

De pronto, se le ocurre una idea. Si él quiere trabajar en un café, como su tío, ¡debe averiguar qué estudió su tío! Lo llama por teléfono y le pregunta.

– Yo estudié muchas cosas – le responde su tío. Empecé y dejé varias carreras, porque ninguna me gustaba. Al final me quedé en la carrera de **Administración de Empresas**, sin estar convencido. Pero gracias a esa carrera aprendí a llevar adelante un negocio, a manejar empleados, a lidiar con los proveedores y muchas otras cosas más que me permitieron comprar este café.

– ¡Gracias, tío! ¡Creo que ya sé lo que quiero estudiar! – le contesta Martín, muy entusiasmado.

– Martín, debes saber que es una carrera que tiene muchas asignaturas que tienen que ver con las matemáticas. ¿Podrás con eso?

– ¡No! Hablando contigo me di cuenta de que yo no quiero comprar un café ni manejar empleados. ¡Yo quiero dibujar! Sobre el café, sobre todo, pero no me vendría mal aprender otras **técnicas**. Me apuntaré en la carrera de Artes.

Vocabulary List

Español	Inglés
el folleto	brochure
la universidad	university, college
la carrera	major
estudiar	to study
el examen	test

leer	to read
Economía	economics
Arquitectura	architecture
Arte	art
Ingeniería	engineering
Educación Plástica	art (subject)
Historia	history
Educación Física	physical education, gym class
Matemática	math
Física	physics
Biología	biology
Administración de Empresas	business administration
la asignatura	subject
la técnica	technique

Summary of the Story in Spanish

Martín está intentando elegir una carrera, aunque no quiere estudiar en la universidad. No le gusta leer ni estudiar y quiere trabajar de barista, lo que viene haciendo en el café de su tío. Sin embargo, su familia lo obliga a elegir una carrera. Sus amigos ya saben qué van a estudiar e intentan convencerlo para que estudie Economía, Arquitectura y Arte. No quiere estudiar Ingeniería ni ninguna carrera que tenga materias como Matemáticas, Física o Biología. Finalmente, decide hablar con su tío dueño del café para averiguar qué estudió él. Pero la carrera que estudió su tío tampoco le interesa. Se decide por Arte, para poder mejorar sus técnicas de dibujo.

Exercises

1. Conecta las siguientes carreras con su traducción en inglés.

   a. Ingeniería   business administration

   b. Arquitectura   engineering

   c. Administración de empresas   art

   d. Arte   architecture

2. ¿Cuál de estas frases no está escrita correctamente?

   a. Joaquín estudiará Arte

   b. La hermana de Martín estudia Ingeniería

   c. A Martín no estudiar le gusta

   d. Martín quiere dibujar

3. Completa este párrafo con las siguientes palabras: *administración de empresas, estudié, arte, arquitectura.*

   Quería construir casas, por eso _____ en la universidad la carrera de _____. Después me di cuenta de que en realidad me gustaba dibujar, entonces me anoté en la carrera de _____. Pero eso tampoco me gustó, así que terminé estudiando _____ para poder abrir mi propio café.

4. Completa las siguientes oraciones.

   a. ¿Qué _____ (lee/estudia) tu hijo?

   b. Mi hijo estudia _____ (ingeniería/asignatura).

   c. Tengo que estudiar, mañana tengo un _____ (folleto/examen)

   d. _____(educación física/examen) es mi asignatura favorita.

5. ¿Cuál de estas oraciones está escrita correctamente?

   a. Debo elegir unas carrera

   b. Debió elegir una carrera

   c. Debo elegir una carrera

   d. Debo elegir una carreras

Comprehension Questions

1. Where does Martín want to work?
2. What has his family told him?
3. What are his favorite subjects?
4. What did Martín's uncle study?
5. What does Martín decide to study?

Summary of the Story in English

Martín is trying to choose a major, even though he doesn't want to study at university. He doesn't like to read or study and wants to work as a barista, which is what he's been doing at his uncle's café. However, his family makes him choose a major. His friends already know what they will study and try to convince him to study economics, architecture, and art. He doesn't want to study engineering or any major that has math-, physics-, or biology-related subjects. Finally, he decides to talk with his uncle, who owns the café to find out what he studied. But his uncle's major doesn't interest him either. He finally decides on art, so he is able to improve his drawing techniques.

Did you know...

In Spain, after the ESO (Educación Secundaria Obligatoria, "Mandatory Secondary School"), you need to sit for an exam to get into university. This exam, called *selectividad* ("selectivity"), is mandatory for everyone who wants to study at a public or private university or tertiary institution.

This entrance examination has two phases. The first one is a general phase, which is mandatory for everyone. The questions of the exam focus on basic high school content, though they may change a bit depending on the autonomous community.

The second phase, which isn't mandatory, is a specific phase. This one consists of 3-4 exams from other high-school subjects, and it is useful to increase the score of the first phase. Generally, students choose high school subjects related to what they want to study.

Since there is limited vacancy to get into each *carrera* (not to be confused with the English word "career," a *carrera* is what people want to study at university, their major), the exam scores will determine which *carreras* one can get into. This is called *nota de corte* ("cut score"), and it's established by each *carrera* and university. Therefore, the *nota de corte* of each *carrera* can change depending on the year or the institution.

Today, the most requested *carreras* in Spain (and, therefore, the ones that require a higher *nota de corte*), are international studies, law, medicine, computer engineering, math, and political science. The medical science *carreras*, like medicine or nursing, have received a higher demand after the COVID-19 pandemic.

Chapter 9: No entiendo – Dealing with Problems

Story in Spanish: El encuentro

1. Michael

Michael mira la hora en su reloj. Todavía tiene veinte minutos hasta la reunión con Lucy y Vincent. Es tiempo suficiente para llegar al Café Gijón. O lo sería, si él supiera dónde está.

La última **esquina** parece familiar. ¿No pasó ya por allí? Michael llegó a Madrid esa misma mañana, desde Israel, y todavía no ha tenido tiempo de **acostumbrarse** a la ciudad. Ni siquiera pudo comprar un chip nuevo para su móvil. Tenía **prisa**. No ve a Lucy y a Vincent desde la universidad, en Estados Unidos, y no fue fácil coordinar ese encuentro. Estaban muy dispersos.

Finalmente, Michael se detiene. Está seguro de que está **perdido**. En la esquina, ve un **estanco** que ofrece, además de tabaco y estampillas, unos cuantos mapas de la ciudad. Decide entrar.

– Hola – dice Michael.

– ¿Puedo ayudarlo? – pregunta el **dependiente**, sin dejar de mirar su móvil.

– Estoy perdido – dice Michael. Su español es limitado, pero afortunadamente recuerda esa frase.

El dependiente levanta la vista.

– ¿A dónde quiere ir? – pregunta.

– Café Gijón – responde Michael.

– Está cerca – dice el dependiente. Camine tres minutos por esta misma calle y se lo encontrará.

Michael se desorienta. No termina de entender las indicaciones.

– Disculpe, no **entiendo** – responde. ¿Puede repetirlo, por favor?

El dependiente se levanta de su silla y sale del estanco. Entonces apunta con su dedo en dirección al norte.

– Por allí – dice. Tres minutos.

– Muchas gracias – responde Michael, y sigue con su camino.

2. Lucy

Lucy está preocupada. La **cinta transportadora** ya dio cuatro o cinco vueltas. Todos los demás pasajeros de su **vuelo** encontraron sus maletas hace rato. Y las suyas todavía no han aparecido.

Mira la **pantalla** sobre la cinta transportadora. Ya no dice "Edimburgo-Madrid", que es el vuelo que ella tomó. Ahora dice "Estambul-Madrid". Es oficial. Su **equipaje** se ha perdido.

Lucy busca el **mostrador** de su aerolínea. Después de caminar durante unos minutos, lo encuentra, al fondo de una larga fila de mostradores. Se acerca a una mujer de rostro amable.

– Buenas tardes – dice Lucy. Mis maletas no aparecieron en la cinta. ¿Cómo puedo **encontrar** mi equipaje?

– ¿En qué vuelo ha venido? – pregunta la mujer.

– El de Edimburgo, de las 10:30 – responde Lucy.

La mujer **teclea** durante unos segundos.

– Sentimos mucho este problema – dice finalmente. Su equipaje debería aparecer dentro de las próximas 24 horas. Fue un pequeño problema de logística; no debería ocurrir, pero ocurre. ¿Quiere que lo **mandemos** al hotel?

– Por favor – dice Lucy.

– Dígame la dirección entonces – contesta la mujer.

Lucy dicta la dirección de su hotel. Piensa que, después de todo, no es un problema tan grande. Ahora no tiene que preocuparse por **desempacar** antes de ir al Café Gijón.

3. Vincent

- Tu tren ya partió, **tío** - dice el empleado.

- No puede ser - responde Vincent. ¿Sevilla-Madrid? ¿El de las 8:10?

- Exacto - contesta el empleado.

- ¡Pero no lo vi! - dice Vincent. ¡Estoy aquí desde las 8!

- Lo sentimos mucho, pero los trenes AVE no esperan a nadie - dice el empleado. Ten en cuenta que, si nos demoramos quince minutos, tenemos que hacer un **reembolso**.

- Lo sé, lo sé - contesta Vincent. Por eso mismo compré estos tickets...

Vincent está intranquilo. Necesita estar en Madrid a la hora del almuerzo. Quedó en encontrarse con Lucy y Michael. Hace años que no los ve. No puede llegar **tarde** justo ese día.

- ¿Hay un bus que pueda tomar? - pregunta Vincent.

- No lo sé - dice el empleado. Pero puedes preguntar en esa **ventanilla**. Allí tienen toda la información.

El empleado **señala** un mostrador al final de la estación. Vincent apura el paso hasta allí.

- Buenos días - dice Vincent. ¿Tienen **boletos** para Madrid?

La empleada está al otro lado de un vidrio. En el centro del vidrio hay una especie de parlante. Vincent ve que la empleada habla a un micrófono, pero apenas **escucha** lo que le dicen.

- Disculpa, pero no te **oigo** - dice Vincent. ¿Podría repetir? Mi español no es tan bueno.

La empleada **revolea los ojos** y se pone de pie. Sale de su oficina y se acerca a Vincent.

- El micrófono siempre funciona mal - dice. Mira, estos son los **horarios**. Hay un bus que sale de aquí mismo dentro de diez minutos. ¿Te interesa?

- ¡Sí! - responde Vincent. ¿A qué hora llegaría a Madrid?

- Oh, cerca de las dos - dice la empleada. Justo para el almuerzo.

Vocabulary List

Español	Inglés
la esquina	corner
acostumbrarse	to get used to
la prisa	hurry
perdido, perdida	lost
el estanco	smoke shop
el dependiente, la dependienta	clerk
entender	to understand
la cinta transportadora	the conveyor
el vuelo	flight
la maleta	bag
la pantalla	screen
el equipaje	luggage
el mostrador	counter
encontrar	to find
teclear	to type
mandar	to send

desempacar	to unpack
el tío, la tía	dude, girl (colloquial)
el reembolso	refund
tarde	late
la ventanilla	window
señalar	to point
el boleto	ticket
escuchar	to listen
oír	to hear
revolear los ojos	to roll your eyes
el horario	schedule

Summary of the Story in Spanish

Michael, Lucy y Vincent fueron compañeros en la universidad, pero ahora viven en lugares muy distantes. Después de muchos años, deciden reunirse en Madrid, en el Café Gijón, a la hora del almuerzo. Sin embargo, cada uno de ellos tiene problemas durante el viaje. Michael se pierde en las calles de Madrid, y tiene que pedirle indicaciones al dependiente de un estanco. Al principio no lo comprende, pero finalmente consigue indicaciones. Lucy descubre que la aerolínea perdió su equipaje, y tiene que hacer un reclamo en el aeropuerto. Finalmente, Vincent pierde su tren de alta velocidad, y debe sacar boletos de urgencia en un bus.

Exercises

1. Completa el diálogo con las siguientes palabras: *perdí, aeropuerto, boleto, aerolínea, tuve, equipaje.*
   - No saben lo que me pasó en el _____ – dice Lucy. La _____ perdió mi _____.
   - ¡No me digas! – responde Vincent. Yo también _____ problemas para llegar hasta aquí.
   - ¿Qué ocurrió? – pregunta Michael.
   - Perdí el tren – dice Vincent. Tuve que comprar un _____ de bus.
   - Qué lástima, Vincent – dice Michael. Yo me _____ en el camino hasta aquí. ¡Pero eso no es nada comparado con ustedes dos!

2. Elige la palabra correcta para completar cada oración.
   a. La aerolínea perdió el (maleta/equipaje).
   b. Michael (se perdió/se pierdó) en el camino al café.
   c. Los trenes de alta velocidad salen en (tiempo/horario).
   d. Lucy habla (bien/bueno) español.

3. ¿Cuál de las siguientes oraciones está escrita de manera incorrecta?
   a. Disculpe, pero no entienda.
   b. ¿Dónde está mi equipaje?
   c. ¿Podría repetir, por favor?
   d. Estoy perdido, ¿puede ayudarme?

4. Elige la oración escrita de manera correcta.
   a. ¿Queda dónde el Café Gijón?
   b. ¿El Café Gijón queda?
   c. ¿Dónde el Café Gijón queda?
   d. ¿Dónde queda el Café Gijón?

5. Une un término de cada columna para formar oraciones.

puede	un	por favor
hay	puedo	maletas
perdí	las	bus
a quién	repetir	llamar

Comprehension Questions

1. Where does Michael come from?
2. Where does Michael ask for directions?
3. What happened to Lucy's luggage?
4. What does the airline say to Lucy?
5. Why does Vincent take a bus?

Summary of the Story in English

Michael, Lucy, and Vincent were university classmates, but now they live in very distant places. After several years, they decide to reunite in Madrid, at the Café Gijón, at lunchtime. However, each of them encounters problems during the trip. Michael gets lost in the streets of Madrid and has to ask for directions from the clerk of a smoke shop. At first, he doesn't understand, but he finally gets the directions. Lucy discovers that the airline lost her luggage, and she has to make a complaint at the airport. Finally, Vincent loses his high-speed train and has to take last-minute bus tickets.

Did you know...

Just like it happened to Lucy, our airline can also lose our luggage. It may have fallen from the conveyor belt and have never left the airport of origin, or it may have gone on another plane to a different destination. For whatever reason, these things are quite common.

If this happens to you, the first thing you need to do is make a complaint before leaving the airport. It's very important that you don't leave the airport without your luggage and without having talked to someone from the airline. That's what Lucy did, and she was very lucky because they sent her luggage to her hotel the next day.

The Madrid airport, Barajas, is really big (so big that it has its own train to move around within), but don't fret. You should look for your airline's counter or, if not, an information counter. There, you should make a complaint if your luggage is missing or if you found it broken or open.

Generally, airlines provide economic compensation for lost elements or for the cost of the elements you will need to buy to replace the loss. To get a reimbursement, they will probably ask you to save all the receipts for everything you've bought. Besides, if your luggage is broken, they may need to give you a new one.

Lastly, a great grandma's advice: always carry extra underwear and hygiene products in your handbag! And, above all, if you take daily medicine, never put it in your checked luggage, always have it with you even if it's a short trip.

Chapter 10: Me duele aquí... - The human body

Story in Spanish: La visita al doctor

Nora y su amiga Patricia están conversando en el banco de una plaza. Es un día **nublado**, pero caluroso.

– Ay, esta humedad es horrible para mi **rodilla** – se queja Nora.

– Dímelo a mí – le responde Patricia. Me duele muchísimo el **ciático**.

– ¿Y el frío de la semana pasada? Me dejó con un **dolor de garganta**...

– Oye, Nora, cuidado con el dolor de garganta, puede ser una **gripe**. Hay muchos virus dando vueltas.

– ¿Tú crees? ¿Debería ir al **médico**?

– Sí, para quedarte tranquila. A nuestra edad... Y yo te acompaño, quiero que me revisen el **corazón**.

– Vale... Además, nunca está de más ir a ver al doctor Sánchez, ¡es tan amable!

– ¡Y tan **buen mozo**! – completa Patricia.

Patricia y Nora se encuentran al día siguiente en el hospital para ir juntas al médico. Son amigas desde hace años, siempre las atiende el mismo doctor y las deja pasar juntas a la consulta. El doctor Sánchez es un hombre alto y **canoso, de edad avanzada**, que usa un **bastón**.

– ¡Nora, Patricia! Qué alegría verlas otra vez, pero ¿no estuvieron aquí la semana pasada? ¿Qué ha pasado?

- Sí, doctor, pero es que me duele muchísimo la rodilla, ¿estará rota? - le pregunta Nora, asustada.

- No, Nora, le tienes que preguntar por el dolor de garganta - la ayuda Patricia.

- Ah, sí, eso también, tengo un dolor fatal en la garganta - agrega Nora.

- Vale, a ver, si quieres te hago una **radiografía** en la rodilla, pero si fuera una **fractura** no podrías caminar, Nora. ¿Hace cuánto te duele la garganta?

- Desde la semana pasada, por el frío.

- Vale, te revisaré. Abre la **boca**, por favor, y di "ah".

- Ahhhhh.

El doctor Sánchez **examina** la garganta de Nora.

- Está un poco **inflamada**, pero estoy seguro de que se soluciona con un rico té con limón y miel. Estás **sana** como un **roble**, no te preocupes. ¿Y tú, Patricia? ¿Quieres que te revise el corazón?

- Sí, por favor. Me dolió el **pecho** hace unos días, y **me quedo sin aliento** al subir las escaleras - responde Patricia.

- Vale, a ver - dice el doctor Sánchez mientras coge su **estetoscopio**. **Respira**, por favor. Ahora intenta **toser**.

Patricia hace lo que el doctor le indica.

- Todo se escucha bien, Patricia. Cuando subas las escaleras, tómate tu tiempo para no quedarte sin aliento. Están las dos impecables, no tienen nada de qué preocuparse.

- Muchas gracias, doctor.

- Sí, muchas gracias. Hasta luego, doctor - lo saluda Nora.

Las dos amigas salen del hospital y regresan caminando juntas.

- Nora, ¿no te ha dicho el doctor que tomes un **jarabe para la tos**? ¿Te ha dicho cuál? - pregunta de pronto Patricia.

- ¿Me ha dicho que tome un jarabe? ¡No lo recuerdo!

- Tendremos que volver mañana - dice Patricia. Si te ha dado un jarabe, debes tomarlo.

- Sí, tienes razón, tendremos que volver mañana - le responde Nora, con una sonrisa cómplice.

Vocabulary List

Español	Inglés
nublado	cloudy
la rodilla	knee
el ciático	sciatic nerve
el dolor de garganta	sore throat
la gripe	flu
médico, médica	doctor
el corazón	heart
buen mozo, buena moza	handsome
canoso, canosa	gray-haired
de edad avanzada	elderly
el bastón	cane
la radiografía	X-ray
la fractura	fracture
la boca	mouth
examinar	to examine
inflamada, inflamado	swollen

sana, sano	healthy
el roble	oak
el pecho	chest
quedarse sin aliento	to be short of breath
el estetoscopio	stethoscope
respirar	to breathe
toser	to cough
el jarabe para la tos	cough syrup

Summary of the Story in Spanish

Nora y Patricia están conversando en una plaza y se quejan de los dolores que tienen. Deciden ir juntas a ver al médico que las atiende siempre, el doctor Sánchez. Se encuentran al día siguiente para ir al hospital. El doctor Sánchez primero atiende a Nora, que teme tener una fractura en la rodilla. La tranquiliza y, además, revisa su garganta. Le dice que no tiene nada grave, que tome un poco de té. Después revisa el corazón de Patricia y también la tranquiliza. Les dice a ambas que están sanas y que no tienen nada por lo que preocuparse. Cuando salen del hospital, Patricia le pregunta a Nora si el doctor le ha dado un jarabe y si le ha dicho qué jarabe debe tomar. Nora se confunde y cree que se ha olvidado del nombre del jarabe. Las amigas deciden volver al día siguiente para preguntarle al doctor sobre el jarabe.

Exercises

1. ¿Cuál de estas oraciones está escrita correctamente?

    a. Me dolor la garganta

    b. Me duele la garganta

    c. Me duelen la garganta

    d. Me dolores la garganta

2. Conecta cada palabra con su traducción en inglés
   a. rodilla   heart
   b. garganta   sciatic nerve
   c. ciático   knee
   d. corazón   throat

3. Completa el siguiente párrafo con las palabras correctas

   Tengo que ir al _____ (bastón/hospital) a que me vea un _____ (médico/roble), porque me _____ (tose/duele) mucho el _____ (estetoscopio/pecho).

4. ¿Cuál de estas oraciones está escrita de manera incorrecta?
   a. La garganta está inflamada
   b. Me duele la gripe
   c. Debo tomar un jarabe para la tos
   d. El médico me examinó el corazón

5. Completa las siguientes oraciones con el adjetivo que corresponda:
   a. El día está _____.
   b. El doctor es muy _____ y _____.
   c. Nora es _____, tiene el pelo gris.

Comprehension Questions

1. Why does Nora's knee hurt?
2. What does Patricia tell Nora about her sore throat?
3. What is Dr. Sánchez like?
4. What does the doctor recommend for Patricia?
5. Why do the friends decide to return the next day?

Summary of the Story in English

Nora and Patricia are talking in a park, complaining about their aches. They decide to go together to see their doctor: Dr. Sánchez. They meet up the next day to go to the hospital. Dr. Sánchez first looks at Nora, who's afraid she has a broken knee. He calms her and also checks her throat. He tells her there's nothing serious wrong, and that she should drink some tea. Then he checks Patricia's heart and also calms her down. He tells both of them that they are healthy and that they have nothing to worry about. When they leave the hospital, Patricia asks Nora if the doctor has given her a syrup and if he has told her what syrup to take.

Nora gets confused and thinks she's forgotten the name of the syrup. Both friends decide to go back the next day to ask the doctor about the syrup.

Did you know...

Most Spaniards use the public health system. This system is managed entirely by the State, and patients do not have to pay for care, hospitalization, or medicine. The system is funded through citizens' taxes, so to use it, you must be a legal resident of the country.

Spain requires tourists to have health insurance that has coverage in the country. Nevertheless, exceptions are made for foreigners in cases of extreme urgency, such as accidents, serious illnesses, or childbirth.

Dental and vision care are not covered in the public health system. This means that patients have to pay for the entire treatment. Alternatively, they can have private health insurance, which covers at least part of it. These private health insurances operate on a monthly fee paid by the patient. Depending on the amount of the fee and the insurer, the patient will have more or less coverage.

While public health works very well, there are people who choose private health insurance, mainly for two reasons: they offer a greater supply of professionals and care centers, and, in addition, they usually have shorter waiting times to get appointments.

Chapter 11: ¡Salud! – Special Occasions

Story in Spanish: Eventos

La boda

Francisco está radiante. Todo se ve perfecto, el salón está impecable y todos sus **seres queridos** están a punto de llegar. Han planeado este día durante meses y por fin ha llegado. Es un precioso día de agosto y hace un **calor** agradable. Ezequiel está en la habitación de al lado. No pueden verse porque es de mala suerte, pero intercambian mensajes.

– ¿Viste quién ha llegado?

– ¡Tu **prima**, Bea! Ha venido desde Segovia, no me lo puedo creer.

– Sí, también, pero yo me refiero a tu **tío**...

– Ah, sí. Y vino con su nueva **esposa**, sus **hijos** y toda la familia.

– Ya veo. ¡Mira, ahí está tu **abuela**! Qué guapa está...

Alguien golpea la puerta en la habitación de Francisco. Su **hermana** le avisa que ya está todo listo y que debe prepararse para bajar.

La **ceremonia** es sencilla pero **emotiva**. Todos están muy emocionados. Francisco y Ezequiel se prometen amor eterno, cuidarse en la salud y la enfermedad y, finalmente, intercambian anillos. "¡**Viva!**", "¡**Olé!**", "¡**Que vivan los novios!**", gritan los invitados. Todo es una fiesta.

Después, llega el momento más esperado: la comida y el baile. Los novios están sentados en su mesa, mientras sus invitados pasan a saludarlos.

- **Enhorabuena**, chicos – dice Luisa, la madre de Ezequiel.

- **Felicitaciones**, hijo – dice emocionado el padre de Francisco.

- ¡**Salud**! ¡Por vosotros! – grita el tío Jorge, que ya ha bebido unas cuantas copas.

- ¡Salud, dinero y amor! – lo corrige Amalia, su sobrina.

Allí están todos sus amigos, colegas y familiares. En la mesa de los amigos de siempre cuentan anécdotas vergonzosas de las que nadie se salva. En otra mesa, Francisco ha puesto, sin querer, a Adriana (su **cuñada**) con Luis (su **exmarido**). Esa mesa no es tan divertida.

Todos bailan, beben y comen. Francisco y Ezequiel bailan juntos toda la noche, muy enamorados. Este es, sin dudas, el mejor día de sus vidas.

La Navidad

Francisco está desesperado. Esta es la primera Navidad que organiza con Ezequiel en su nueva casa y todo está saliendo mal. Los invitados han llegado y la comida todavía no está lista, ha discutido con Ezequiel y, para colmo, no ha podido comprar ningún **regalo**.

Observa a su familia mientras controla el **pavo** en el **horno**. Su madre discute de política con el tío de Ezequiel. Su abuela no habla con nadie, pero grita "¡**Feliz Navidad**!" a todos los que pasan por al lado.

Sus hermanas están encerradas en el **lavabo**, maquillándose y sacándose fotos. Su padre sigue atentamente los movimientos de Ezequiel, que ordena la casa discretamente:

- ¡**Felices fiestas**, tía! – exclama mientras patea debajo del sillón un par de **pantuflas**. Gracias por venir, Antonio – dice con una sonrisa mientras recoge unas tazas sucias.

Finalmente, Francisco llama a todos a la mesa: la comida está lista. Todos se acomodan haciendo mucho ruido, y el abuelo guarda un **bocata** que había sacado del bolsillo a escondidas.

- ¡FRANCISCO! – grita Ezequiel desde la cocina.

- ¿Qué pasa?

- ¿Tú has controlado el pavo?

- Sí...

- ¿Lo has probado?

- Bueno, no...

- ¿Lo has mirado?

- Bueno, no...

– ¡El horno estaba apagado! ¡Este pavo está crudísimo!

Ezequiel sale de la cocina.

– Familia, sé que todos estáis muy hambrientos, pero deberéis esperar un poco más... hasta que llegue la pizza.

Sin dudas, esta no será la mejor Navidad de sus vidas.

Vocabulary List

Español	Inglés
los seres queridos	loved ones
el calor	warmth
el primo, la prima	cousin
el tío, la tía	uncle, aunt
el esposo, la esposa	husband, wife
los hijos, las hijas	children
el abuelo, la abuela	grandfather, grandmother
el hermano, la hermana	brother, sister
la ceremonia	ceremony
emotivo, emotiva	touching
¡Viva!	Hurrah!
¡Olé!	Bravo!
¡Qué vivan los novios!	Long live the grooms!

Enhorabuena	Congratulations
Felicitaciones	Congratulations
Salud	Cheers / To your health
la cuñada	sister-in-law
el exmarido	ex-husband
el regalo	the present
el pavo	the turkey
el horno	oven
Feliz Navidad	Merry Christmas
el lavabo	bathroom
Felices fiestas	Happy holidays
las pantuflas	slippers
el bocata	sandwich

Summary of the Story in Spanish

En la primera parte, Ezequiel y Francisco están a punto de casarse. Ven llegar a los invitados: todos sus seres queridos están allí. La ceremonia es muy emotiva y luego todos felicitan a los recién casados. La fiesta es muy divertida, todos bailan, beben y comen. En la segunda parte, unos meses después, Ezequiel y Francisco celebran la primera Navidad en su casa. Las cosas no salen bien. La casa está desordenada y la comida no está lista. Mientras Francisco cocina, Ezequiel ordena la casa, intentando que los invitados no noten nada. Cuando están por sentarse a comer, Ezequiel descubre que el horno estaba apagado y que el pavo está crudo. Deciden pedir una pizza.

Exercises

1. Conecta cada término con su significado.

    a. prima   children

    b. esposo   sister-in-law

    c. hermano   cousin

    d. hijos   grandfather

    e. cuñada   husband

    f. abuelo   brother

2. Completa este diálogo con las siguientes palabras: *regalos, enhorabuena, feliz Navidad, ¡viva!, felices fiestas.*

    A: Hola, Paula, ¡_____ _____!

    B: ¡_____ _____, Camila! ¿Has recibido _____?

    A: ¡Sí! Me han regalado una casa de muñecas. ¿Y tú?

    B: ¡_____! A mí me regalaron un par de zapatos.

    A: ¡_____!

3. Selecciona la manera correcta de escribir la siguiente palabra.

    a. felisitasiones

    b. felicitaciones

    c. felicitasiones

    d. felisitaciones

4. Indica si estas oraciones son verdaderas o falsas.

    a. El hijo de mi tía es mi sobrino

    b. El papá de mi mamá es mi abuelo

    c. La hermana de mi novia es mi prima

    d. El hermano de mi papá es mi tío

5. Selecciona de la historia tres maneras distintas de felicitar a una pareja recién casada.

Comprehension Questions

1. What's the weather like on the day of the wedding?

2. How do Ezequiel and Francisco talk before the wedding?

3. Why is Francisco desperate during Christmas dinner?

4. Who's arguing about politics before Christmas dinner?

5. What happened to the turkey?

Summary of the Story in English

In the first part, Ezequiel and Francisco are about to get married. They watch the guests arrive: all their loved ones are there. The ceremony is very touching, and then everyone congratulates the newlyweds. The party is very fun, everyone dances, drinks, and eats. In the second part, a few months later, Ezequiel and Francisco celebrate their first Christmas at home. Things don't go okay. The house is messy, and the food is not ready. While Francisco cooks, Ezequiel tidies the house, trying not to let the guests notice. When they are about to sit down to eat, Ezequiel discovers that the oven was off and that the turkey is raw. They decide to order a pizza.

Did you know...

In Spain, weddings are similar to those in other cultures: the bride usually wears a white dress and the groom an elegant suit. However, there's a big difference with US weddings: traditional Spanish weddings are catholic celebrations, which means that they are officiated by a priest or clergyman.

Another difference from American weddings is they have *padrinos*. Instead of having bridesmaids and groomsmen, in Spain, the groom and bride are joined by a *padrino* (which could be translated as "godfather") and a *madrina* (which could be translated as "godmother"), which are generally the bride's father and the groom's mother.

Another Spanish custom shared by other countries is throwing rice at the newlyweds. It is said that this symbolizes a desire for prosperity for the new couple so that they may never starve. In the last few years, rice has been replaced by rose petals (to make less mess!).

Spanish weddings are very exciting... and fun! After the religious ceremony comes the party! Generally, the bride and groom and their respective parents sit at the main table while the rest of the guests are distributed at other tables. Typically, the receptions are done at night and finish very late, even in the early morning. During the party, there is food, music, and live shows.

Lastly, a Spanish wedding custom is the tie cut. At the party, the groom's friends cut his tie and divide the pieces among the guests. Sometimes, the pieces are even sold to the guests to raise money for the newlyweds. A similar tradition is that the bride throws the flower bouquet backward; superstition says that the woman who catches it is the next to be married.

Chapter 12: Lo que hice hoy – What I Did Today

Story in Spanish: El faro

Manolo se despertó, **miró** el reloj y soltó un grito. ¡Eran casi las nueve de la mañana! Se levantó, **se cepilló los dientes**, se vistió rápidamente y salió corriendo de su casa. No había tiempo para ducharse.

Esperó el autobús en la parada. Cuando **llegó**, se subió, **pagó** su boleto y se sentó en uno de los asientos que había al fondo. Luego, sacó su móvil del bolsillo y leyó las noticias del día.

«Una gran tormenta dejó árboles caídos e **inundaciones** en Santander», decía. Manolo se preocupó. Santander no estaba lejos del pueblo.

El autobús llegó al puerto. Manolo se bajó y **caminó** los doscientos metros que lo separaban de su trabajo. Cuando llegó al **faro**, vio a Concepción, la cuidadora nocturna. Ella miraba su reloj, impaciente.

- Manolo, ¡por fin llegas! – dijo Concepción. Te esperé un buen rato.

- Lo siento, Concepción. No sonó mi **despertador** esta mañana. ¿Alguna novedad?

- Sí: parece que se acerca una tormenta. Llamé al departamento de meteorología y me dijeron que comenzará por la tarde.

- Siempre me ponen nervioso las tempestades – dijo Manolo.

- Pero ¡qué dices! Si eres el mejor farero de España – respondió Concepción con una sonrisa. Se puso el abrigo y se marchó.

Manolo **subió** los 250 escalones que lo separaban de la cúpula del faro y empezó a trabajar. Al mediodía, **bajó** a comprar comida a la tienda de abastos del puerto, un pequeño comercio atendido por un hombre viejo y barbudo llamado Tristán.

- Aquí tienes tu sándwich de **mariscos**, como siempre - le dijo Tristán. ¿Así que Concepción está aprendiendo a manejar las máquinas de la cúpula?

- ¿Cómo? - preguntó Manolo, desconcertado. No, Concepción es la cuidadora nocturna.

- Entonces... ¿quién está allá arriba? - preguntó Tristán, señalando a través de la ventana de su tienda.

Manolo se dio media vuelta y miró hacia arriba. Era cierto: en la cúpula del faro había una silueta.

Le pagó a Tristán y **corrió** en dirección al faro. «Quizá Concepción se olvidó algo y regresó a buscarlo. O a lo mejor es un turista demasiado curioso», pensó mientras subía la escalera.

Cuando llegó a la cúpula del faro, vio a una joven muchacha sonriente.

- ¡Mar! - dijo Manolo.

- Hola, papá - saludó Mar, y corrió a abrazarlo.

- ¿Qué estás haciendo aquí?

- Quise darte una sorpresa - explicó Mar. **Volé** desde Sevilla esta misma mañana. Necesitaba un fin de semana cerca del océano.

- ¡Gracias por esta hermosa sorpresa! - le dijo Manolo.

Manolo cortó por la mitad su sándwich de mariscos. Él y su hija **almorzaron** y **conversaron** durante horas mientras miraban el océano. Mar le contó que le iba muy bien en la universidad, y que estaba planeando mudarse a un **piso** en el centro junto a una compañera.

Al atardecer, llegó la tormenta. Primero, despacio; luego, más fuerte: las **gotas** de lluvia golpearon los cristales del faro. Abajo, el mar estaba revuelto. Por suerte, no había ningún barco en el área. La única tarea de Manolo era avisar a las embarcaciones que evitaran la zona. La lluvia se detuvo cerca de las seis de la tarde, justo cuando terminaba el turno de Manolo.

Él y Mar bajaron la escalera del faro.

- Bueno, ¿qué quieres hacer ahora? - le preguntó Manolo. ¿Ir al cine? ¿Dar un paseo?

Mar miró el cielo. Todavía estaba muy nublado.

– Creo que **me apetece** ir a casa.

Esa noche, Manolo y Mar pidieron pizza, vieron una película en la tele y jugaron a los naipes. Cuando Manolo se acostó, pensó en que su hija estaba creciendo. Él se estaba haciendo mayor. Sonrió: guardaría ese día tan especial por siempre en su memoria.

Vocabulary List

Español	Inglés
mirar	to look at
cepillarse los dientes	to brush one's teeth
esperar	to wait
llegar	to arrive
pagar	to pay
la inundación	flood
caminar	to walk
el faro	lighthouse
el despertador	alarm
subir	to go up
bajar	to go down
el marisco	seafood
correr	to run

volar	to fly
almorzar	to have lunch
conversar	to talk, to converse
el piso	apartment
la gota	drop
Me apetece...	I would like...

Summary of the Story in Spanish

Manolo es un farero español que vive en un pueblo cerca de Santander, España. Un día, mientras espera que llegue una tormenta, recibe una sorpresa: la visita de Mar, su hija, que vive y estudia en Sevilla. Él y Mar pasan un día especial comiendo un sándwich de mariscos, mirando el océano y poniéndose al día. Luego, miran desde lo alto del faro la lluvia y el mar revuelto. Al final del día, ven una película, comen pizza, juegan a los naipes y se van a dormir.

Exercises

1. Completa el siguiente texto con las siguientes palabras: *bebimos, compré, duché, salí, llegué, levanté, pedí, comimos.*

Ayer me _____ temprano. Después de desayunar, fui al gimnasio. Luego, me _____ y me fui a trabajar. En la oficina, cerré un nuevo trato con un cliente, así que mi jefe me felicitó. Durante el mediodía, salí a almorzar con mis compañeros y _____ tortilla de patatas. Cuando _____ del trabajo, me fui al centro comercial y _____ un poco de ropa. Por la noche, fui a festejar el cumpleaños de un amigo y _____ barbacoa. También _____ un poco de vino blanco. Luego, _____ a casa y me acosté.

2. Primero, lee la rutina de un día en la vida de Sabrina, una joven española.

7:00	Levantarse
7:15	Yoga
7:45	Desayuno
8:00	Prepararse para ir a trabajar
9:00	Entrar al trabajo
10:40	Bocadillo de media mañana
14:00	Almuerzo
17:00	Salir del trabajo
18:00	Clase de pintura
19:30	Llegar a casa
20:00	Mirar el capítulo de una serie
21:00	Cenar
23:00	Acostarse

Ahora, responde verdadero o falso:

a. Sabrina hace yoga justo después de desayunar.

b. Sabrina mira el capítulo de una serie a las ocho de la noche.

c. Sabrina tiene clase de teatro a las seis de la tarde.

d. Sabrina sale del trabajo a las cinco de la tarde.

3. ¿En qué momento del día suelen realizarse cada una de las siguientes actividades? *Despertarse, dormirse, levantarse, cenar, acostarse, desayunar, llegar a casa, ir a trabajar, ducharse, relajarse después del trabajo, cocinar la cena, vestirse para ir a trabajar.*

Por la mañana	Por la tarde/noche
Despertarse	*Llegar a casa*

4. Las siguientes frases están escritas de forma incorrecta. ¿Puedes corregirlas?

   a. Miguel se lebanta a las ocho de la mañana.

   b. Manuela se hacuesta a las diez de la noche.

   c. Los domingos, la familia Pérez hace el haseo de la casa.

   d. Los sábados, Ramón sale a bever una copa.

5. Lee el siguiente diálogo y responde las preguntas.

Francisco: ¡Hola, Sonia! ¿Quieres ir a desayunar conmigo?
Sonia: ¡Hola, Francisco! Ya he desayunado. Cada mañana, suelo tomar un café con churros en el bar que hay enfrente. Pero ¡podemos cenar esta noche!

Francisco: Esta noche no puedo. Los martes tengo clase de esgrima. ¿Mañana?
Sonia: Mañana soy yo la que no puede: los miércoles tengo que ir a la autoescuela por la tarde y a mi clase de flamenco por la noche.
Francisco: ¿Y los viernes? ¿Tienes alguna actividad?
Sonia: Este viernes tengo que cuidar a mi sobrina, ¡pero estoy libre por la noche!

Francisco: Estupendo. Entonces, ¡cenamos el viernes!

   a. ¿Cuándo tiene clases de esgrima Francisco?

   b. ¿Qué desayuna Sonia todos los días?

c. ¿Qué clases tiene Sonia los miércoles?

d. ¿Qué hace Sonia este viernes?

Comprehension Questions

1. What happened in Santander?
2. Why was Manolo late for work?
3. Who is Tristán?
4. Who was in the lighthouse cupola?
5. What did Manolo and Mar do at night?

Summary of the Story in English

Manolo is a Spanish lighthouse keeper who lives in a village near Santander, Spain. One day, while waiting for a storm to arrive, he receives a surprise: a visit from Mar, his daughter, who lives and studies in Seville. He and Mar spend a special day eating a seafood sandwich, watching the ocean, and catching up. Then they look out from the top of the lighthouse at the rain and the rolling sea. At the end of the day, they watch a movie, eat pizza, play cards and go to sleep.

Did you know...

In Spain, people's life rhythm is *a bit late* in comparison to other countries. In general, Spanish people get up at around 7 a.m. and have coffee and a light snack for breakfast, like toast with Iberian ham and olive oil, a pastry, or a slice of potato *tortilla*. Then, they get ready and go to work.

While the adults go to work, the children go to school (which is called *colegio*, but they affectionately call it *el cole*). School begins at 08:30 h and goes on until 15 h (that is, 3 p.m. Remember that people use 24-hour clocks in Spain!). After school, children sometimes do extracurricular activities, like English, sports, and music.

Spanish people have lunch at around 15 h. Sometimes (especially on weekends and non-working days), they do the *sobremesa*, a resting period after lunch in which people stay at the table chatting and drinking coffee.

Nap time is very common in small towns and medium-sized cities. It's a period of some hours in which the majority of shops close their doors, and their owners rest for a while. In general, nap time is between 14 h and 16 h.

In Spain, people also have a *merienda* at around 18 h. This food consists of a snack made of cold cuts (like *chorizo*) and a cup of some infusion or chocolate milk, which is especially popular among children.

Long days, mild climate, and night leisure results in Spanish people dining very late, nearly 22 h. In general, dinner is lighter than lunch. It's also common to have some drinks and walk around the city after dinner, especially if one doesn't work the next day.

Chapter 13: Mis planes – My Future Plans

Story in Spanish: El diario

Querido diario:

Hoy la profesora Muñoz me ha dicho que **interpretaré** a Julieta en la **obra de teatro** de la escuela "Romeo y Julieta: el musical". Cuando recibí la noticia, no lo podía creer. Mis padres me han felicitado y el próximo sábado haremos una gran fiesta en casa para celebrarlo. Vendrán mi tía Antonia y mis primos, Pedro e Ignacio.

Estoy muy feliz de interpretar a la **protagonista,** pero también estoy un poco nerviosa. Tendré que aprenderme un guion muy largo y tendré que cantar. Además, la profesora Muñoz es muy exigente: seguramente me marcará cada **error.** Ella querrá que la obra salga **genial.**

Me encantaría ser actriz profesional en un futuro. Aún no se lo he dicho a mis padres, pero se lo diré el sábado, durante la fiesta que daremos en casa. Mi **sueño** es ser una actriz reconocida, ¡como Penélope Cruz! Quiero hacer películas y series en España y en todo el mundo, porque viajar es una de mis **metas.**

¡Y hablando de viajar...! La noticia sobre el papel protagonista no ha sido la única sorpresa de hoy. Mi tía Antonia me ha enviado un mensaje esta mañana y me ha escrito: "Laura, te diré algo que te pondrá muy contenta. En invierno nos iremos de vacaciones a Sudamérica, y queremos que tú y tu hermana vengáis con nosotros".

¡**Qué pasada**! Iremos a Argentina, Chile y Brasil. Pasaremos por sitios increíbles como las **cataratas** del Iguazú, la Patagonia y la **selva** amazónica. **Partiremos** en diciembre y el viaje durará cerca de un mes. Será muy divertido, porque mi hermana y yo nos llevamos muy bien con nuestros primos Pedro e Ignacio. ¡Estoy deseando!

Ahora debo irme. Esta noche, mi amiga Sara festejará su cumpleaños en su casa y hará una **pijamada**. Seguramente, veremos una película y jugaremos a algún juego. La mamá de Sara hará **bocadillos** para todas. Pero no nos acostaremos muy tarde, porque mañana tenemos que ir al colegio y tenemos un examen de **mates**.

Vocabulary List

Español	Inglés
interpretar	to interpret
la obra de teatro	A play
el protagonista, la protagonista	main role
el error	mistake
genial	great
el sueño	dream
la meta	goal
¡Qué pasada!	What a blast!
las cataratas	waterfalls
la selva	rainforest
la pijamada	sleepover

partir	to leave
el bocadillo	snack
mates	math

Summary of the Story in Spanish

En su diario íntimo, Laura cuenta que su profesora de teatro, la señora Muñoz, la ha elegido para interpretar a Julieta en la obra escolar "Romeo y Julieta: el musical". Laura está contenta, aunque está un poco nerviosa porque tendrá que aprenderse un guion muy largo. Para festejar la noticia, la familia hará una fiesta el sábado.

Por otro lado, Laura y su hermana han sido invitadas a un viaje por Sudamérica junto a su tía Antonia y sus primos Pedro e Ignacio. Irán a Argentina, Chile y Brasil en un viaje que durará un mes.

Por último, Laura tiene que prepararse para la fiesta de cumpleaños de su amiga Sara: una pijamada. Allí, verán una película, jugarán a juegos y comerán bocadillos hechos por la madre de Sara.

Exercises

1. ¿Puedes completar los espacios en blanco con los verbos correspondientes conjugados en futuro simple?

    a. (Viajar - Yo): _____ a Italia en marzo.

    b. (Estudiar - Tú): Sé que _____ mucho para ese examen.

    c. (Salir - Ella): Rosa _____ a cenar con sus amigas.

    d. (Ir - Nosotros): _____ a dar un paseo al atardecer.

2. Completa los espacios en blanco en el siguiente diálogo. Usa las formas conjugadas de los verbos *ver, aprobar, ser, probar, tener* y *montar*.

    A: Hola, David. ¿Estás bien? Pareces tenso.

    B: Hola, Alberto. Estoy un poco nervioso, porque mañana por la mañana _____ mi examen final de la carrera de Gastronomía.

    A: Entonces, ¿pasado mañana ya _____ un chef profesional?

    B: Así es. Bueno, si apruebo el examen, claro.

    A: Por supuesto que lo _____. Ya _____ que pronto _____ tu propio restaurante... ¡y yo _____ tu deliciosa comida!

3. Ahora, responde las siguientes preguntas sobre el ejercicio anterior.

    a. ¿Cuándo tiene su examen David?

    b. ¿En qué se convertirá David?

    c. ¿Qué piensa Alberto sobre el futuro de David?

4. ¿Cuál de las siguientes frases está bien escrita?

    a. David será un cosinero profesional.

    b. David será un cocinero profecional.

    c. David será un cosinero profesional.

    d. David será un cocinero profesional.

5. Elige la palabra correcta en cada caso.
El _____ (sueño/meta) de mi hija menor es ser veterinaria. Dice que _____ (curarán/curará) a todos los animales de la ciudad. Mi otra hija, la mayor, tiene la _____ (meta/sueña) de ser arquitecta. Dice que _____ (construirá/construiré) edificios por todo el mundo. Hagan lo que hagan, si le ponen pasión y cariño, estoy segura de que ambas _____ (estarán/serán) muy buenas en lo suyo.

Comprehension Questions

1. What will Laura do to celebrate having been chosen for the leading role?

2. What's Laura's dream?

3. What's one of Laura's goals?

4. What places will Laura visit in the winter?

5. What are Laura's plans for the night?

Summary of the Story in English

In her diary, Laura writes down that her drama teacher, Mrs. Muñoz, has chosen her to play Juliet in the school play "Romeo and Juliet: The Musical." Laura is happy, although she's a little nervous because she will have to study a very long script. To celebrate the news, her family will have a party on Saturday.

On the other hand, Laura and her sister have been invited on a trip to South America with her aunt Antonia and her cousins Pedro and Ignacio. They will travel to Argentina, Chile, and Brazil on a month-long trip.

Finally, Laura has to get ready for her friend Sara's birthday party: a sleepover. There, they will watch a movie, play games, and eat snacks made by Sara's mother.

Did you know...

Spain is a country that is always looking to the future. For example, it's one of the pioneer countries in the production of green hydrogen. Green hydrogen is a strong renewable source of energy that doesn't harm the planet when it's produced or when it's used.

The problem with green hydrogen is that it's very expensive to generate. Luckily, Spain is one of the countries that can produce it at a not-so-high price. At this moment, several projects related to this topic are underway.

On top of this, Spanish people are also at the leading age when it comes to technology. For example, the Mobile World Congress (MWC) has been taking place in Barcelona since 2006. This congress gathers companies, designers, users, and investors in mobile communications and is where news and developments in robotics, computer science, and artificial intelligence are presented, among other things.

What can we expect from our mobile phones in the future? Will Spain manage to neutralize carbon, along with other countries of the European Union, by 2050? We will have to wait and see!

Appendix I: Translation & Answer Sheet

Translations

Chapter 1

Short story: The Birthday

Lucía is thrilled. Today is the birthday of Javier, her son, who lives in Seville. She is sitting in front of the computer, about to buy plane tickets to go visit him. But she wants to confirm the dates with him. She knows he works a lot and doesn't want to bother him. When she phones him, the conversation doesn't go too well.

"Hello, Javi!"

"Good morning, mom."

"Happy birthday! How are you?"

"Fine, but I'm busy now, mom. Can we talk later?"

"Yes, of course. So long."

"Goodbye."

Lucía hangs up, hoping to speak with his son again in the evening and, thus, confirm her trip. After work, she calls him again.

"Good afternoon, Javi. Can you talk now?"

"What's up, mom? Kind of."

"I just thought I'd surprise you and visit you, but I wanted to talk to you before buying the tickets to know which dates you think are best."

"I can't talk now, mom. I'll call you later. See you tomorrow."

Javier hangs up without waiting for a reply. Lucía gets worried. Does her son don't love her anymore? He didn't even say, "How nice, mom, I'll call you later, sleep tight, I love you, kisses..." None of that!

Lucía calls him again, but Javier's phone is off, so she leaves him a message.

"Good evening, Javi. I'm sorry I couldn't find you. What a nice day for your birthday, wasn't it? It's been incredibly sunny here in Madrid. Ok, Javi, I can see you're busy. Don't worry: I'll cancel the trip to Seville. Call me when you can. Talk to you tomorrow. Bye!

Lucía prepares dinner, thinking about Javier and how weird he's acting. That's why he wants to visit him: to see how he's doing, where he lives, what he is eating... While she's thinking about it, her doorbell rings.

"Who is it?"

"Good evening. I have a delivery for Mrs. Lucía Suárez."

"From whom?"

"I don't know, but it comes from Seville."

Lucía runs to open the door, thrilled. And when she opens it, she crashes, face-to-face, with her son.

"Hi, mom! Surprise!"

Chapter 2

Short story: The Interview

The interviewer opens the door. He allows the previous candidate to leave, a tall young man with a short beard. They shake hands firmly. Then, the young man leaves the waiting room, and the interviewer greets Carmen.

"Come in," says the interviewer.

Carmen enters the office. It's spacious and has good lighting. She sits down in a wooden chair that's not very comfortable. The interviewer walks to the other side of the desk to face her.

"My name is Javier Alonso," says the interviewer, extending his hand. Carmen takes it and gives him a handshake. "You are Carmen Pérez Hernández, ¿right?"

"Fernández," answers Carmen, shyly.

"What was that?" asks Javier.

"My last name is Fernández," says Carmen. "I'm Carmen Pérez Fernández."

"Oh, I'm sorry," says Javier. "I must have misread your résumé."

Javier goes through the papers on his desk. Finally, he puts Carmen's résumé right on top of his computer's keyboard.

"Here it is," says Javier. "Pérez Fernández, yes. Do you mind if we fill out some information? Your résumé is very good, but we need more information."

"No problem," replies Carmen.

"How old are you?" asks Javier.

"Thirty-two," answers Carmen.

"Very good," says Javier. "Where do you live?"

"In Alcorcón," answers Carmen.

"Excellent, so you are just a few minutes away by car," says Javier. "Let's continue with the rest. Here it says that you studied at Universidad Politécnica de Madrid.

"Yes, I got a degree in Computer Science and Engineering five years ago," says Carmen. "Then, I did an MBA at Universidad Complutense.

"Very good, that's the end of the education part," says Javier. "Tell me about your work experience."

"My first job was in Telefonía Móvil, while I was studying. Junior programmer," answers Carmen. "I was there for three years. Then I spent five years in a small video game studio, San Isidro. There I had to do a bit of everything, programming tasks as well as managing tasks. That's why I did the master's degree".

"And after that?" asks Javier

"I worked at Banco Industrial," answers Carmen. "Up until a few months ago."

"And why are you interested in working here at Data S. A.?" asks Javier.

"I think it's a great opportunity for me," says Carmen. "I'm at a point in my career in which I'm looking for more responsibilities. I want to make a project grow and feel it's my own. And I think I can do that in Data S. A."

"Very well. Okay, we are almost done," says Javier. "I only need you to tell me a bit about yourself. Do you have any hobbies, any interests that you'd like to share?"

"I really like climbing," answers Carmen. "Normally, I go to a climbing wall in Leganés. But every two other weeks, more or less, I take the car to Sierra de los Gredos. I prefer climbing outdoors."

"I've always wanted to start climbing," says Javier. "I never did it; I don't know why."

"Well, if you are still interested in Leganés, there's an excellent wall," says Carmen. "It's called Vértigo."

"I'll keep that in mind!" says Javier. "Thank you for your time, Carmen. We'll call you next week to let you know our decision."

"Thank you, Javier," answers Carmen.

Chapter 3

Story: Jobs and Professions

1 - Francisco, the teacher

Francisco teaches History at a high school in the center of Madrid for a living. He loves passing his knowledge on to his students. His classes are usually really interesting, and Francisco opens the debate for all his students to say what they think.

2 - Roberto, the bus driver

Roberto's job is driving a bus in Granada. The part he enjoys the most about his job is talking with tourists and recommending places of interest, like the Alhambra castle or the mountain ranges. What he likes the least about being a driver is when he has to take the night shift: Roberto loves getting home early to be with his cats.

3 - Mónica, the businesswoman

Mónica is a successful businesswoman: she is the marketing manager of the best-selling fashion magazine in all of Barcelona. Mónica's favorite moment is when she closes a deal with a client. Despite her busy life, Mónica also enjoys simple things, like a walk around the park or a good talk with her friends.

4 - Pedro, the baker

Pedro opens his bakery every morning at seven o'clock. Some say that his are the best cakes in all of Murcia. When there are few clients, Pedro seizes the opportunity to organize the merchandise, clean the store or contact the suppliers. It's a lonely job, but luckily, he gets on well with Fernanda, the owner of the bookstore across the street.

5 - Marta, the doctor

Marta is a young pediatrician who works at a hospital in Valencia. She *loves* her job: healing children is what makes her the happiest in the world. The bad thing about her job is that she has to be on call for many hours and has to leave her little girl with a babysitter.

6 - Fernando, the waiter

Fernando is a waiter at a bar with views of the sea in Palma de Mallorca. He generally waits tables, although sometimes he has to be behind the bar. At first, he wasn't a very good bartender, but now he is an expert: He prepares the best drinks in the Balearic Islands!

Example Dialogue

Martín: Hi! Sorry to bother you, but can you tell me the wifi password for this coffee shop?

Paula: Of course, the password is the name of the café; that is to say, "Flamenco." And you don't bother me at all. In fact, maybe talking with someone might help me regain inspiration.

Martín: Inspiration? Let me guess: are you a writer?

Paula: Not exactly. I'm a journalist. I work for an online newspaper.

Martín: That sounds interesting. You surely have to do many interviews, research, and articles.

Paula: Yes, it's part of my job. I love it! It's just that I'm a bit blocked right now. I've been asked to write a column for the culture section, but I can't think of anything... Anyway, what do you do?

Martín: I'm an artist. I studied Arts at University, and I did classical painting for a living for years. However, right now, I focus more on digital collage. I discovered that it's one of the art fields that excites me the most. This weekend I will be exhibiting some of my works here in Madrid.

Paula: Hey... I think I have the perfect article for the cultural section. Would you mind granting me an interview?

Chapter 4

Story: Memories

The doctor finishes examining Rafael and says:

"You can go home today. But keep in mind that everything will be harder. He doesn't remember anything before the accident."

Rafael listens to the words, but he doesn't understand them. He's disoriented. He knows he's with his wife and parents, but he doesn't recognize them.

"Shall we, darling?" says Ana, his wife.

Rafael realizes that they are all very excited. He's heard them saying they hope that once Rafael sees his things, he will begin to remember. They arrive at a simple house with stone walls and large windows.

It's a small house. In the dining room, there's a green armchair, worn-out over the years. The TV is resting on an old marble table. Rafael stares at it for a while.

"Do you remember it?" his mother asks. "It's the table from your grandparents' house."

Rafael nods. He doesn't want to disappoint his mother, but the truth is that he is watching an ant that is walking on the table.

He goes over the place with his eyes. On a bookshelf, besides books, he finds several photographs. In most of them, he appears next to Ana, his parents, or other people he doesn't know.

His parents go to the kitchen to make coffee, and Ana goes with him to their room. They start taking things out of the suitcase.

"How long have I been in the hospital?" Rafael asks.

"Three weeks, honey," Ana replies as she takes out of the suitcase two sweaters, a computer, a mobile phone, a mobile phone charger, a toothbrush, and a blanket. "Do you want to have something to eat? A drink?"

"A glass of water would be nice," Rafael says.

"Sure. I'll get it, "Ana replies, and leaves the bedroom.

Rafael stays alone in an unfamiliar room. The bed sheets are soft, and the pillows look comfortable.

In front of him, there's a wooden wardrobe. Suddenly, he's sure of something: if he opens that wardrobe, he'll find, in the last drawer, an old cardboard box. Excited, he runs to the closet, opens the last drawer, and there it is. He opens it without knowing what's inside. Disappointed, he discovers that it's a sewing box: there are needles, thread, pins, and buttons. None of that brings any memories. When he's about to put it away, a white button catches his attention, and he grabs it without knowing why.

He goes down to meet his family, fiddling with the button. Ana sees it and starts crying.

"Do you remember that button, Rafa?"

Rafael looks at her and sees a very clear image in his head: they are in that same dining room, Rafael has a ring in his hand, and he goes down on one knee, but when he does, a button on his shirt shoots out and hits Ana in the nose. They both start laughing, and Ana exclaims:

"Okay, I'll marry you, but don't hit me!"

Rafael starts crying too; he's beginning to remember.

Chapter 5

Story: The Wedding

Paulina and her mother, Gloria, walk through a sidewalk in Madrid. Suddenly, they stop in front of a shop window. It's a store devoted to wedding dresses. Paulina takes out her phone and confirms that they've arrived at the right address. Then, they go in. Adriana, one of the shop assistants, welcomes them.

"Good morning, my name is Adriana," she says. "Can I help you?"

"Yes, thank you," answers Gloria. "Look, my daughter is getting married in a few months, and we're looking for a simple dress. It will be an intimate party."

"Nothing too ornate, please," says Paulina. "It's not my style."

"Ok," answers Adriana. "I'm sure we'll find something. Come with me, please."

Adriana guides Gloria and Paulina to the back of the store. There, they have three racks with different dress designs. Adriana takes one and shows it to Paulina.

"Something like this?" asks Adriana.

"Yes, although... Well, not exactly," answers Paulina. She looks at herself in the mirror with the dress over her torso.

"It's gorgeous," says Gloria.

"I'm not saying it's ugly," answers Paulina. "It just isn't for me. What other options do you have?"

"If you want, you can try one of these on," says Adriana while she takes another dress. "They are from our new collection. It's modest yet elegant. But if it was black, you could wear it to a gala."

Paulina takes the dress and looks at it thoroughly. A shadow crosses her eyes, and then she looks at her mother.

"The new collection?" asks Paulina. "I don't think..."

"Go on, try it on," answers Gloria. "At least to see how it fits you."

"I guess it can't do any harm," says Paulina. "Adriana, do you have a size 40?"

"Of course," answers Adriana. "Here, this will do."

Paulina gets into the fitting room with the dress and spends a few minutes there. When she gets out, she has a surprised expression on her face, almost stunned.

"It's...," says Paulina. She can't finish the sentence.

"It's really cute," finishes Gloria. "Let me look at the back... Yes, it's really cute."

"It's perfect," answers Paulina.

"How much does it cost?" asks Gloria.

"Well, as I said, it's a design from our latest collection," answers Adriana. "That means that the price is... isn't cheap."

"We can keep on looking," says Paulina.

"No, Pauli, the dress is perfect," answers Gloria. "Let's not give up so easily. How much are we talking about?"

"Two thousand three hundred euros," says Adriana. She tries to soften the news with a smile, but she isn't successful.

Gloria lets out a sigh. Paulina leaves the dress immediately on one of the racks. She's afraid of breaking it by accident.

"I guess we can stretch..." says Gloria after a few seconds.

"Mom, no," answers Paulina. "It's very expensive. It's really beyond our budget."

"I know, Pauli," says Gloria. "But you'll get married only once. Well, at least once. But we don't know if there will be another one."

Paulina smiles a bit. Her mom never understood what she saw in Arturo. She doesn't dislike him; it's just that she thinks he's a bit bland. But she's more than willing to respect her daughter's decision.

"I'm sorry to interrupt," says Adriana suddenly. "I... Well, I have an offer to make you."

"What?" asks Paulina.

"The thing is that sellers have a discount, you know," says Adriana. "An employee discount. Pretty big. About thirty percent, I think. We can only use it once a year, and I will turn one year working here in two weeks, so..."

"You would do that for me?" says Paulina, suddenly thrilled.

Adriana shrugs.

"You said the dress was perfect," she answers.

"Thank you!" says Paulina while she hugs Adriana. "Thank you very much!"

"You're welcome; it's my pleasure," says Adriana, slightly uncomfortable. "But I have one condition."

At that moment, Paulina lets go of Adriana and distances herself. Suddenly, she feels the shadow of doubt again.

"You have to invite me to the wedding!" says Adriana finally.

"Of course, you are invited!" answers Paulina. "Write down the date right now, please."

Chapter 6

Story: The Tourist

Sebastián walks around the Gothic Quarter, disoriented and tired. His travel bag is heavy, and the weather is very warm. He's spent several days in Barcelona, but he has not yet become familiar with the old town. It looks like a maze: it is full of narrow streets, passages, and alleys.

"Whoever designed the city probably had fun thinking about the number of tourists that were going to get lost," Sebastián thinks, smiling, and he leaves the bag on the floor for a moment to take some air.

Then, a man dressed in a suit walks by. "He has to be a local," Sebastián thinks. "What kind of tourist wears a suit on the street?"

"Excuse me, sir," says Sebastian. "I need to get to the airport. Can you tell me how to get there?"

"Of course," replies the man. "You need to take the subway and a bus. Keep walking down this street until you see the subway station of line 3. Take the subway and get off at Plaza España. There, you will find the bus stop of the bus line that goes to the airport."

"Thank you very much." Sebastián walks in the direction the man told him.

He gets to the subway without any problems, he gets off at Plaza España, and then he takes the bus. Fortunately, the journey is quick. It's Sunday morning, and there's not much traffic in Barcelona.

When he gets to his destination, he's faced with another problem. The airport is too big! He looks at his watch: it's eight a.m., and his flight leaves at nine o'clock. He still needs to check in and drop his bags off. And on top of that, he's starving because he hasn't had any breakfast yet.

Sebastián approaches the information desk. There's a woman on the other side.

"Good morning, madam," he says. "I need to check in and drop my bags off. Where are the counters?"

"Where are you flying, sir?"

"I'm going to Madrid with Fluffy Clouds airline."

"You have to go up two floors. You can use the escalator."

"And where's the escalator?"

"About two hundred meters in a straight line. You can also use the elevator, which is located at the end of that hallway."

"Thank you very much. Oh! One more thing... Can you tell me where there's a cafeteria?"

"Of course. There is a food court on the third floor of the airport. However, I advise you to hurry, or you'll miss your flight!"

Sebastián thanks the woman and runs towards the escalator. There will be time to have some chocolate and churros in Madrid!

Chapter 7

Story: The Friend

Lisa is the first one to arrive at the restaurant. She sits at a table by the window; five minutes later, Gloria arrives. Lisa and Gloria were friends when they were little, but they stopped seeing each other for a long time. This is the first time they get together to have lunch in ten years. They have a lot to talk about.

"Do you want to look at the menu?" Lisa asks Gloria. "The specialty of the place is pasta; I think they don't have other dishes."

"No, it's not okay; I know what I want," answers Gloria, beckoning the waiter with a gesture. "Well, tell me about you!"

Before Lisa can answer, the waiter arrives.

"I'd like to order the ravioli with filleto sauce, please," orders Lisa.

"I want grilled fish," says Gloria.

"We don't serve fish, ma'am," the waiter says.

"Okay, but I have to eat fish, so go and ask if they can cook fish for me now," replies Gloria as she waves the waiter away. "Well, Lisa, honey, how are you?"

Lisa is a little disgusted by her friend's attitude, but she doesn't want to make a scene, so she continues talking.

"Well, I'm working in a bookstore and..."

"Oh!" Gloria interrupts, "I love bookstores. Whenever I'm in one, I try not to buy everything, but it's very difficult! Did you know my father worked in a bookstore once? Is yours specialized in something? My father's had mostly books about cooking and traveling; what are those called? Well, I don't know, but they are really magical places, aren't they?"

As Gloria speaks, the waiter arrives and tells her that, indeed, they don't serve fish. She can order something from the menu. Gloria, without looking at the menu, orders a serving of paella.

"We don't serve paella, ma'am. We serve pasta and some beef dishes, but we don't have any fish."

Gloria makes a gesture of disgust.

"Okay, don't bring me anything; I'll share what she's ordered."

Lisa is so appalled by her friend's attitude that she doesn't dare to say anything. She's starving, but she doesn't want to contradict her; she wants the lunch to end as soon as possible. Gloria keeps talking and talking until the food arrives. Lisa tries to prong a ravioli, but Gloria takes the plate from her, tries one, and calls the waiter:

"This is cold. Go heat it up, now."

Lisa blushes; she can't believe her friend's bad manners. She tries to say something, but Gloria's already talking again:

"I tried to work, you know? But it wasn't my thing; it was very difficult for me to keep a schedule, to be told what I have to do... You know, I'm a very independent woman."

The waiter comes back with the dish of steaming ravioli. It's very hot. Lisa can't even get one in her mouth, and neither can Gloria. Nevertheless, she calls the waiter again.

"This doesn't have any salt; it's disgusting. My friend and I are leaving because of the lousy service. Thanks for nothing!" says Gloria, getting up. "Shall we?"

Lisa is watching the scene, stunned.

"No, Gloria, thank you, I'll stay here and eat the ravioli... But see you later, sweety; I hope you are good!"

When Gloria leaves, offended, Lisa looks at the waiter:

"I apologize for my friend's behavior! Could you bring me the check, please? I'll leave you a good tip, you can be sure."

Chapter 8

Story: A Hard Choice

Martín is sitting in his room, surrounded by brochures from different universities. His mother told him he can't leave until he makes a decision. All of his schoolmates have already decided on the majors they will study, but he still hasn't.

Martín doesn't like to study. During the summer, he worked in his uncle's café as a barista, and he wants to do that for a living. He enjoys drawing on the coffee foam, serving customers, and talking to them. He doesn't want to study for exams. He doesn't like to read or do his homework. But his family has told him that he has to choose a major; it's mandatory.

His friends are no help either, they're very confident about their majors and want to convince him, but he doesn't like any of them.

"You should study economics like me," repeats his friend Pedro. "Then, one day, we could be presidents."

"No, you should study architecture! We will make beautiful buildings, museums, cathedrals...," his friend Paula tries to convince him.

"Martín, don't listen to them; come study art with me. We will learn a bit of everything, and then you can do the thing you like the most." His friend Joaquín is the one who resembles him the most, but art doesn't spark his interest either.

His sister is studying engineering, so that major is ruled out. He doesn't want to do the same thing as her.

He needs to decide now: the exams to get into university are next month, and he needs to start getting ready. His favorite subjects at school are arts, history, and physical education. He hates math, physics, and biology.

Suddenly, he comes up with an idea. If he wants to work at a café, like his uncle, he needs to find out what his uncle studied! He calls him over the phone and asks.

"I studied many things," answers his uncle. "I started several majors because I didn't like any of them. Finally, I ended up doing business administration; I'm not sure why. But thanks to that major, I learned to carry my business forward, manage employees, deal with suppliers, and many other things that allowed me to buy this café.

"Thanks, uncle! I think I know what I want to study now!" answers Martín, very excited.

"Martín, you should know that it is a major with many math-related subjects. Will you be able to handle that?"

"No! Talking with you, I realized that I don't want to buy a café or manage employees. I want to draw! On coffee, mainly, but it wouldn't be a bad idea to learn other techniques. I will sign up for art.

Chapter 9

Story: The Meeting

1. Michael

Michael looks at the time on his watch. He still has twenty minutes before his meeting with Lucy and Vincent. That's enough time to get to Café Gijón. Or it would be if he knew where he was.

The last corner looks familiar. Didn't he pass it already? Michael got to Madrid that very morning, from Israel, and he has not yet had time to get used to the city. He couldn't even buy a new chip for his phone. He was in a hurry. He hasn't seen Lucy and Vincent since university in the United States, and it wasn't easy to arrange the meeting. They were very scattered.

Finally, Michael stops. He's sure he's lost. On the corner, he sees a smoke shop that offers, besides tobacco and stamps, a few city maps. He decides to go in.

"Hello," says Michael.

"Can I help you?" asks the clerk, keeping his eyes on his phone.

"I'm lost," says Michael. His Spanish is limited, but luckily, he remembers that phrase.

The clerk looks up.

"Where do you want to go?" he asks.

"Café Gijón," answers Michael.

"It's nearby," says the clerk. "Walk through this same street for three minutes, and you'll find it."

Michael gets disoriented. He doesn't completely understand the directions.

"I'm sorry, I don't understand," he answers. "Can you repeat that, please?"

The clerk gets up from his chair and goes out of the smoke shop. Then, he points with his finger toward the north.

"There," he says, "three minutes."

"Thank you very much," answers Michael, and he goes on his way.

2. Lucy

Lucy is worried. The conveyor has already gone around four or five times. The rest of the passengers from her flight found their bags a while ago. And hers haven't appeared yet.

She looks at the screen above the conveyor. It doesn't say "Edinburgh-Madrid" anymore, which is the flight she took. Now it says "Istanbul-Madrid." It's official. Her luggage is lost.

Lucy looks for her airline's counter. After walking for a few minutes, she finds it at the end of a long row of counters. She gets close to a kind-faced woman.

"Good afternoon," says Lucy. "My bags didn't appear on the belt. How can I find my luggage?"

"Which flight did you arrive on?" asks the woman.

"The one from Edinburgh, at 10:30," answers Lucy.

The woman types for a few seconds.

"We're very sorry about this problem," she says finally. "Your luggage should turn up in the next 24 hours. It was a small logistics problem; it shouldn't happen, but it does. Do you want us to send it to the hotel?

"Please," says Lucy.

"Tell me the address, then," answers the woman.

Lucy dictates the hotel address. She thinks that, after all, it isn't such a big problem. Now she doesn't have to worry about unpacking before going to Café Gijón.

3. Vincent

"Your train left, dude," says the employee.

"No way," answers Vincent. "Seville-Madrid? The 8:10 one?

"Exactly," answers the employee.

"But I didn't see it," says Vincent. "I've been here since 8!"

"I'm really sorry, but the AVE trains wait for no one," says the employee. "Bear in mind that if we are delayed for over fifteen minutes, we have to give you a refund."

"I know, I know," answers Vincent. "That's exactly why I bought these tickets..."

Vincent is uneasy. He needs to be in Madrid by lunchtime. He agreed to meet Lucy and Michael. It's been years since the last time he saw them. He can't be late that day.

"Is there a bus I can take?" asks Vincent.

"I don't know," says the employee. "But you can ask at that window. They have all the information there."

The employee points to a counter at the end of the station. Vincent picks up the pace up to there.

"Good morning," says Vincent. "Do you have tickets to Madrid?"

The employee is on the other side of the glass. In the center of the window, there's a kind of speaker. Vincent sees that the employee speaks into a microphone, but he barely listens to what she says.

"I'm sorry, I can't hear you," says Vincent. "Could you repeat that? My Spanish isn't so good."

The employee rolls her eyes and stands up. She leaves her office and gets closer to Vincent.

"The microphone always malfunctions," she says. "Look, these are the schedules. There's a bus that leaves from here in ten minutes. Are you interested?"

"Yes!" answers Vincent. "When does it get to Madrid?"

"Oh, at about two," says the employee. "Right on time for lunch."

Chapter 10

Story: A Visit to the Doctor

Nora and her friend Patricia are talking on a park bench. It's a warm but cloudy day.

"Oh, this humidity is horrible for my knee," Nora complains.

"Tell me about it," replies Patricia. "My sciatic nerve hurts a lot."

"What about last week's cold? I was left with a sore throat..."

"Hey, Nora, be careful with that sore throat; it might be the flu. There's a lot of viruses going around."

"Do you think so? Should I go to the doctor?"

"Yes, so you don't have to worry about it. At our age... And I'll go with you; I want to have my heart checked."

"Okay... Besides, it's always good to go see Dr. Sánchez; he's so kind!"

"And so handsome!" finishes Patricia.

Patricia and Nora meet up the next day at the hospital to go to the doctor together. They have been friends for years, and they go to the same doctor, who allows them to come into his office together. Dr. Sánchez is a tall, gray-haired, elderly man who uses a cane.

"Nora, Patricia! Good to see you again, but weren't you here last week? What's happened?"

"Yes, doctor, but my knee hurts a lot, is it broken?" asks Nora, frightened.

"No, Nora, you have to ask him about the sore throat," says Patricia.

"Oh, yes, that too; I have a terrible sore throat," adds Nora.

"Okay, let's see, if you want, I'll do an X-ray on your knee, but if it was a fracture, you wouldn't be able to walk, Nora. How long have you had a sore throat?"

"Since last week, because of the cold weather."

"Okay, I'll take a look at it. Open your mouth, please, and say 'ah.'"

"Ahhhhh."

Dr. Sánchez examines Nora's throat.

"It's a little swollen, but I'm sure you can heal it with a nice lemon and honey tea. You're healthy as an oak, don't worry. What about you,

Patricia? Do you want me to check your heart?"

"Yes, please. My chest hurt a few days ago, and I end up out of breath when I climb the stairs," replies Patricia.

"Okay, let's see," says Dr. Sánchez as he grabs his stethoscope. "Take a breath, please. Now try to cough."

Patricia obeys the doctor.

"Everything sounds good, Patricia. When you climb the stairs, take your time, so you don't run out of breath. You are both perfect; you have nothing to worry about."

"Thank you so much, doctor."

"Yes, thank you very much. See you soon, doctor," says Nora.

The two friends leave the hospital and walk back together.

"Nora, didn't the doctor tell you to take cough syrup? Did he tell you which one?" Patricia asks suddenly.

"Did he tell me to take a syrup? I don't remember!"

"We'll have to come back tomorrow," Patricia says. "If he prescribed a syrup, you should take it."

"Yes, you're right; we'll have to come back tomorrow," Nora replies with a conspiratorial smile.

Chapter 11

Story: Events

The wedding

Francisco is beaming. Everything looks perfect, the living room is spotless, and all his loved ones are about to arrive. They've planned this day for months, and it has finally arrived. It's a beautiful August day, and it's pleasantly warm. Ezequiel is in the room next door. They can't see each other because it's bad luck, but they exchange messages.

"Have you seen who's arrived?"

"Your cousin, Bea! She's come all the way from Segovia; I can't believe it."

"Yes, too, but I mean your uncle..."

"Oh, yes. And he came with his new wife, his children, and the whole family."

"I see. Look, there's your grandma! She looks beautiful..."

Someone knocks on the door of Francisco's room. His sister tells him that everything is ready and that he has to get ready to go down.

The ceremony is simple but touching. Everyone's very moved. Francisco and Ezequiel promise each other that they will love each other forever and take care of each other in sickness and health, and finally, they exchange rings. "Hurrah!", "Bravo!", "Long live the grooms!" call the guests. It's a party.

Then comes the most awaited moment: the food and the dancing. The grooms are seated at their table, and guests come to greet them.

"Congratulations, boys," says Luisa, Ezequiel's mother.

"Congratulations, son," Francisco's father says, moved.

"To your health!" shouts uncle Jorge, who's already had a few drinks.

"May you have health, money, and love!" Amalia, his niece, corrects him.

All their friends, colleagues, and family are there. At their table, their closest friends tell embarrassing anecdotes from which no one is safe. Also, Francisco has unconsciously sat Adriana (his sister-in-law) at the same table as Luis (her ex-husband). That table is no fun at all.

Everyone dances, drinks, and eats. Francisco and Ezequiel dance together all night long, very much in love. This is, without a doubt, the best day of their lives.

Christmas

Francisco is desperate. This is the first Christmas he and Ezequiel organize in their new house, and everything is going wrong. The guests have arrived, and the food is not ready; he has argued with Ezequiel, and, on top of all, he couldn't buy any gifts.

He looks at his family while watching the turkey in the oven. His mother is having an argument about politics with Ezequiel's uncle. His grandmother isn't talking to anyone, but she's yelling "Merry Christmas!" to everyone who passes by.

His sisters are locked in the bathroom, putting on makeup and taking pictures. His father is closely following Ezequiel's moves – who is arranging the house discreetly.

"Happy holidays, aunt!" he exclaims as he kicks a pair of slippers under the armchair. "Thanks for coming, Antonio," he says with a smile as he picks up some dirty cups.

Finally, Francisco calls everyone to the table: the food is ready.

Everyone sits down, making a lot of noise, and grandpa puts away a sandwich he had sneaked out of his pocket.

"FRANCISCO!" Ezequiel shouts from the kitchen.

"What's wrong?"

"Have you watched the turkey?"

"Yes..."

"Have you tried it?"

"Well, no..."

"Have you looked at it?"

"Well, no..."

"The oven was off! The turkey is raw!"

Ezequiel comes out of the kitchen.

"Dear family, I know you're all very hungry, but you'll have to wait a little longer... until the pizza arrives."

This is definitely not going to be the best Christmas of their lives.

Chapter 12

Story: The Lighthouse

Manolo woke up, looked at the clock, and let out a scream. It was almost nine in the morning! He got up, brushed his teeth, got dressed quickly, and ran out of his house. There was no time for a shower.

He waited for the bus at the stop. When it arrived, he got on, paid for his ticket, and sat in one of the back seats. Then, he got his phone out of his pocket and read the news of the day.

"A great storm left fallen trees and floods in Santander," it said. Manolo got worried. Santander wasn't far from his town.

The bus got to the port. Manolo got down and walked the two-hundred meters that separated him from his job. When he got to the lighthouse, he saw Concepción, the night keeper. She looked at her watch, impatient.

"Manolo, you're finally here!" said Concepción. "I waited for you for a long while."

"I'm sorry, Concepción. My alarm didn't go off this morning. Any news?"

"Yes: it seems like a storm is coming. I called the meteorology department, and they told me that it would start in the afternoon."

"Storms always make me nervous," said Manolo.

"But what are you saying? If you're the best lighthouse keeper in all of Spain," answered Concepción with a smile. She put her coat on and left.

Manolo went up the 250 steps that separated him from the cupola and started working. At midday, he went down to buy food at the grocery store in the harbor, a small shop run by an old, bearded man called Tristán.

"Here's your seafood sandwich, as usual," said Tristán. "So, Concepción is learning to operate the cupola's machines?"

"What?" asked Manolo, puzzled. "No, Concepción is just the night keeper."

"Then... Who is up there?" asked Tristán, pointing through his store window.

Manolo turned around and looked up. It was true: there was a silhouette in the lighthouse cupola.

He paid Tristán and ran to the lighthouse. "Maybe Concepción forgot something and came back to look for it. Or perhaps it's an overly curious tourist," he thought while he went up the stairs.

When he got to the lighthouse cupola, he saw a young smiling girl.

"Mar!" said Manolo.

"Hey, dad," greeted Mar and ran to hug him.

"What are you doing here?"

"I wanted to surprise you," explained Mar. "I flew from Seville this very morning. I needed a weekend by the ocean."

"Thanks for this lovely surprise!" said Manolo.

Manolo cut his seafood sandwich in half. He and his daughter had lunch and talked for hours while looking at the ocean. Mar told him that she was doing really well at university and that she was planning on moving to an apartment downtown with a classmate.

At sundown, the storm arrived. First, slowly, then stronger: the raindrops hit the lighthouse glass. Underneath, the sea was disturbed. Luckily, there were no boats in the area. Manolo's only task was to tell boats to avoid the area. The rain stopped at around six in the afternoon, exactly when Manolo's shift ended.

Mar and he went down the lighthouse stairs.

"Well, what do you want to do now?" asked Manolo. "Go to the movies? Go for a walk?"

Mar looked at the sky. It was still cloudy.

"I think I would like to go home."

That night, Manolo and Mar ordered pizza, watched a movie on TV, and played cards. When Manolo went to bed, he thought that his daughter was growing up. He was getting older. He smiled: he would hold that special memory in his mind forever.

Chapter 13

Story: The Diary

Dear Diary,

Today Professor Muñoz told me that I will play Juliet in the school play "Romeo and Juliet: The Musical." When I got the news, I couldn't believe it. My parents have congratulated me, and next Saturday, we will throw a big party at home to celebrate. My aunt Antonia and my cousins Pedro and Ignacio will come.

I'm very happy to have the lead role, but I'm also a little nervous. I'll have to learn a very long script, and I'll have to sing. In addition, Professor Muñoz is very demanding: she will surely mark all my mistakes. She'll want the play to go wonderfully.

I'd love to be a professional actress in the future. I haven't told my parents yet, but I'll tell them on Saturday, during the party we're having at home. My dream is to be a renowned actress like Penelope Cruz! I want to be in films and shows in Spain and around the world because traveling is one of my goals.

And speaking of traveling...! The news about my starring role was not the only surprise today. My aunt Antonia texted me this morning and wrote: "Laura, I'll tell you something that will make you very happy. In winter, we will go on vacation to South America, and we want you and your sister to come with us."

What a blast! We'll go to Argentina, Chile, and Brazil. We'll visit incredible sites such as the Iguazu Falls, Patagonia, and the Amazon rainforest. We will leave in December, and the trip will last about a month. It'll be so much fun because my sister and I get along so well with our cousins Pedro and Ignacio. I can't wait!

Now I must go. Tonight, my friend Sara is celebrating her birthday at her house; she's having a sleepover. We'll probably watch a movie and play a game. Sara's mom will make snacks for everyone. But we're not going to go to bed very late, because tomorrow we have to go to school and we have a math test.

Answer Sheet
Chapter 1

1.
a. Buenas tardes   Good afternoon
b. Buenos días   Good morning
c. Buenas noches Good evening

2.
Hasta mañana, adiós, hasta luego, chao.

3.
c. Qué lindo día

4.
A: Mari, ¡Hola!
B: Buenas tardes, Pedro.
A: ¿Cómo estás?
B: Estoy bien. ¿Y tú?
A: Ahora un poco ocupada. Después hablamos. ¡Adiós!
B: Hasta luego.

5.
Hola, buenas tardes, buenas noches.

Comprehension Questions
1. Javier lives in Seville.
2. Visiting him in Seville.
3. Because he is busy.
4. Because she is afraid, he doesn't love her anymore.
5. Javier.

Chapter 2

1.

b. Javier es entrevistador en una empresa.

2.

A: ¿Cuál es tu <u>nombre</u>? – pregunta Javier.
B: Pérez Fernández – <u>responde</u> Carmen.
A: ¿Sabes una cosa? – dice Javier. Mi madre <u>se llama</u> Carmen.
B: Es un <u>nombre</u> muy común – contesta Carmen.

3.

a. Carmen <u>tiene</u> treinta y dos años.

b. Hernández no <u>es</u> el apellido correcto.

c. La oficina es <u>amplia</u>.

d. Carmen quiere <u>el</u> trabajo.

4.

d. Nombre, te llamas.

5.

b. En Alcorcón.

Comprehension Questions

1. His office is spacious and has good lighting

2. She studied at Universidad Politécnica de Madrid and at Universidad Complutense.

3. Her last job was at Banco Industrial.

4. No, he hasn't.

5. It's called Vértigo.

Chapter 3

1.

a. Mónica es <u>empresaria</u>.

b. Marta deja a su hija al cuidado de una <u>canguro</u>.

c. Al principio, Fernando no era muy buen <u>coctelero</u>.

d. Paula, la <u>periodista</u>, hace muchos reportajes.

2.

a. Panadero   Panadería

b. Chófer   Autobús

c. Gerenta de marketing   Revista de modas

d. Camarero   Bar

3.

c. Norma se dedica a cantar en bares del centro de la ciudad.

4.

Mi hijo está estudiando <u>derecho</u> porque quiere convertirse en un gran <u>abogado</u>. Toma clases en la <u>facultad</u> de leyes. Su sueño es trabajar en un <u>bufete</u>. Quién sabe: ¡quizá algún día llegue a ser <u>juez</u>!

5.

a. Lucía <u>trabaja</u> en una empresa de cosméticos.

b. Marcelo se <u>dedica</u> a reparar muebles.

c. Marisa está <u>empleada</u> en un restaurante.

d. Tomás es <u>periodista</u>.

Comprehension Questions

1. Talking with tourists and recommending places of interest.

2. Mónica also enjoys simple things, like a walk around the park or a good talk with her friends.

3. In Murcia.

4. At a hospital in Valencia.

5. She is a journalist.

Chapter 4

1.

a. Rafael se sienta en su <u>cama</u>.

b. En la biblioteca hay <u>libros</u> y <u>fotografías</u>.

c. En el último <u>cajón</u> Rafael encuentra un <u>costurero</u>.

d. Rafael coge un <u>botón</u> color <u>blanco</u>.

2.

b. Pared de piedra.

3.

Agujas e hilo.

4.

a. Cepillo de dientes	Toothbrush
b. Mármol	Marble
c. Anillo	Ring
d. Maleta	Suitcase

5.

a. Había un sillón <u>verde</u>.

b. El botón era <u>blanco</u>.

c. Encontró muchas <u>fotografías</u> suyas.

d. La mesa era <u>vieja</u>.

Comprehension Questions

1. He lost his memory.
2. Because there was an ant walking on top of it.
3. Ana is his wife.
4. Because he's sure he'll find an old cardboard box in it.
5. He remembers his proposal.

Chapter 5

1.

c. Paulina casará pronto

2.

– ¿Cuánto <u>cuestan</u> estos zapatos? – pregunta Paulina.

– ¿Los blancos? – responde Adriana. Cincuenta euros.

– ¡Son muy <u>baratos</u>! – contesta Paulina. ¿Puedo <u>probármelos</u>, por favor?

– No hay problema – dice Adriana. ¿Qué <u>talla</u> eres?

– Ocho – contesta Paulina.

– Aquí tienes – responde Adriana. ¿Quieres pasar al <u>probador</u>?

– No, <u>gracias</u> – contesta Paulina. Puedo ponérmelos aquí mismo, frente al <u>espejo</u>.

3.

c. La oferta es tentadora.

4.

a. Paulina se casará con Arturo.

b. Adriana trabaja en una tienda de ropa.

c. Gloria está emocionada por la boda.

d. El vestido es nuevo.

5.

c. Menos de un año.

Comprehension Questions

1. They are looking for a wedding dress.

2. Because it's from the new collection.

3. That he's a bit bland.

4. Her employee discount.

5. That they invite her to the wedding.

Chapter 6

1.

El metro es uno de los medios de transporte más veloces. El de Madrid fue inaugurado en 1919 y tiene 12 líneas y 276 estaciones. En algunas estaciones de la red del metro de Madrid se puede realizar trasbordo con trenes y con autobuses.

2.

viajar	en	avión
pedir	una	indicación
tomar	un	autobús
llegar	al	aeropuerto

3.

c. Quisiera saber cuándo se construyó la Sagrada Familia.

4.

A: ¿Me diría cómo llego al centro de la ciudad?

B: Sí, puede ir a pie o tomarse un medio de transporte. ¿Qué prefiere?

A: Lo segundo, por favor.

B: Vale. Puede tomar el autobús número 35. La parada está en esa esquina.

A: De acuerdo, ¡muchas gracias!

5.

b. ¿En qué parada tengo que bajarme?

Comprehension Questions

1. Because it is full of narrow streets, passages, and alleys.
2. Two: the subway and a bus.
3. Because it's Sunday morning.
4. At nine o'clock.
5. On the third floor of the airport.

Chapter 7

1.

Quisiera pedir un pescado, por favor. Si es posible, lo quisiera sin sal.

2.

b. ¿Podrías traerme la cuenta, por favor?

3.

a.	Carne	beef
b.	Almuerzo	lunch
c.	Pescado	fish
d.	Propina	tip

4.

c. Propina te dejaré.

5.

Voy a pedir la especialidad del restaurante, me han dicho que sus pastas son muy sabrosas. Pero no debes pedir el pescado, es asqueroso. Se lo diré cuando traiga la cuenta.

Comprehension Questions

1. She wants fish.
2. In a bookstore.
3. The pasta.
4. That it's cold and it doesn't have salt.
5. A good tip.

Chapter 8

1.

e.	Ingeniería	engineering
f.	Arquitectura	architecture
g.	Administración de empresas	business administration
h.	Arte	art

2.

c. A Martín no estudiar le gusta.

3.

Quería construir casas, por eso <u>estudié</u> en la universidad la carrera de <u>Arquitectura</u>. Después me di cuenta de que en realidad me gustaba dibujar, entonces me anoté en la carrera de <u>arte</u>. Pero eso tampoco me gustó, así que terminé estudiando <u>administración de empresas</u> para poder abrir mi propio café.

4.

a. ¿Qué <u>estudia</u> tu hijo?

b. Mi hijo estudia <u>ingeniería</u>.

c. Tengo que estudiar, mañana tengo un <u>examen</u>.

d. <u>Educación física</u> es mi asignatura favorita.

5.

c. Debo elegir una carrera.

Comprehension Questions

1. In a coffee shop.
2. That is mandatory for him to study a major.
3. Arts, history, and physical education.
4. Business administration.
5. Art.

Chapter 9

1.

- No saben lo que me pasó en el <u>aeropuerto</u> - dice Lucy. La <u>aerolínea</u> perdió mi <u>equipaje</u>.

- ¡No digas! - responde Vincent. Yo también <u>tuve</u> problemas para llegar hasta aquí.

- ¿Qué ocurrió? - pregunta Michael.

- Perdí el tren - dice Vincent. Tuve que comprar un <u>boleto</u> de bus.

- Qué lástima, Vincent - dice Michael. Yo me <u>perdí</u> en el camino hasta aquí. ¡Pero eso no es nada comparado con ustedes dos!

2.

a. La aerolínea perdió el <u>equipaje</u>.

b. Michael <u>se perdió</u> en el camino al café.

c. Los trenes de alta velocidad salen en <u>horario</u>.

d. Lucy habla <u>bien</u> español.

3.

a. Disculpe, pero no entienda.

4.

d. ¿Dónde queda el Café Gijón?

5.

puede	repetir	por favor
hay	un	bus
perdí	las	maletas
a quién	puedo	llamar

Comprehension Questions

1. Michael comes from Israel.

2. At a smoke shop.

3. It got lost.

4. That there was a logistics problem and her luggage should turn up in the next 24 hours.

5. Because he missed his AVE train from Seville to Madrid.

Chapter 10

1.

b. Me duele la garganta

2.

a. rodilla	knee

b. garganta   throat

c. ciático   sciatic nerve

d. corazón   heart

3.

Tengo que ir al <u>hospital</u> a que me vea un <u>médico</u>, porque me <u>duele</u> mucho el <u>pecho</u>.

4.

b. Me duele la gripe

5.

a) El día está nublado.

b) El doctor es muy amable y buen mozo.

c) Nora es canosa, tiene el pelo gris.

Comprehension Questions

1. Due to the humidity.

2. To be careful because it could be the flu.

3. Dr. Sánchez is a tall, gray-haired, elderly man who uses a cane.

4. To take her time when climbing the stairs.

5. Because they forgot whether Nora should take cough syrup or not.

Chapter 11

1.

a. prima   cousin

b. esposo   husband

c. hermano   brother

d. hijos   children

e. cuñada   sister-in-law

f. abuelo   grandfather

2.

A: Hola, Paula, ¡feliz Navidad!

B: ¡<u>Felices fiestas</u>, Camila! ¿Has recibido <u>regalos</u>?

A: ¡Sí! Me han regalado una casa de muñecas. ¿Y tú?

B: ¡Viva! A mí me regalaron un par de zapatos.

A: ¡Enhorabuena!

3.

b. felicitaciones

4.

a. Falso

b. Verdadero

c. Falso

d. Verdadero

5.

Enhorabuena, felicitaciones, salud, viva, olé, qué vivan los novios.

Comprehension Questions

1. It's pleasantly warm.

2. They exchange messages.

3. Because the house is a mess, the food isn't ready, and he had a fight with Ezequiel.

4. Francisco's mother and Ezequiel's uncle.

5. It's raw.

Chapter 12

1.

Ayer me <u>levanté</u> temprano. Después de desayunar, fui al gimnasio. Luego, me <u>duché</u> y me fui a trabajar. En la oficina, cerré un nuevo trato con un cliente, así que mi jefe me felicitó. Durante el mediodía, salí a almorzar con mis compañeros y <u>pedí</u> tortilla de patatas. Cuando <u>salí</u> del trabajo, me fui al centro comercial y <u>compré</u> un poco de ropa. Por la noche, fui a festejar el cumpleaños de un amigo y <u>comimos</u> barbacoa. También <u>bebimos</u> un poco de vino blanco. Luego, <u>llegué</u> a casa y me acosté.

2.

a. Falso

b. Verdadero

c. Falso

d. Verdadero

3.

Por la mañana	Por la tarde/noche
Despertarse	*Llegar a casa*
Levantarse	*Relajarse después del trabajo*
Desayunar	*Cocinar la cena*
Ducharse	*Cenar*
Vestirse para ir a trabajar	*Acostarse*
Ir a trabajar	*Dormirse*

4.

a. Miguel se <u>levanta</u> a las ocho de la mañana.

b. Manuela se <u>acuesta</u> a las diez de la noche.

c. Los domingos, la familia Pérez hace el <u>aseo</u> de la casa.

d. Los sábados, Ramón sale a <u>beber</u> una copa.

5.

a. Los martes.

b. Café con churros.

c. Autoescuela (clases para conducir) y flamenco.

d. Tiene que cuidar a su sobrina.

Comprehension Questions

1. There was a storm that left fallen trees and floods.

2. Because his alarm didn't go off.

3. The owner of the grocery store in the harbor.

4. Mar, Manolo's daughter.

5. They ordered pizza, watched a movie on TV, and played cards.

Chapter 13

1.

a. <u>Viajaré</u> a Italia en marzo.

b. Sé que <u>estudiarás</u> mucho para ese examen.

c. Rosa <u>saldrá</u> a cenar con sus amigas.

d. <u>Iremos</u> a dar un paseo al atardecer.

2.

A: Hola, David. ¿Estás bien? Pareces tenso.

B: Hola, Alberto. Estoy un poco nervioso, porque mañana por la mañana <u>tendré</u> mi examen final de la carrera de Gastronomía.

A: Entonces, ¿pasado mañana ya <u>serás</u> un chef profesional?

B: Así es. Bueno, si apruebo el examen, claro.

A: Por supuesto que lo <u>aprobarás</u>. Ya <u>verás</u> que pronto <u>montarás</u> tu propio restaurante... ¡y yo <u>probaré</u> tu deliciosa comida!

3.

a. Mañana por la mañana.

b. En un chef profesional.

c. Que tendrá su propio restaurante.

4.

d. David será un cocinero profesional.

5.

El <u>sueño</u> de mi hija menor es ser veterinaria. Dice que <u>curará</u> a todos los animales de la ciudad. Mi otra hija, la mayor, tiene la <u>meta</u> de ser arquitecta. Dice que <u>construirá</u> edificios por todo el mundo. Hagan lo que hagan, si le ponen pasión y cariño, estoy segura de que ambas <u>serán</u> muy buenas en lo suyo.

Comprehension Questions

1. She'll throw a big party at her home.

2. To be a renowned actress.

3. To travel.

4. She'll visit the Iguazu Falls, Patagonia, and the Amazon rainforest in Argentina, Chile, and Brazil.

5. She is going to a sleepover at her friend's place.

Appendix II: Vocabulary Reference

In this section, you'll find all the vocabulary we have seen in the short stories organized in alphabetical order. Next to each term, you'll find the type of word, the phonetic transcription, the definition, and the number of the page where you can find the word. Since most words have more than one meaning, we have chosen here the definition that applies to the use of the word in the short story you've read.

¡Olé!
(interjection) [o̞ˈle̞]
¡Bravo! Used to cheer and encourage. 77

¡Qué pasada!
(phrase) [ke̞ pãˈsäðä]
What a blast! Used to express that something is amazing. 93

¡Que vivan los novios!
(phrase) [ke̞ ˈbibän lo̞s̬ ˈno̞βio̞s̬]
Long live the grooms! Used to congratulate a couple on
their wedding day. 77

¡Viva!
(interjection) [ˈbibä]
Hurrah! Used to cheer and acclaim. 77

¿Cómo estás?

(phrase) ['komo̞ es'täs]

How are you? As in English, it can be used to ask someone how they are feeling, but it's also a somewhat informal way of saying hello.

¿Dónde está...?

(phrase) ['do̞nde̞ es'täs]

Where is...? Used to ask about the whereabouts of something or someone.

¿Dónde queda?

(phrase) ['do̞nde̞ 'ke̞ɾä]

Where is...? Used to ask where something is located.

¿Hacia dónde se dirige?

(phrase) ['äsiä 'do̞nde̞ se̞ di'ɾixe̞]

Where are you flying? Formal way to ask someone where they are traveling to.

¿Podría indicarme cómo ir?

(phrase) [po̞'dɾiä indi'kärme̞ 'ko̞mo̞ iɾ]

Can you tell me how to get there? Formal way of asking directions to a location.

¿Puede decirme dónde hay...?

(phrase) [pu'e̞de̞ de̞'siɾme̞ 'do̞nde̞ äi]

Can you tell me where there's...? Formal way of asking where something is located.

¿Puedes hablar ahora?

(phrase) ['pue̞de̞s ä'blär ä'o̞ɾä]

Can you talk now? A way to ask someone if this is a good time to talk to them.

¿Qué tal?

(phrase) [ke̞ täl]

What's up? Colloquial way of greeting someone or asking how they are doing.

¿Quién es?

(phrase) [ˈkien es]

Who is it? A way to answer the phone or the doorbell............. 6

abrazar

(verb) [äbɾäˑθäɾ]

to hug. To hold in your arms. 36

abuelo/a

(noun) [äˑbuelo]

grandfather, grandmother. The father or mother of a
person's parents... 76

acera

(noun) [äˑseɾä]

sidewalk. The side of the street that's reserved for people
to walk in. 33

acostumbrarse

(verb) [äkostumˈbräɾse]

to get used to. To get the habit of doing something. 60

Adiós

(interjection) [äˑdios]

goodbye. The usual way of saying goodbye. 5

Administración de Empresas

(noun) [ädministräˑsion de emˈpɾesäs]

business administration. A university degree that studies the
organization of assets and wealth in a company....................... 56

aeropuerto

(noun) [äeɾoˈpueɾto]

airport. A place where airplanes land and take over that usually
has a service area for passengers... 42

aguja

(noun) [äˑguxä]

needle. A small and pointed instrument usually made of steel
used for stitching, knitting or sewing... 27

---

alfiler

(noun) [älfiˈleɾ]

pin. A thin metallic nail used to fasten things together, usually dresses, headdresses or other ornaments.

almohada

(noun) [älmoˌˈädä]

pillow. Cover filled with soft material used to support the head when sleeping.

almorzar

(verb) [älmoɾˈθäɾ]

to have lunch. To eat something at noon.

almuerzo

(noun) [älˈmueɾθo]

lunch. The midday meal.

amplio/a

(adjective) [ˈämplio]

spacious. That its extent is wide and vast.

anillo

(noun) [äˈniʎo]

ring. A round piece usually made of metal used to embellish the fingers.

apagar

(verb) [äpäˈgäɾ]

to turn off. To make the fire, light, electricity or flow of something stop.

apellido

(noun) [äpeˌˈʎido]

last name. The name shared by all members of a family.

apretón de manos

(noun) [äpɾeˌˈton deˌ ˈmänos]

handshake. The action of two people clasping each other's right hand.

armario

(noun) [äɾˈmäɾio̞]

wardrobe. Piece of furniture with doors, shelves and hangers to store clothes and other objects. 27

Arquitectura

(noun) [äɾkite̞kˈtuɾä]

architecture. Discipline that studies the design and construction of buildings. 55

Artes

(noun) [ˈäɾte̞s̞]

art. Study of the skills necessary to produce a work of art 55

asentir

(verb) [äs̞e̞ɲˈtiɾ]

to nod. To admit that what another person has stated before is true moving the head up and down. 26

asignatura

(noun) [äs̞ignäˈtuɾä]

subject. Each one of the courses of study in an educational center. 55

asqueroso/a

(adjective) [äs̞ke̞ˈɾo̞s̞o̞]

disgusting. Something that generates repulsion or rejection because of its taste or appearance. 49

atónito/a

(adjective) [äˈto̞ɲito̞]

stunned. To be surprised or scared of a strange object or event. 34

bajar

(verb) [bäˈxäɾ]

to go down. To move downwards. 85

barato

(adjective) [bäˈɾäto̞]

cheap. That has a low or lower than normal price. 35

bastón

(noun) [bäs'toɲ]

cane. Element used for support when walking......................... 70

Bien

(adverb) [bieɲ]

fine. In good health, not sick. 4

billetes de avión

(noun) [bi'ʎeṭe̯ de̯ a˜'bioɲ]

plane ticket. The ticket that entitles you to board and travel in a plane... 4

Biología

(noun) [bioḷo̯'xiä]

biology. School subject based on the science that studies all the living beings on the planet. 55

blanco/a

(adjective) ['bläŋko̯]

white. That has the color of milk or snow. 27

boca

(noun) ['bokä]

mouth. Cavity in the face where the teeth and tongue are located. 70

bocadillo

(noun) [bo̯kä˜'diʎo̯]

snack. A light refreshment, usually eaten between meals. 93

bocata

(noun) [bo̯'kätä]

sandwich. The name given in Spain to sandwiches or open sandwiches. 78

boda

(noun) ['bo̯dä]

wedding. Ceremony through which two people are united in marriage. 36

boleto

(noun) [boˌˈleto]

ticket. An electronic or physical document that shows that you have paid a fare or admission. 63

bonito/a

(adjective) [boˌˈnito]

cute. That is attractive or pretty. 34

botones

(noun) [boˌˈtoɲ]

button. In clothing, a rounded piece that's passed through a loop to fasten it. 27

buen mozo/a

(adjective) [bueɲ ˈmoˌθo]

handsome. A good-looking person. 70

buenas noches

(phrase) [ˈbueɲäs ˈno̯tʃe̯s]

Good evening. It's used both as a greeting and a farewell after sunset. 6

Buenas tardes

(phrase) [ˈbueɲäs ˈtäɾde̯s]

Good afternoon. It's used as a greeting between noon and sunset, usually in formal settings and with strangers. 5

Buenos días

(phrase) [ˈbueɲo̯s ˈdiäs]

Good morning. It's used to greet known or unknown people in the morning, usually until noon. 4

caja de cartón

(noun) [ˈkäxä̈ de̯ käɾˈtoɲ]

cardboard box. A container made of cardboard that serves to store or transport things. 27

cajón

(noun) [käˈxoɲ]

drawer. Receptacle that fits into a specific hole in a cupboard, table, chest of drawers, or other piece of furniture. 27

caliente

(adjective) [kaˈli̯ente̞]

hot. Something at a very high temperature 49

calor

(noun) [kaˈlo̞ɾ]

heat. High temperature. 76

cama

(noun) [ˈkäma]

bed. A piece of furniture designed to sleep in it. 26

camarero/a

(noun) [kämäˈɾe̞ɾo̞]

waiter, waitress. Person whose job is to serve drinks and food in restaurants, bars or other similar establishments. 19

caminar

(verb) [kämiˈnäɾ]

to walk. To advance by foot. 84

camisa

(noun) [käˈmisä]

shirt. A garment that covers the torso, which is buttoned in the front and generally has a collar and sleeves. 27

canguro

(noun) [käŋˈɡuɾo̞]

babysitter. A person, usually young, who cares for small children in the absence of their parents. 19

canoso/a

(adjective) [käˈno̞so̞]

gray-haired. Who has gray hair. 70

cargador

(noun) [käɾɡäˈdo̞ɾ]

charger. An electrical device for charging batteries. 26

carne
(noun) ['kär̃ne]
beef. Flesh of a cow that is served as a meal. 48

caro/a
(adjective) ['kär̃o]
expensive. That has a high or higher than normal price. 35

carrera
(noun) [ka'r̃er̃a]
major. Course of determined years to obtain a college
degree. 54

casarse
(verb) [ka'sär̃se]
to get married. Of two people, to join in marriage. 35

catarata
(noun) [kätä'r̃atäs]
fall. A big waterfall. 93

cepillarse los dientes
(verb) [sepi'ʎär̃se los 'dieṇtes]
to brush one's teeth. To clean one's teeth with a brush. 84

cepillo de dientes
(noun) [se'piʎo de 'dieṇtes]
toothbrush. Brush used to clean one's teeth. 26

ceremonia
(noun) [ser̃e'monia]
ceremony. A formal act dictated by law, statute or custom. 77

Chao
(phrase) [tʃäo]
bye. A colloquial way of saying "goodbye." 6

ciático
(noun) ['siätiko]
sciatic nerve. Nerve located in the back of the hip. 69

cinta transportadora
(noun) ['sintä tränspor̃tä'dor̃a]

conveyor. A non-stop moving belt.

cliente/a

(noun) ['kliɛ̯nte̯]

client. Someone who buys in a store, or who uses the
services of a professional or company.

coche

(noun) ['koʧe̯]

car. Automobile used to transport people, with no more than
seven seats.

coctelero/a

(noun) [ko̯kte̯'leɾo̯]

bartender. Someone whose job is to serve drinks at a bar,
pub or club.

compartir

(verb) [ko̯mpäɾ'tiɾ]

to share. Make someone else part of something that is yours.

con firmeza

(adverb phrase) [ko̯n fiɾ'me̯θä̯]

firmly. In a firm way.

conductor/a

(noun) [ko̯nduk'toɾ]

driver. Someone in charge of driving a motor vehicle.

conversar

(verb) [ko̯nbe̯ɾ'sä̯ɾ]

to talk, to converse. Of two or more people, to exchange
ideas through speech.

corazón

(noun) [ko̯ɾä̯'θo̯n]

heart. Muscle located in the chest that pumps blood to the
body.

correr

(verb) [ko̯'re̯ɾ]

to run. To walk quickly so that, between one step and the next, both feet are in the air for a moment. 85

corto/a

(adjective) ['koɾto]

short. Having little length, or less length than others. 11

costar

(verb) [ko̞s'täɾ]

to cost. To be worth. 35

costurero

(noun) [ko̞stu'ɾeɾo]

sewing box. Box or basket where sewing materials are
stored. 27

cuenta

(noun) ['kueɲtä]

check. Paper where the dishes and their values are added
up to pay at the end of a meal in a restaurant. 49

cuñada

(noun) [ku'ɲädä]

sister-in-law. Both the wife of someone's sibling and the
sister of someone's spouse. 77

daño

(noun) ['däɲo]

harm. The act of damaging. 34

de edad avanzada

(phrase) [de̞ e̞'däd äβän'θädä]

elderly. Used to refer to a person of an older age. 70

de madera

[de̞ mä"deɾä]

wooden. Object made of wood. 27

dedicarse a

(verb) [de̞di'käɾse̞ ä]

to do for a living. To develop an activity as an occupation or
profession. 18

dejar un mensaje

(verb) [de̩ˈxäɾ un me̩ɲˈsäxe̩]

to leave a message. When you call someone and they don't answer, you can leave a recorded voice message on their answering machine for them to listen to later. 6

dependiente/a

(noun) [de̩pe̩ɲˈdie̩nte̩]

clerk. Someone whose job is serving customers in a store. 61

descuento

(noun) [de̩sˈkue̩nto̩]

discount. A reduction made to the price of something. 36

desempacar

(verb) [de̩se̩mpäˈkäɾ]

to unpack. To remove the contents of a suitcase. 62

despertador

(noun) [de̩spe̩ɾtäˈdo̩ɾ]

alarm. A signal, usually a loud noise, used to wake up. 85

destino

(noun) [de̩sˈtino̩]

destination. Point of arrival of a journey. 42

disculpe

(interjection) [disˈkulpe̩]

excuse me. Used to politely interrupt someone 41

dolor de garganta

(noun) [do̩ˈlo̩ɾ de̩ gäɾˈgäntä]

sore throat. Unpleasant sensation in the throat, usually related to a cold or the flu. 69

Economía

(noun) [e̩ko̩no̩ˈmiä]

economics. Science that studies the administration of goods and services. 55

Educación Física

(noun) [e̩dukäˈsio̩ɲ ˈfisikä]

physical education. School subject that teaches sports and
physical exercises... 55

Educación Plástica

(noun) [e̩dukaˈsioɲ ˈplästikä]

art (subject). School subject where you learn abilities such as
drawing, painting and sculpting....................................... 55

emocionada

(adjective) [e̩mosio̩ˈnädo̩]

thrilled. To be very pleased and excited about something. 4

emotivo/a

(adjective) [e̩mo̩ˈtibo̩]

touching. That has the ability to move someone. 77

empresario/a

(noun) [e̩mpɾe̩ˈsärio̩]

businessman, businesswoman. Someone who owns or
directs an industry, business or company................................. 18

encongerse de hombros

(verb) [e̩ŋko̩ˈxeɾse̩ de̩ ˈo̩mbɾo̩s]

to shrug. To raise the shoulders to show indifference or
uncertainty. 36

encontrar

(verb) [e̩ŋko̩ɲˈträɾ]

to find. To come upon someone or something that you
were or weren't looking for... 62

enhorabuena

(interjection) [e̩no̩ɾäˈbue̩ɲä]

way to go. Used to congratulate someone. 77

entender

(verb) [e̩ɲte̩ɲˈdeɾ]

to understand. To have a clear idea or to know about something.
.... 61

entrevistador/a

(noun) [e̩ntɾe̩βistäˈdoɾ]

interviewer. A person who conducts interviews. 11

equipaje
(noun) [e̞ki'päxe̞]

luggage. The set of personal belongings that are taken on trips. 61

error
(noun) [e̞'ro̞ɾ]

mistake. Misguided or wrong action. 92

escalar
(verb) [e̞ska̠'la̠r]

to climb. To go up a steep slope or to a great height. 13

escaparate
(noun) [e̞ska̠pa̠'ɾa̠te̞]

shop window. The exterior space of a store, usually closed with glass, where the goods are displayed. 33

escritorio
(noun) [e̞skɾi'to̞ɾio̞]

desk. A piece of furniture with a horizontal surface, used especially to write, draw or read. 11

escuchar
(verb) [e̞sku'tʃa̠r]

to listen. To pay attention to what is being heard. To pay attention to what is being heard. 63

espalda
(noun) [e̞s'pa̠lda̠]

back. The rear part of the human body, expanding from the shoulders to the waist. 34

especialidad
(noun) [e̞spe̞sia̠li'da̠d]

speciality. The best dish in a restaurant. 47

espejo
(noun) [e̞s'pe̞xo̞]

mirror. A glass surface that reflects the objects in front of it. ... 34

esperar

(verb) [eˌspeˌˈɾäɾ]

to wait. To expect someone to arrive or something to
happen. 84

esposo/a

(noun) [eˌsˈpoˌso]

husband, wife. The person someone is married to. 76

esquina

(noun) [eˌsˈkinä]

corner. The point where converging streets meet.................... 60

estación de metro

(noun) [eˌstä˘sioɲ deˌ ˈmeˌtɾo]

subway station. The place where the subway usually stops. 41

estanco

(noun) [eˌsˈtäŋko]

smoke shop. A store where stamps, tobacco and matches
are sold. 60

estetoscopio

(noun) [eˌsteˌtoˌsˈkopioˌ]

stethoscope. Medical device used to amplify and listen to
the sounds of the chest and other body parts. 71

estirarse

(verb) [eˌstiˈɾäɾse]

to strech. To extend one's limits to reach more. 35

estoy ocupado

(verb) [eˌsˈtäɾ oˌkuˈpädo]

to be busy. Not to have time because you are engaged in
some other activity.. 5

estudiar

(verb) [eˌstuˈdiäɾ]

to study. To attend classes at some educational place or to
read and prepare oneself for a test. 54

examen

(noun) [ek̯ˈsämen̠]

test. A group of questions or problems designed to evaluate someone's knowledge or abilities. 54

examinar

(verb) [eksämiˈnär]

to examine. To corroborate the patient's health by means of medical examinations. 70

exmarido

(noun) [ek̯smä¨ɾido̯]

ex husband. The man to whom someone used to be married. 77

fechas

(noun) [ˈfet̠ʃä]

date. The time when something is done or takes place. 4

felices fiestas

(phrase) [fe̯ˈlise̯s ˈfie̯stä̈s]

happy holidays. Used during the holidays, it refers to both Christmas and New Year. 78

felicitaciones

(interjetion) [fe̯lisitä¨sio̯ne̯s]

congratulations. Used to express joy and acknowledgment in someone else's good fortune. 77

feliz Navidad

(phrase) [fe̯ˈliθ näbiˈdä̈d]

merry Christmas. Used to wish people a merry Christmas, both close friends and strangers. 78

fiesta

(noun) [ˈfie̯stä]

party. A gathering of people to celebrate something or have fun. 33

Física

(noun) [ˈfisikä]

physics. School subject that teaches the properties of matter and energy. 55

folleto

(noun) [foˈʎeto]

brochure. Piece of paper, usually promotional, that has information about something.. 54

fotografía

(noun) [fotoˈɣɾafia]

photograph. An image obtained by photography. 26

fractura

(noun) [frakˈtuɾa]

fracture. What happens when a bone breaks. 70

frío/a

(adjective) [ˈfrio]

cold. Something at a very low temperature. 48

genial

(adjective) [xeˈnial]

great. Pleasant, causing delight or joy. 92

gota

(noun) [ˈgota]

drop. Small portion of a liquid, with a spheroidal shape. 86

gripe

(noun) [ˈgɾipe]

flu. Contagious disease that usually causes fever, cough and sore throat... 69

guardias

(noun) [ˈguaɾdia]

on call. A service that ensures the continuity of basic services outside regular hours... 19

Hablamos mañana

(phrase) [aˈblamos maˈɲana]

Talk to you tomorrow. Phrase used to say farewell to someone and assuring them that you will speak the next day. 6

Hasta luego

(phrase) ['ästä 'luego]

So long. Phrase used to say farewell to someone you hope to

Hasta mañana

(phrase) ['ästä 'mä'ɲänä]

Until tomorrow. Phrase used to say farewell and that entails
that you will see or communicate with the addressee the

hermano/a

(noun) [eɾ'mäno]

brother, sister. A person related to another through shared

hijos/as

(noun) ['ixos]

hilo

(noun) ['ilo]

thread. Group of filaments twisted together and used for sewing.

Historia

(noun) [is'toɾiä]

history. School subject where you learn about important past

Hola

(interjection) ['oɭä]

horario

(noun) [o̞'ɾäɾio]

schedule. Timetable or program that indicates the time

horno

(noun) ['oɾno]

humeante

(adjective) [umeˌˈänte]

steaming. Something that is so hot that smoke or steam comes out of it. 49

inflamado/a

(adjective) [inflä ˈmädo]

swollen. That is larger than its usual size, reddened or irritated. 70

Ingeniería

(noun) [inxeɲieˌˈɾiä]

engineering. A set of mathematical and physical knowledge applied to the design and construction of machines, buildings, objects, software, hardware, etc. 55

interpretar

(verb) [inteɾpɾeˌˈtäɾ]

to play. To execute a role in a dramatic play. 92

inundación

(noun) [inundä¨sioɲ]

flood. Overflowing body of water on normally dry land. 84

jarabe para la tos

(noun) [xä ˈɾäbeˌ ˈpärä lä toʂ]

cough syrup. Medicine in drinkable form given for sore throats and coughs. 71

lavabo

(noun) [lä¨bäbo]

toilet. Used to refer both to the bathroom and the sink alone. 78

leer

(verb) [leeˌɾ]

to read. To interpret a text. 54

librería

(noun) [libɾeˌˈɾiä]

bookstore. A place that sells books. 19

libro

(noun) [ˈlibɾo]

book. A written text comprised of many pages and bind together. 26

llegar

(verb) [ʎeˈgaɾ]

to arrive. To reach a destiny. 84

maestro/a

(noun) [maˈestɾo]

teacher. Person who teaches others about a subject. 18

maleta

(noun) [maˈleta]

suitcase. Bag with a handle used to carry clothes and objects, especially during trips. 26

mandar

(verb) [manˈdaɾ]

to send. To dispatch a package or message through a means of communication. 62

manta

(noun) [ˈmanta]

blanket. Piece of a fabric used to warm and cover oneself. 26

marisco

(noun) [maˈɾisko]

seafood. Sea animals, especially crustaceans and mollusks, that are eaten. 85

mármol

(noun) [ˈmaɾmol]

marble. More or less crystalized and compact stone, usually used for tables, counters or other surfaces. 25

Más o menos

(phrase) [mas o ˈmenos]

Kind of. Approximately. 5

Matemáticas

(noun) [maːteˈmaːtikaːs]

mates

(noun) [ˈmaːteˌs]

Me apetece...

(phrase) [meˌaːpeˈteˌse]

médico/a

(noun) [ˈmeˌdikoˌ]

mercadería

(noun) [meˌɾkaːdeˌˈɾiaː]

mes

(noun) [meˌs]

mesa

(noun) [ˈmeˌsaː]

meta

(noun) [ˈmeˌtaː]

mirar

(verb) [mi'ɾäɾ]

to look. To direct one's view towards an object.

morir de hambre

(phrase) [mo'ɾiɾ de̞ 'ämbɾe̞]

be starving. Used in a figurative sense to express that one is very hungry.

mostrador

(noun) [mo̞s̪tɾä˜do̞ɾ]

counter. Kind of table or similar furniture where things are displayed for buyers to see. It can also be used to refer to a surface where business is conducted.

móvil

(noun) ['mo̞βil]

mobile phone. Portable device used in a celular system.

muchacho/a

(noun) [mu'tʃätʃo̞]

young man/woman. Person of a young age.

Necesito llegar a...

(phrase) [ne̞s̪e̞'sito̞ ʎe̞'gäɾ ä]

I need to get to the... Phrase used to ask someone for directions to a place.

nublado

(adjective) [nu'βlädo̞]

cloudy. When the sky has clouds.

obra de teatro

(noun) ['o̞βɾä de̞ te̞'ätɾo̞]

play. A dramatic representation of a story or action, generally presented on a stage.

oferta

(noun) [o̞'fe̞ɾtä]

offer. Proposal that can be accepted or rejected.

oír

(verb) [o̞'iɾ]

to hear. To perceive something with one's ears........................ 63

oración

(noun) [oɾaˈsio̞n]

sentence. groups of words or phrases that form a syntactic
unit. 34

ordenador

(noun) [oɾde̞naˈdoɾ]

computer. Electronic device that processes and stores data....... 4

ordenar

(verb) [oɾde̞'naɾ]

to order. To request food in a restaurant................................... 47

pagar

(verb) [paˈgaɾ]

to pay. To give something, especially money, in return for
goods or services. 84

palestra

(noun) [paˈle̞stɾa]

climbing wall. Wall specially designed to be climbed, generally
simulating a rocky surface... 13

panadería

(noun) [panade̞'ɾia]

bakery. Place where bread is made and sold. 19

pantalla

(noun) [pan'taʎa]

screen. Surface where images and text appear in electronic
devices. 61

pantuflas

(noun) [pan'tuflas]

slippers. Comfortable usually low-cut footwear used at
home.. 78

---

parada del autobús

(noun) [pä'räda'del äuto'bus]

bus stop. Designated place where buses stop.

pared de piedra

(noun) [pä'red de̗ 'piedr̯ä]

stone wall. Fence or wall usually made with rough stones.

parrilla

(noun) [pä'riʎä]

grill. Device, usually made of iron, used for cooking directly on the fire.

partir

(verb) [pär'tir]

to leave. To start walking or to be on one's way to a destination.

pasar

(verb) [pä'sär]

to come in. To enter a place.

pavo

(noun) ['päbo̗]

turkey. Flesh of a large bird typically served as food during holidays.

pecho

(noun) ['petʃo̗]

chest. Central area of the human body, where the heart and lungs are located.

pediatra

(noun) [pe̗'diätr̯ä]

pediatrician. Doctor specialized in the care of children.

percheros

(noun) [pe̗rtʃe̗ro̗]

rack. Structure for hanging clothes.

perdido/a

(adjective) [pe̗r'dido̗]

lost. Used to refer to a person who is disoriented, does
not know where he is or where he is going. 60

pescado

(noun) [peṣˈkädo]

fish. Flesh of an animal that lives in the water, served as a
meal. 47

pijamada

(noun) [pijäˉmädä]

sleepover. Used to refer to an activity, usually for children,
where several guests spend the night in the same place............ 93

pinchar

(noun) [pinˈtʃäɾ]

to prog. To grab a piece of food with a fork. 48

piso

(noun) [ˈpiso]

apartment. Colloquial way of referring to a dwelling in a
building. 86

plato

(noun) [ˈpläto]

dish. A specific prepared meal. It is also used to refer to the
element on which the food is placed. 47

por favor

(phrase) [poɾ fäˉboɾ]

please. Phrase to add after asking for something cordially....... 33

porción

(noun) [poɾˈsioɲ]

serving, piece. Individual ration of a meal............................... 48

precio

(noun) [ˈpreṣio]

price. Monetary value of something. 35

presupuesto

(noun) [preṣuˈpueṣto]

budget. Money available for a specific purpose. 35

primo/a

(noun) ['pɾimo]

cousin. The child of your parent's brother or sister. 76

prisa

(noun) ['pɾisa]

hurry. When something is done too fast or when you are
in a rush. 60

probador

(noun) [pɾo̞'baðo̞]

fitting room. The room to put on clothes in a clothing store. .. 34

probar

(verb) [pɾo̞'baɾ]

to try. To put on clothes to see how they fit. 34

propina

(noun) [pɾo̞'pina]

tip. Additional money given to the waiter at a restaurant,
coffee shop or bar. 49

protagonista

(noun) [pɾo̞taɣo̞'nista]

main role. Character who plays the most important role in a
play, film or book. 92

Que duermas bien

(phrase) [ke̞ 'dueɾmas bie̞n]

Sleep tight. A way of wishing someone a good night's sleep,
usually used with someone close. 5

Qué lindo día

(phrase) [ke̞ 'lindo̞ 'dia]

What a nice day. Expression used to refer to a day with
pleasant weather. 6

quedarse sin aliento

(phrase) [ke̞'daɾse̞ sin a'lie̞nto̞]

to be short of breath. Difficulty breathing or feeling a lack
of air, generally due to physical exertion. 71

radiografía

(noun) [rädioɡɾäˈfiä]

X-ray. Photograph of the interior of the human body obtained by means of x-rays. 70

ravioles

(noun) [räˈbioɹes̩]

ravioli. Stuffed pasta, usually square, which is cooked in boiling water. 47

reembolso

(noun) [re̞e̞mˈboɹso̩]

refund. Return of a payment. 62

regalo

(noun) [re̞ˈɡälo̩]

gift. Something a person gives to another as a gesture of affection or gratitude, without expecting anything in return. 78

rendirse

(verb) [re̞ɲˈdiɾse̞]

to give up. To accept defeat or stop trying something. 35

respirar

(verb) [re̞spiˈɾäɾ]

to breathe. To inhale and exhale air. 71

revisar

(verb) [re̞biˈsäɾ]

to go through. To observe something carefully and attentively. 12

revolear los ojos

(verb) [re̞βo̞ˈle̞äɾ lo̞s̩ ˈo̞xo̞s̩]

to roll your eyes. To show disgust or disagreement by moving the eyes upwards. 63

roble

(noun) [ˈro̞βle̞]

oak. Tree of strong wood, used to speak of a healthy or strong person. 71

rodilla

(noun) [roˈdiʎäs]

knee. Part of the body than joins the thigh to the lower part
of the leg. 69

sábanas

(noun) [ˈsäbänä]

sheet. Each of the pieces of fabric used to cover the
mattress. 26

sal

(noun) [säl]

salt. Substance used for seasoning and preservation of food.... 49

sala de espera

(noun) [ˈsälä̈ deˌ esˈpeɾä]

waiting room. A place for people to wait................................. 11

salsa fileto

(noun) [ˈsälsä̈ fiˈleto]

filetto sauce. Italian pasta accompaniment based on crushed
tomatoes.. 47

salud

(interjection) [säˈlud]

cheers / to your health. A common way to toast....................... 77

sano/a

(adjective) [ˈsäno]

healthy. Who is in good health, free from disease. 71

Se encuentra...

(phrase) [seˌ eɲˈkueɲtɾä]

is located in... A way to indicate the position of something...... 42

selva

(noun) [ˈselbä]

rainforest. Vast tropical terrain populated with trees and
vegetation. 93

semana

(noun) [seˈmänä]

week. The period of seven consecutive days, from
Monday to Sunday. 13

señalar

(verb) [seɲaˈlar]

to point. To use a finger or a gesture to indicate the location
of something. 63

sentir

(verb) [senˈtir]

to feel. To experience physical or emotional sensations. 13

seres queridos

(noun) [ˈseɾeˌs keˈɾidoˌs]

loved ones. A way of referring to family or friends, those we
love. 76

sillón

(noun) [siˈʎoɲ]

armchair. Cushioned chair with armrests. 25

soso/a

(adjective) [ˈsoˌso]

bland. Without taste or grace. 35

suave

(adjective) [ˈsuabe]

soft. A texture that is pleasant to the touch, not rough. 26

subir

(verb) [suˈbir]

to go up. To use stairs or an elevator to go from bottom to
top. 85

sueño

(noun) [ˈsueɲo]

dream. A wish or hope about the future. 92

suspiro

(noun) [susˈpiro]

sigh. Noisily blowing air out of the mouth, usually to express
some emotion. 35

---

talla

(noun) [taˈʎä]

size. The measurements of something, usually a piece of clothing. 34

tarde

(adverb) [ˈtärde]

late. After the due time or schedule. 63

Te quiero

(phrase) [te̞ ˈkie̞ɾo]

I love you. Phrase used to express love or care to someone. 5

teclado

(noun) [te̞ˈklädo]

keyboard. Where the computer keys are located. 12

teclear

(verb) [te̞ˈkle̞äɾ]

to type. To write on a computer or any keyboard. 62

técnica

(noun) [ˈte̞knikä]

technique. Set of skills or procedures needed to develop certain sciences or arts. 56

tienda

(noun) [ˈtie̞ndä]

store. Place where merchandise is sold. 19

tío/a

(noun) [tio]

uncle, aunt or dude, girl. Your mother's or father's brother (uncle) or sister (aunt). Also used to call someone, colloquially. 62

tomar el autobús

(verb) [to̞ˈmäɾ e̞l äuto̞ˈbus]

to take the bus. To travel by bus or to get on the bus. 42

toser

(verb) [to̞ˈse̞ɾ]

to cough. To take air out of the lungs with force and noise, often an involuntary movement. 71

turno nocturno

(noun) [ˈtuɾno̞ no̞kˈtuɾno]

Part 2: Intermediate Spanish Short Stories

Take Your Vocabulary and Culture Awareness to the Next Level

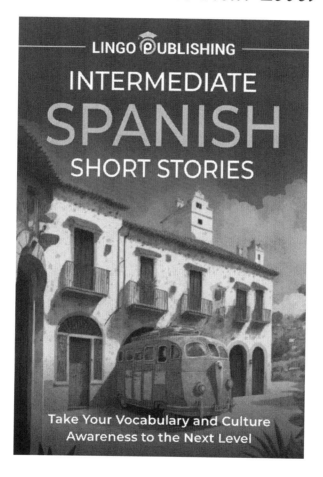

Introduction

¡Hola! Are you an intermediate Spanish speaker who wants to learn more vocabulary in a fun way? Have you understood Spanish grammar so far but can't seem to memorize long lists of words? Do you want to read real conversations that show you how the language is spoken? Well, then, you've got the perfect book in your hands!

With this intermediate-level book of short stories, you will be able to learn Spanish in the most entertaining way! Throughout, we will focus on a group of friends, their interests, problems, plans, and daily life so that you can see how native speakers really use the language.

Learning a new language doesn't have to be boring. With this book, you will learn by reading stories with real-life dialogues in Spanish! But this isn't merely a collection of short stories; you will find everything you need to understand the gist of the story and the words included in it.

In each chapter, you will find the story, a vocabulary list with all the words that may be unfamiliar to you at this level, a summary of the story in Spanish, and a summary of the story in English. Additionally, you will get a short quiz to complete and some reading comprehension questions to check your understanding – and even some interesting facts about Spain!

With all of this information in each chapter, we recommend that you first read the story in its entirety, then pay attention to the vocabulary list and look up any unfamiliar words to you. Then, read the story again with the vocabulary in mind, paying attention to how the new words are used in context. Then, you can go on to read the summary of the story in

Spanish to make sure you've understood things correctly and focused on the important parts.

After all of this, you can move on to the exercises and comprehension questions that will tell you whether or not you have understood the story. After you've finished the exercises and questions, check your answers using the answer key from Appendix I. If your results aren't what you hoped for, try reading the story in Spanish again and then the summary in Spanish and English. After this second read-through, you can try doing the exercises again to learn if your comprehension has improved. You will also be able to find an English translation of all short stories in Appendix I in case you need them.

Finally, before moving on to the next chapter, read the "Did you know...?" section to learn a bit more about Spanish culture and some fun facts.

Now that you're ready to make the most out of this book, how about getting started? *¡Comencemos!*

Chapter 1: ¡Bienvenido a España! - Welcome to Spain!

Story in Spanish: La confusión

Santiago Martínez llega al aeropuerto de Badajoz a las ocho de la mañana. Lo acompañan sus padres, su hermana menor y su mejor amigo, Luis. Están algo **ajustados de tiempo**, así que caminan rápidamente y llegan hasta el mostrador para **despachar** el **equipaje** de Santiago. Luego, se dirigen hacia la puerta catorce, que es desde donde sale el **vuelo**.

- Bueno, hijo, **¡que tengas un buen viaje!** – dice el señor Martínez y le da un cálido abrazo - . Estudia mucho... Pero también diviértete. Haz buenos amigos.

- ¡Pero no me cambies por otro amigo! – le dice Luis, sonriente, y le entrega un papel doblado - . Toma, aquí tienes un mapa de Madrid. He marcado en él los lugares más emblemáticos de la ciudad. Te extrañaré. Iré a visitarte en cuanto pueda.

- Os espero en Madrid a todos – responde Santiago - . Beatriz, mi nueva **compañera de vivienda**, me ha enseñado algunas fotos del **piso**. Es muy grande. Hay una **habitación para invitados**, así que podéis venir a visitarme cuando queráis. – Santiago se da media vuelta y se dispone a saludar a su madre... ¡que está hecha un mar de **lágrimas**! - . ¡Mamá, no **llores**!

- Lo siento, cariño – dice la señora Martínez. Su maquillaje se ha corrido - . Es que has crecido tan rápido... No puedo creer que te estés **marchando** a estudiar una carrera a la gran ciudad.

Santiago abraza a su madre y luego a su hermana menor.

- ¡Adiós! – dice Santiago. Mira por última vez a su familia, con una sonrisa, y le entrega su **pasaje** a la empleada de la **aerolínea**.

El viaje en avión es sorprendentemente corto, de unos cuarenta y cinco minutos. Santiago apenas ha leído unas cuantas páginas de su libro (uno sobre dinosaurios que le ha regalado Luis), cuando el capitán anuncia por **altavoz:**

- **Damas y caballeros,** aterrizaremos en el aeropuerto internacional de Madrid-Barajas en diez minutos. La temperatura fuera es de veinte grados centígrados, con **cielo despejado.** Muchas gracias por volar con nosotros.

Barajas es... *enorme.* Un poco **aturdido,** arrastrando su pesada **maleta** y con una gran **mochila** en su espalda, Santiago se abre paso entre las personas que corren para no perder su vuelo. Un rato después, encuentra una gran puerta de cristal que da al exterior. Cuando sale, ve una **fila** de taxis blancos esperando y se sube a uno.

- Buenos días – saluda Santiago – . Tengo que ir a la calle Rosas, número 56.

- Vale – responde el **taxista,** y comienza a **conducir** – . ¿Vienes de muy lejos?

- De Montijo, un pequeño pueblo cerca de Badajoz – le explica Santiago.

- Eres muy joven. Pareces tener la edad de mi hija. Supongo que vienes a estudiar.

- Así es. He venido para estudiar Paleontología en la Universidad Central de Madrid.

- ¿Paleontolo... qué?

- Es la ciencia que estudia los fósiles.

- Entonces, ¿descubrirás dinosaurios? – pregunta el taxista.

- Bueno, ¡eso espero!

- Qué interesante. Mi hija también comenzará a estudiar en la Universidad Central de Madrid este año. Estudiará **Bibliotecología.** Casi tan emocionante como descubrir dinosaurios.

- Bibliotecología era mi segunda opción – responde Santiago – . ¡Me encanta leer!

- Os llevaríais bien – responde el taxista.

El taxista sigue conduciendo por las calles de Madrid y Santiago mira por la ventana. Son las diez de la mañana y la ciudad está en su momento de mayor actividad. Las calles están **llenas de gente**. Todos caminan **con prisa**, como si estuvieran **llegando tarde** a algún sitio. La arquitectura de los edificios es bellísima.

Entonces, Santiago se da cuenta de que algo anda mal. Hace casi **media hora** que está en el taxi. Según sus **cálculos**, el viaje desde el aeropuerto hasta su nueva casa era mucho más corto. Además, está **atravesando** el **centro de la ciudad**, y se suponía que no era necesario.

El taxista **detiene** el **coche** frente a un **edificio** enorme. Ese lugar no tiene absolutamente nada que ver con lo que él ha visto en las fotos que le ha enviado Beatriz, su futura compañera de piso.

– Bueno, hemos llegado – dice el taxista.

– ¿Está seguro de que es aquí? – pregunta Santiago, nervioso. ¡Lo último que quiere es perderse en una de las ciudades más grandes de Europa nada más llegar!

– Sí: calle Rosas, número 56.

Santiago paga y se baja del taxi, que se aleja calle arriba. **Alza** la cabeza y contempla el edificio, que debe tener unas veinte **plantas**. Definitivamente, está en el lugar incorrecto. Entonces, decide sacar su **móvil** del **bolsillo** y llamar a Beatriz.

– ¡Hola, Beatriz! Soy Santiago Martínez.

– ¡Ah, mi nuevo compañero de piso! – dice Beatriz de buen humor –Te estoy esperando. ¿Está todo bien? Pensé que llegarías más **temprano**.

– Sí... Bueno, en realidad no. Creo que le he dicho mal la **dirección** al taxista.

– ¿Dónde estás?

– En la calle Rosas, número 56.

Del otro lado del teléfono, Beatriz suelta una carcajada:

– ¡Estás en la otra punta de la ciudad!

– ¿Cómo?

– La dirección del piso es calle Ríos Rosas, número 56.

– ¡No puede ser! ¿Y ahora qué hago?

Santiago mira su equipaje. Atravesar toda la ciudad con una mochila **pesadísima** y una maleta a cuestas no es muy tentador... pero no tiene otra opción.

– Descuida, iré a buscarte en mi coche – le dijo Beatriz, divertida – . Llegaré en media hora.

– Vale. Muchas gracias, Beatriz. Nos vemos.

Santiago suspira y se sienta en el **cordón de la acera** a esperar. Está un poco **avergonzado,** pero ¡por suerte Beatriz parece muy simpática!

Vocabulary List

Español	Inglés
ajustado / ajustada de tiempo	short on time
despachar	to drop off
el equipaje	luggage
el vuelo	flight
¡Qué tengas un buen viaje!	Have a nice trip!
la compañera / el compañero de vivienda / piso	roommate
el piso	apartment
la habitación para invitados	guest room
la lágrima	tear
llorar	to cry
marcharse	to leave

el pasaje	ticket
la aerolínea	airline
el altavoz	speaker
damas y caballeros	ladies and gentlemen
el cielo despejado	clear sky
aturdido / aturdida	stunned
la maleta	suitcase
la mochila	backpack
la fila	row
el / la taxista	taxi driver
conducir	to drive
Bibliotecología	Librarianship
lleno / llena de gente	filled with people
con prisa	hurriedly
llegar tarde	to be late
la media hora	half an hour
el cálculo	estimate

atravesar	to go through
el centro de la ciudad	city center
detener	to stop
el coche	car
el edificio	building
alzar	to lift
el móvil	mobile phone
el bolsillo	pocket
temprano	early
la dirección	address
pesadísima / pesadísimo	really heavy
el cordón de la acera	sidewalk curb
avergonzado / avergonzada	embarrassed

Summary of the Story in Spanish

Santiago Martínez vive en Montijo, un pueblo cerca de Badajoz, pero viaja en avión a Madrid para estudiar Paleontología en la Universidad Central de Madrid. Cuando llega al aeropuerto Madrid-Barajas, toma un taxi y le dice al taxista la dirección del piso que compartirá con una chica llamada Beatriz. Cuando llegan a la dirección, Santiago se baja del taxi, pero está seguro de que ese no es el lugar correcto, así que llama a Beatriz. ¡Santiago se ha equivocado de dirección y está al otro lado de la ciudad! Por fortuna, Beatriz se ofrece a ir a buscarlo hasta allí en coche y Santiago se sienta a esperarla.

Exercises

1. Cuando llegan al aeropuerto, Santiago y su familia corren porque...

   a. está lleno de gente.

   b. están ajustados de tiempo.

   c. no quieren perder el tiempo.

2. ¿Cuál de las siguientes frases es correcta?

   a. ¡Qué tengas un bien viaje!

   b. ¡Qué tengas un viaje buen!

   c. ¡Qué tengas un buen viaje!

3. Completa las siguientes oraciones:

   a. Luis es el mejor _____ de Santiago.

   b. Beatriz es la compañera de _____ de Santiago.

   c. Luis sube a un _____.

4. ¿Qué ve Santiago por la ventana? Elige la respuesta correcta.

   a. Las calles vacías.

   b. Gente caminando lento.

   c. Edificios bellísimos.

5. ¿A cuál de estas direcciones tenía que ir Santiago?

   a. Calle Ríos Rosas, número 56.

   b. Calle Rosas, número 56.

   c. Calle Rozas, número 56.

Comprehension Questions

1. ¿Quiénes acompañan a Santiago al aeropuerto?

2. ¿Dónde vivirá Santiago en Madrid y con quién?

3. ¿Qué estudiará Santiago?

4. ¿Qué hace Santiago cuando se da cuenta del error?

5. ¿Cómo irá Beatriz a buscar a Santiago?

Summary of the Story in English

Santiago Martínez lives in Montijo, a town near Badajoz, but he flies to Madrid to study Paleontology at the Universidad Central de Madrid. When he gets to Madrid-Barajas airport, he takes a taxi and tells the driver the address of the apartment he will share with a girl named

Beatriz. When they arrive at the address, Santiago gets out of the taxi, but he is certain that it isn't the right place, so he calls Beatriz. Santiago had the wrong address and is on the other side of the city! Luckily, Beatriz offers to pick him up there by car, and Santiago sits down to wait for her.

Did you know...?

Spanish is the official language of Spain, and it is the most widely spoken language in the country. However, some of the autonomous communities that make up Spain have other co-official languages: Catalan and Aranese in Catalonia, Basque in the Basque Country, Valencian (a variety of Catalan) in the Valencian community, and Galician in Galicia. In addition to the official languages, Spain also has many non-official languages spoken in different regions: Aragonese in Aragon, Asturian in Asturias, and Leonese in Castile and Leon.

Lastly, in Spain, there are also many dialects like Andalusian, Canarian, Cantabrian, Eonavian, Benasquese, Fala, and Extremaduran. In fact, since Santiago comes from Montijo, which is in the autonomous community of Extremadura, he speaks the Extremaduran dialect, which would be noticeable, above all, in his pronunciation.

Chapter 2: Hogar, Dulce Hogar – Home Sweet Home

Story in Spanish: La compañera de piso

Beatriz es una chica muy carismática... ¡y **charlatana**! Ha estado hablando durante todo el viaje sin parar un segundo. Santiago se ha enterado de muchas cosas de su vida: tiene treinta años, está trabajando como **camarera** en un restaurante y ha nacido en Málaga. Vive en Madrid desde hace unos diez años.

- Este es el edificio – dice Beatriz, **aparcando** el coche frente al portal del número 56. Ríos Rosas es una calle hermosa, con **adoquines** y edificios bajos. Es **silenciosa**, a pesar de que hay una **transitada** avenida a pocos metros.

- Es un edificio muy **antiguo**, ¿no? – pregunta Santiago cogiendo sus maletas y mirando su nuevo hogar – . Diría que de la década del 20.

- No sé de qué década es, pero sí, es *muy* antiguo – confirma Beatriz – . El **ascensor** tiene un millón de años. A veces no funciona, así que espero que no te moleste subir tres pisos por las **escaleras** de vez en cuando. Bueno... casi siempre.

Santiago mira su pesadísimo equipaje. Está cansado y hambriento, pero solo tiene que hacer un esfuerzo más. Pronto, podrá desplomarse en su **cama** y descansar un rato.

- Supongo que no será un problema – responde al final.

Entre los dos, suben el equipaje por las escaleras. Finalmente, exhaustos, llegan hasta el apartamento.

- Bueno, ¡bienvenido a casa! - dice Beatriz.

La **sala** es **amplia** y **luminosa**. Hay un sofá grande de color rojo con muchos **almohadones encima**. **Enfrente**, hay un gran televisor. **Entre** el sofá y el televisor hay una **mesa de café** de estilo industrial. **Contra la pared**, hay una **estantería** con algunos libros. Por todos lados hay muchas plantas muy bonitas. Un poco más allá, hay una gran mesa de madera con cuatro sillas **alrededor**. **En el centro** de la mesa hay un enorme **florero**. También hay un pequeño **balcón** con vistas a la calle.

Todo está muy limpio y ordenado.

- Esta es la sala y el **comedor** - explica Beatriz - . Es mi parte favorita de la casa. Los jueves por la noche, aquí me reúno con mis amigos para ver películas. Así que, si no tienes otros planes, puedes unirte a nosotros. Esta semana toca noche de terror.

- ¡Me encantaría! - responde Santiago.

- Guay - dice Beatriz - . Bueno, sigamos. Voy a mostrarte el cuarto de baño.

- Espera. ¿Y ese **cuadro**? - Santiago está señalando una enorme pintura de estilo realista. Representa a una mujer de cabello negro y rizado y ojos grises y muy expresivos - . Es increíble. ¿Lo has comprado, o venía con la casa cuando la alquilaste?

- Ninguna de las dos cosas. Lo he pintado yo misma.

- ¡No puedo creerlo! ¿Eres pintora?

- Oh, claro que no. Es solo un **pasatiempo**. Un tonto pasatiempo, en realidad. No soy más que una aficionada.

- Yo creo que eres una excelente artista.

- Gracias - responde Beatriz.

Santiago puede ver que se está sonrojando.

- ¡De nada!

Beatriz se pone en marcha nuevamente. Le enseña a Santiago el **cuarto de baño**, que tiene una **ducha**, un **lavabo** y un **inodoro**, y luego lo conduce hasta la **cocina**. La cocina tiene un **microondas**, un **horno**, una **cafetera**, una **tostadora**, un **lavavajillas** y una **nevera**. Del otro lado de la cocina hay una pequeña **lavandería** que cuenta con una **lavadora** y una **secadora**.

- Bueno, creo que eso es todo - dice Beatriz.

- ¿Y mi **habitación**? - pregunta Santiago.

- ¡Oh, por supuesto! Lo había olvidado. Ven, sígueme.

Beatriz conduce a Santiago por un **pasillo**. Hay algunos otros cuadros, todos muy bonitos, colgados contra las paredes. Santiago se pregunta si estos también los ha pintado Beatriz. Finalmente, Beatriz abre la última puerta del pasillo.

- Este es tu dormitorio - dice Beatriz.

Es un ambiente pequeño, pero práctico: tiene una cama, un **escritorio** y un gran **armario**. Lo mejor de todo es que tiene una ventana desde la que se ve un bonito parque.

- Mi dormitorio está al lado. Hay dos habitaciones más. Una de ellas estará disponible para alojar a nuestras visitas. La otra será para otro compañero de piso. He puesto un anuncio en un foro de internet, y me han escrito unas cuantas personas... pero creo que ya tengo a la indicada. Vendrá este fin de semana.

- ¡Me muero de ganas por conocerla! - responde Santiago.

- Seguro nos llevaremos bien - dice Beatriz - . Una última cosa: debes saber que soy *demasiado* **ordenada**.

- ¿De verdad? - pregunta Santiago esperando que eso no sea un problema. No puede decirse que él sea desordenado, pero definitivamente no es un obsesivo del orden.

- Mi sugerencia es que mantengamos lo más ordenados posible los lugares comunes: la sala, la cocina y el cuarto de baño.

- Vale - responde Santiago.

- Por supuesto, no tienes que preocuparte por Lila. Yo me encargaré de comprar su alimento y de mantener su caja limpia.

- ¿Lila? - pregunta Santiago, desconcertado - . ¿Quién es Lila?

En ese mismo momento, un enorme gato blanco salta desde un mueble cercano y aterriza en los brazos de Santiago.

- ¡Mira, le has caído bien! - dice Beatriz.

Vocabulary List

Español	Inglés
charlatán / charlatana	chatty
el camarero / la camarera	waiter / waitress
aparcar	to park
el adoquín	cobblestone
silencioso / silenciosa	quiet
transitado / transitada	busy
antiguo / antigua	old
el ascensor	elevator
las escaleras	stairs
la cama	bed
la sala	living room
amplio / amplia	wide
luminoso / luminosa	bright
el almohadón	cushion
encima	on top
enfrente	in front of

entre	between
la mesa de café	coffee table
contra la pared	against the wall
la estantería	shelf
alrededor	around
en el centro	in the center
el florero	flower vase
el balcón	balcony
el comedor	dining room
el cuadro	painting
el pasatiempo	hobby
el cuarto de baño	bathroom
la ducha	shower
el lavabo	sink
el inodoro	toilet
la cocina	kitchen
el microondas	microwave

el horno	oven
la cafetera	coffee maker
la tostadora	toaster
el lavavajillas	dishwasher
la nevera	fridge
la lavandería	laundry room
la lavadora	washing machine
la secadora	drier
la habitación	bedroom
el pasillo	corridor
el escritorio	desk
el armario	closet
ordenado / ordenada	tidy

Summary of the Story in Spanish

Beatriz habla todo el camino hasta la casa y Santiago aprende más cosas sobre ella. Una vez que llegan, Beatriz explica que el ascensor no siempre funciona, así que tienen que subir por las escaleras. Beatriz le enseña a Santiago la sala, el comedor, el baño, la cocina, la lavandería y, al final, su dormitorio. Beatriz le explica que llegará otra compañera de piso el fin de semana y que es demasiado ordenada y quiere que mantengan las áreas comunes tan limpias como puedan. Santiago descubre que también vivirá con Lila, un gato.

Exercises

1. Señala el elemento que no pertenece a la sala:
   a. Estantería
   b. Inodoro
   c. Almohadones

2. ¿Dónde está la estantería?
   a. Enfrente del sofá
   b. En el centro de la mesa
   c. Contra la pared

3. ¿Cuál de estos objetos se puede encontrar en la cocina?
   a. Lavavajillas
   b. Ducha
   c. Escritorio

4. La habitación de Santiago es...
   a. Grande y espaciosa
   b. Pequeña y práctica
   c. Demasiado pequeña

5. ¿Quién es Lila?
   a. El gato de Beatriz
   b. La nueva compañera de piso
   c. La mejor amiga de Beatriz

Comprehension Questions

1. ¿Cómo es la calle Ríos Rosas?
2. ¿Qué hay entre la mesa y el televisor?
3. ¿Qué hace Beatriz los jueves por la noche?
4. ¿Cuál es el pasatiempo de Beatriz?
5. ¿Santiago es desordenado?

Summary of the Story in English

Beatriz talks all the way to the house, and Santiago learns more about her. Once they arrive, Beatriz explains that the elevator doesn't always work, so they take the stairs. Beatriz shows Santiago the living room, dining room, bathroom, kitchen, laundry room, and, lastly, his bedroom. Beatriz explains that another roommate will be arriving on the weekend and that she's too tidy and wants them to keep the common areas as tidy as possible. Santiago finds out that he will also be living with Lila, a cat.

Did you know...?

Of course, rent prices vary throughout Spain, but the average for a 4-bedroom apartment with the characteristics of Beatriz's is around 2,000 EUR / month, and the price per m2 in Madrid is around 13 EUR. However, it should be noted that Madrid is the most expensive city to live in, while Extremadura (where Santiago is from) is one of the cheapest areas.

In Spain, rental contracts usually last for five years, and the deposit shouldn't exceed two months' rent. As for the requirements, you will be required to present your work contract and last three payslips (or you will be asked to prove your financial means another way), your NIE (foreigner's identity number), and your passport. If you rent through an agency, you will be asked for a reservation fee equivalent to a month's rent (which the agency must return).

Chapter 3: Una Visita del Primo Pedro – A Visit from Cousin Pedro

Story in Spanish: ¿Cómo está la familia?

Beatriz abre los ojos. Anoche ha tenido que trabajar en el **turno nocturno** del restaurante, así que está muy cansada. Entonces, se da cuenta de que su móvil lleva sonando un buen rato. Mira la **pantalla del teléfono**: se trata de un número **desconocido**.

– ¿Hola? – pregunta, y **da un bostezo**.

– Hola, ¿hablo con Beatriz Gutiérrez? – pregunta la voz de un hombre desde el otro lado.

– Sí... ¿quién es?

– Soy Pedro – responde el hombre.

Beatriz hace un esfuerzo para pensar en quién es Pedro. Todavía sigue un poco dormida, pero está segura de que ninguno de sus amigos se llama así.

– Creo que estás equivocado – dice Beatriz, y se dispone a **colgar la llamada**.

Justo en ese momento, el hombre dice:

– ¡Pedro Gutiérrez! ¡Tu primo!

¡El primo Pedro! Por supuesto, no le ha **reconocido** la voz. No lo ve desde hace muchos años. Aunque los dos estaban muy unidos de pequeños porque tienen la misma edad, han **perdido contacto** cuando

Beatriz se mudó de Málaga a Madrid.

— Primo Pedro, ¿cómo estás? — pregunta Beatriz —. ¿Está todo bien? ¿Sigues viviendo en Málaga?

— Sigo viviendo en Málaga, sí, aunque ahora estoy en Madrid. He venido por **negocios**. Tengo el vuelo de regreso a Málaga esta tarde, pero he pensado que podía visitarte antes de marcharme.

— Claro — responde Beatriz —. ¿Quieres **almorzar** en casa hoy?

— Excelente. ¿A la una **en punto**?

— ¡A la una en punto!

Beatriz cuelga la llamada y se levanta de la cama. Luego, va hasta la habitación de Santiago. El chico está sentado en su escritorio mientras lee un libro con el **ceño fruncido**, muy concentrado.

— Buenos días, Santi.

— ¡Hola, Bea! ¿Cómo estás?

— Muy bien. Oye, en algunas horas vendrá a comer Pedro, un primo a quien no veo desde hace algunos años. He pensado que puedo cocinar **ajoblanco malagueño**, una receta de mi abuela. ¿Te **apuntas**?

— Suena delicioso... pero no puedo — dice Santiago con tristeza —. Tengo que ir a la universidad. El **próximo** lunes comienzan las clases, así que tengo que **inscribirme** a mis **asignaturas**.

— Por supuesto — dice Beatriz —. Te guardaré una porción.

— Eso me encantaría — responde Santiago.

Poco después de que Santiago se vaya, **suena** el **timbre**. Desde el **telefonillo**, Beatriz le abre la puerta de la calle a su primo. Al minuto, aparece Pedro en la puerta del piso. Es un joven alto, con el cabello **bien peinado** y con un **pulcro** traje negro. Además, tiene un **maletín** en su mano. Es un **hombre de negocios**. ¡Todo lo contrario a Beatriz, que viste de forma muy **casual** y está llena de tatuajes!

— ¡Primo Pedro! — saluda Beatriz, y ambos se dan un breve abrazo —. No te he visto desde la **boda** de mi hermano Manolo. Ven, pasa. El almuerzo está servido. He hecho ajoblanco malagueño.

— ¡Como el que hacía la abuela! — dice Pedro, mientras se sienta a la mesa —. Siempre has sido una gran cocinera, prima.

— Jamás podría igualar la receta de la abuela — responde Beatriz con una sonrisa, sentándose también —. Bueno, cuéntame, Pedro. ¿Cómo estás?

- Bien, Bea. Sigo trabajando en el estudio de arquitectos. He venido a Madrid para reunirme con algunos inversores.

- ¿Y cómo está todo por Málaga?

- Muy bien. Tengo muchas novedades. ¿Recuerdas a María, mi **novia**? Bueno, vamos a casarnos en junio.

- **¡Enhorabuena!**

- Muchas gracias. Espero que puedas venir. Haremos una gran boda en la playa.

- Por supuesto. Allí estaré. ¿Y cómo están los **hijos** de tu **hermana** Sandra?

- **¡Preciosos y enormes!** - responde Pedro - . Andrés va a cumplir siete años pronto. **Habla hasta por los codos.** Está en esa etapa en la que pregunta absolutamente *todo* lo que se le ocurre. «Mamá, ¿por qué debo comer verduras?», «mamá, ¿cuánta sal hay en el mar?». - Pedro y Beatriz ríen a carcajadas - . La pequeña Fernanda cumplió cinco años el mes pasado. Le ha pedido a Sandra y al padre, Miguel, que la apunten a clases de fútbol. Le encanta el deporte.

- ¿Y tus padres cómo están? - pregunta Beatriz - . No he visto a los tíos Antonio y Francisca desde hace mucho tiempo.

- Ellos están bien - responde Pedro - . Mamá sigue trabajando en el hospital. Papá continúa **al frente del** estudio de arquitectos familiar. Ya está viejo: ¡tiene el pelo **canoso**! Sandra y yo le decimos que es momento de **jubilarse.** Que se dedique a descansar y viajar. Que nosotros dos podemos hacernos cargo de la empresa. Pero ¡él insiste con seguir trabajando!

- Pero tu padre siempre fue muy jovial - dice Beatriz - . La última vez que lo vi, parecía una persona de cuarenta años. Además, los Gutiérrez somos personas muy **enérgicas.**

- Eso es verdad - dice Pedro - . Bueno, Beatriz, cuéntame algo de ti. ¿Cómo estás? ¿Sigues pintando esos cuadros maravillosos?

- Sí, de vez en cuando - responde Beatriz, ligeramente sonrojada - . Aunque no me dedico a eso. Trabajo en un restaurante que queda a pocas calles de aquí. La verdad es que estoy bien. Me gusta mi empleo, tengo muchos amigos y ¡estoy enamorada de Madrid!

- ¿Quién no? - dice Pedro - . Nunca te aburres en Madrid. Teatros, conciertos, parques... Siempre hay cosas para hacer aquí. Me gustaría venir más seguido, pero tengo mucho trabajo allá en Málaga - En ese

mismo momento, el móvil de Pedro empieza a sonar. – ¿Me disculpas?
– Claro.

Pedro se lleva el móvil a la oreja.

– ¿Hola? Sí, soy yo. Ajá. Claro. Es una lástima. ¿Y no tienen...? Ya veo. Bueno, muchas gracias por avisarme. – Cuelga. Parece algo **preocupado**.

– ¿Está todo bien? – pregunta Beatriz.

– Más o menos. Han cancelado mi vuelo de regreso a Málaga, y no hay otro hasta mañana por la tarde. – Pedro se levanta de la silla – . Creo que será mejor que me marche, Bea. Debo buscar un hotel para pasar la noche.

– ¿Un hotel? – pregunta Beatriz – . ¡Nada de eso, primo! Te puedes quedar en casa. Hay una habitación para invitados. Allí estarás **cómodo**.

– Pero ¿no es mucha molestia?

– Claro que no. ¡Somos familia!

Vocabulary List

Español	Inglés
el turno nocturno	night shift
la pantalla del teléfono	phone's screen
desconocido / desconocida	unknown
dar un bostezo	to yawn
colgar la llamada	to hang up the phone
reconocer	to recognize
perder contacto	to lose contact
el negocio	business

almorzar	to have lunch
en punto	o'clock
el ceño fruncido	furrowed brow
el ajoblanco malagueño	a popular Spanish cold soup made of bread, almonds, and garlic
apuntarse	to be up for it
próximo / próxima	next
inscribirse	enroll
la asignatura	subject
sonar	to ring
el timbre	doorbell
el telefonillo	intercom
bien peinado / peinada	well-groomed
pulcro / pulcra	smart
el maletín	briefcase
el hombre de negocios / la mujer de negocios	businessman / businesswoman
casual	casually

la boda	wedding
la novia	girlfriend
¡Enhorabuena!	Congratulations!
el hijo / la hija	son / daughter
la hermana / el hermano	sister / brother
precioso / preciosa	beautiful
enorme	very big
hablar hasta por los codos	to talk someone's ear off
al frente de	in charge of
canoso / canosa	with gray hair
jubilarse	to retire
enérgico / enérgica	vigorous
preocupado / preocupada	worried
cómodo / cómoda	comfortable

Summary of the Story in Spanish

Beatriz recibe una llamada sorpresa. Su primo Pedro, a quien no ve hace mucho tiempo, está en Madrid por negocios. Su vuelo sale por la tarde, así que lo invita a almorzar. Beatriz también invita a Santiago a sumarse al almuerzo, pero tiene que ir a la universidad a inscribirse a las asignaturas. Cuando llega Pedro, le cuenta sobre su vida: va a casarse con su novia María, sus sobrinos están grandes, sus padres están bien. Por su parte, Beatriz le cuenta que sigue pintando, que trabaja de camarera y que es muy feliz en Madrid. En ese momento, Pedro recibe una llamada y se entera que su vuelo ha sido pospuesto hasta el día siguiente, por lo que Beatriz lo invita a quedarse a pasar la noche en su casa.

Exercises

1. Señala el adjetivo que no describe el aspecto de Pedro:
   a. Pulcro
   b. Casual
   c. Bien peinado

2. ¿Quién es María?
   a. La hermana de Pedro
   b. La sobrina de Pedro
   c. La novia de Pedro

3. ¿Qué miembro de la familia hacía ajoblanco?
   a. La abuela
   b. La tía
   c. El padre

4. Santiago no puede sumarse al almuerzo porque...
   a. Ese día empiezan las clases
   b. Está estudiando
   c. Tiene que inscribirse a las asignaturas

5. ¿Dónde va a pasar la noche Pedro?
   a. En casa de su prima Beatriz
   b. En su casa en Málaga
   c. En un hotel

Comprehension Questions

1. ¿Por qué Beatriz está cansada al principio de la historia?
2. ¿Por qué Beatriz y Pedro estaban unidos de pequeños?
3. ¿Desde cuándo no se veían Beatriz y Pedro?
4. ¿Qué edad tiene Fernanda? ¿Y Andrés?
5. ¿Qué le gusta a Pedro de Madrid?

Summary of the Story in English

Beatriz receives a surprise phone call. Her cousin Pedro, whom she hasn't seen for a long time, is in Madrid for business. His flight leaves in the afternoon, so she invites him for lunch. Beatriz also invites Santiago to join them for lunch, but he has to go to university to enroll in classes. When Pedro arrives, he tells Beatriz about his life: he's going to marry his girlfriend María, his niece and nephew are grown up, and his parents are doing well. For her part, Beatriz tells him that she is still painting, that she works as a waitress, and that she's very happy in Madrid. Then, Pedro gets a phone call and learns that his flight has been postponed until the next day, so Beatriz invites him to stay the night at her house.

Did you know...?

Spain is well-known for its cuisine, which includes many world-famous dishes and ingredients, such as Iberian ham, *tortillas*, and *paellas*. But it's not only Spanish food that is different; its dining customs are different too. For example, when it comes to eating out, it's very unusual to go to a single restaurant and stay there for a long time. Spanish people – especially in cities – prefer to *ir de tapas*, which means having a drink with a small dish at one bar, often standing up, and then walking to another one. It's something like a pub crawl, but with the difference that the focus is more on eating than on drinking. However, the most traditional drink, in this case, is the *caña*: a small glass of beer, usually a half-pint.

This tradition is so institutionalized that, in most places, if you order a *caña*, the waiter will also bring you a *tapa* ¡on the house! However, the content of the *tapa* varies greatly. Some are generous, others are not, and it can be anything from a piece of *tortilla* to a few slices of ham, olives, squid rings... you name it!

Chapter 4: Haciendo Turismo – Going Sightseeing

Story in Spanish: Una mañana en Madrid

El sábado, Santiago está decidido a salir a **recorrer** la ciudad. Solo faltan dos días para que comiencen las clases en la universidad, y cree que luego no va a tener mucho tiempo para **pasear**.

Mientras desayuna, recibe una llamada. Es Bea.

- Hola, Santi. Ya estoy en el trabajo: hoy me ha tocado cubrir el **turno de la mañana**. Quería contarte que esta tarde, a las tres, llegará nuestra nueva compañera de piso, y me ha pedido que la **vaya a buscar** a la **estación de trenes** de Atocha. ¿Te gustaría venir conmigo?

- Claro, Bea - dice Santiago - . Iré a recorrer la ciudad, pero estaré allí a las tres en punto.

- Vale. ¡Que te diviertas!

En ese mismo momento, el móvil de Santiago se apaga. Entonces, recuerda que la noche anterior se ha olvidado de **enchufarlo** a la corriente y ahora se ha quedado sin batería.

«¡Qué problema!», piensa Santiago. «Esto significa que no podré consultar el GPS... y Madrid es gigante».

Entonces, recuerda que, en Montijo, su mejor amigo Luis le ha dado un mapa de Madrid antes de despedirlo. Tras buscarlo durante un rato, lo encuentra en uno de los **bolsillos laterales** de su mochila. En el mapa, Luis ha marcado algunos de los lugares más importantes de Madrid.

Santiago se viste con ropa ligera y gafas de sol y sale a la calle, dispuesto a comenzar su aventura madrileña.

Su primera **parada** es el Museo de Ciencias Naturales. Según el mapa, queda bastante cerca de su vivienda. Efectivamente, solo tarda un **cuarto de hora** en llegar. El museo es hermoso y tiene la colección paleontológica más grande que Santiago ha visto en su vida. Está tan entusiasmado observando los fósiles de dinosaurios que pasa dos horas allí dentro.

Cuando sale del museo, se dirige al parque del Retiro, su segunda parada. Según el mapa, está a un par de kilómetros de allí... ¡pero no tiene ni idea de cómo llegar!

– Disculpe, señora – le dice a una mujer que pasa por allí – , quiero ir al parque del Retiro. **¿Podría indicarme cómo llegar?**

– Claro, querido. Tienes que tomar el autobús de la línea 14.

– ¿Dónde está la parada?

– Justo allá, enfrente de la farmacia.

– Vale. ¿Y dónde tengo que bajarme?

– Cuando veas la Fuente de Cibeles. Es un viaje muy corto, de unos diez minutos.

– ¿Y sabe cuánto cuesta el **billete de autobús?**

– Un euro con cincuenta – responde la mujer.

– ¡Muchas gracias, señora!

Siguiendo las **indicaciones** de la mujer, Santiago llega al Retiro sin ninguna dificultad. Se trata de un parque gigantesco lleno de interesantes plantas y árboles. También hay muchos monumentos como estatuas y edificios. ¡Incluso hay un palacio hecho totalmente de cristal!

Después del paseo, Santiago está exhausto, así que decide parar en un pequeño restaurante para almorzar algo.

– Buenos días, chaval – dice el camarero – . **¿Qué te pongo?**

– **¿Qué me recomienda**, señor?

– La **especialidad de la casa** es el cocido madrileño. Es un guiso con garbanzos, verduras, carne y embutidos.

– Perfecto, pediré eso. Y para beber, póngame un buen vaso de **zumo** de naranja, por favor. Necesito recargar energías para seguir recorriendo la ciudad.

Después de almorzar, Santiago consulta el mapa que le ha dado Luis. Uno de los sitios turísticos más cercanos de su ubicación es el Palacio de Oriente, así que se encamina hacia allí. Afortunadamente, llega a las puertas del palacio justo a tiempo para sumarse a una **visita guiada**. La guía es una mujer joven y simpática.

- Mi nombre es Carmen y seré vuestra **guía turística** esta tarde en el Palacio de Oriente - dice - . Esta es la residencia oficial de los **reyes** de España, aunque actualmente no viven aquí. Vamos a entrar. Seguidme.

Santiago entra en el palacio junto al grupo de turistas, maravillado con lo que ve. La guía turística resulta ser muy buena y sabe muchísimo acerca del palacio y de todo Madrid. Santiago aprende, por ejemplo, que el palacio es uno de los más grandes del mundo: tiene 3500 habitaciones y duplica el tamaño del palacio de Buckingham en Londres. También aprende que desde el edificio parten numerosos **túneles subterráneos** que lo conectan con diferentes puntos de la capital española.

- Bueno - dice la guía turística después de un rato - . Ya van a ser las dos y media. Es hora de hacer una pausa para que comáis algo y os refresquéis. Nos veremos en la Plaza de la Armería en media hora.

- ¿Has dicho que ya son las dos y media? - pregunta Santiago, asombrado.

¡Ha **quedado con** Beatriz para ir a recoger a su nueva compañera de piso! Al no llevar su móvil encima y no tener ningún **reloj**, ha perdido por completo la **noción del tiempo**. Mientras todos los turistas empiezan a irse, Santiago se acerca a Carmen.

- He olvidado que tengo que hacer una cosa. Tengo que estar en la estación de trenes de Atocha en media hora. ¿Sabes cuál es la ruta más rápida, Carmen?

- Claro. Tienes que tomar la línea 2 del metro en la estación Ópera. Está justo enfrente de un gran supermercado. Baja en la estación Sol y haz trasbordo con la línea 1 del metro. Cuatro paradas más tarde, te tienes que bajar en la estación Valdecarros. ¡Y eso es todo! Llegarás a Atocha en veinte minutos.

- Vale, Carmen. ¡Muchas gracias!

Santiago sale a toda prisa del palacio, intentando memorizar todas las indicaciones que le ha dado Carmen.

Vocabulary List

Español	Inglés
recorrer	to explore
pasear	to walk around
el turno de la mañana	morning shift
ir a buscar	to pick up
la estación de trenes	train station
enchufar	to plug
el bolsillo lateral	side pocket
la parada	stop
el cuarto de hora	fifteen minutes
¿Podría indicarme cómo llegar?	Could you tell me how to get there?
el billete de autobús	bus ticket
las indicaciones	directions
¿Qué te pongo?	What can I get you?
¿Qué me recomienda?	What do you recommend?
la especialidad de la casa	specialty of the house

el zumo	juice
la visita guiada	guided tour
el / la guía turístico / turística	tour guide
los reyes	monarchs
el túnel subterráneo	underground tunnel
quedar con	to arrange to meet
el reloj	watch
la noción del tiempo	sense of time

Summary of the Story in Spanish

Santiago decide salir a recorrer la ciudad, ¡pero se olvidó de cargar el móvil! Por suerte, su amigo Luis le ha regalado un mapa de Madrid en el que ha marcado varios sitios de interés. Primero, Santiago visita el Museo de Ciencias Naturales y queda maravillado con los fósiles. Luego, pide indicaciones para llegar al parque del Retiro y logra llegar sin problemas. Después de recorrer la ciudad, se sienta a comer cocido madrileño en un restaurante. Por último, visita el Palacio Oriente y se suma a una visita guiada. Sin embargo, a las dos y media se da cuenta de que había quedado con Beatriz para buscar a su nueva compañera de piso, así que pide indicaciones para llegar a la estación Atocha.

Exercises

1. ¿Dónde encontró el mapa que le regaló Luis?
    a. En el bolsillo lateral de la mochila.
    b. En el bolsillo trasero de la mochila.
    c. En el bolsillo delantero de la mochila.

2. ¿Cuánto tarda en llegar al Museo de Ciencias Naturales?
    a. 1 hora.
    b. 30 minutos.
    c. 15 minutos.

3. ¿Cuáles de estas cosas encuentra Santiago en el parque del Retiro?

    a. Un palacio.

    b. Mucha gente.

    c. Fósiles.

4. ¿Cuál de las siguientes no es una característica del Palacio de Oriente?

    a. Tiene 3,500 habitaciones.

    b. Triplica el tamaño del palacio de Buckingham.

    c. Está conectado a túneles subterráneos.

5. Santiago ha perdido la noción del tiempo porque...

    a. no lleva el móvil.

    b. perdió el mapa.

    c. quedó sorprendido con la visita.

Comprehension Questions

1. ¿Qué pasó con el celular de Santiago?

2. ¿A quién le pregunta cómo llegar al parque del Retiro?

3. ¿Qué pide Santiago en el restaurante?

4. ¿Dónde se debe encontrar Santiago con Beatriz?

5. ¿Cuántas líneas de metro debe tomar Santiago para encontrarse con Beatriz? ¿Cuánto tardará?

Summary of the Story in English

Santiago decides to go out and explore the city, but he forgot to charge his phone! Luckily, his friend Luis has given him a map of Madrid on which he's marked several sites of interest. First, Santiago visits the Museum of Natural Sciences and is amazed by the fossils. Then, he asks for directions to El Retiro park and manages to get there without any problems. After exploring the city, he sits to eat *cocido madrileño* in a restaurant. Finally, he visits the Oriente palace and joins a guided tour. However, at half past two, he realizes that he had arranged to meet Beatriz to pick up their new roommate, so he asks for directions to Atocha station.

Did you know...?

Like most European cities, Madrid is very old. Its origins are more than unclear: they may be Roman or Muslim and date back to the first or the ninth century. In any case, it didn't start out as a big city. Madrid grew slowly over the years, from a small fortress to a decent-sized town, and it wasn't until the sixteenth century that it became the capital of Spain.

It was a long time ago, but many things from that era remain. Most of Madrid's historic neighborhoods, such as Barrio de las Letras, La Latina, or Lavapiés, with their curved, narrow, and erratic streets, retain the flair of the Middle Ages. But the city had its reforms, too. Many of them are associated with the eighteenth century and the Bourbon dynasty, and, more specifically, with one king in particular: Carlos III, known as "the Best Mayor of Madrid."

Many of the places Santiago visits in the short story were built or reformed by Carlos III. He was the first one to open the Buen Retiro park to the public and also the first king to live in the Oriente Palace. He also commissioned the construction of the Cibeles Fountain and of the buildings that later became the Museo del Prado and the Museo Reina Sofía, the two largest museums in the city. In short: although the layout and the characteristic atmosphere of the city are medieval or baroque, the main monuments of Madrid are mostly from the Enlightenment period, that is, from the eighteenth century.

Chapter 5: La Maestra de la Cocina – The Master Chef

Story in Spanish: Paellas, migas extremeñas y ensaladas mediterráneas

Patricia Solano, la nueva compañera de piso de Beatriz y Santiago, tiene veinticinco años y ha venido desde Barcelona. Beatriz y Santiago le han hecho un recorrido por todo el piso.

- Es un piso muy bonito y muy bien **ubicado** - dice Patricia - . Aunque la parte que más me ha gustado, sin dudas, ha sido la cocina. ¡Está muy bien **equipada**!

- ¿Eso quiere decir que te gusta cocinar? - pregunta Santiago.

- ¿Estás **bromeando**? ¡Soy **cocinera** profesional! - dice Patricia.

- ¿De verdad? - pregunta Beatriz.

- Claro. No **pasaréis hambre** mientras yo viva en esta casa. Me encanta cocinar para mí y para los demás. Es mi pasión.

- ¡Qué excelente noticia! - dice Santiago - . Yo soy bastante malo en la cocina. Bea, en cambio, es muy buena. El otro día preparó un ajoblanco malagueño que estaba delicioso.

- Una receta de mi abuela - confirma Beatriz, sonriente.

- Me encantaría probarla - dice Patricia.

- ¿Y en qué trabajas, Patri? - pregunta Santiago.

- Durante los últimos tres años, fui **jefa de cocina** en un importante hotel en Barcelona. Me marché porque el **ambiente laboral** no era bueno. Actualmente estoy **desempleada**. Si sabéis de algún **curro**, os **agradeceré** que me lo mencionéis.

– Claro – dice Beatriz – . En el restaurante en que trabajo hay buen clima. Mis compañeros son muy **guays**, y mis **jefes** son personas **justas**. Voy a preguntarles si necesitan gente.

– Perfecto – dice Patricia – . Bueno, entonces, decidme: ¿qué comida os gusta? Me gustaría ir conociendo vuestras preferencias para saber qué cocinar.

– A mí me gusta todo – dice Santiago – . Me encanta el **pescado**, por ejemplo. Adoro la **paella**. También me flipan el **gazpacho** y las migas extremeñas.

– ¿Migas extremeñas? – pregunta Patricia – . Nunca las he preparado. ¿Qué llevan?

– Llevan **pan** del día anterior, **pimientos** verdes y rojos, **huevos**, **ajo**, chorizo, **panceta** y condimentos. ¡Ah! Y **aceite de oliva**. Mi madre hace las mejores migas extremeñas de todo Badajoz. Le preguntaré cuál es su receta secreta.

– Muy bien. ¿Y a ti, Bea? ¿Qué te gusta comer? – pregunta Patricia.

– Yo soy **vegetariana**. Me encanta la **ensalada** mediterránea, con **tomate, lechuga, zanahoria** y **aceitunas**. También me gusta la **tortilla de patatas**. Y las **croquetas de queso**.

– ¿Y preferís la comida **frita** o **al horno**?

– Al horno – dice Bea – . La comida **con demasiado aceite** me hace doler el **estómago**.

– A mí me gusta la comida de ambas formas – dice Santiago.

Patricia sonríe y pregunta:

– ¿Hay algo que *no* te guste, Santi?

Santiago piensa durante un momento, y luego responde, con una sonrisa:

– ¡Me parece que no!

Vocabulary List

Español	Inglés
ubicado / ubicada	located
equipada / equipado	equipped
bromear	to kid
la cocinera / el cocinero	cook
pasar hambre	to starve
la jefa de cocina / el jefe de cocina	head chef
el ambiente laboral	work environment
desempleada / desempleado	unemployed
el curro	job
agradecer	to appreciate
guay	cool
el jefe / la jefa	boss
justa / justo	fair
el pescado	fish

la paella	a dish made with round-grain rice, green beans, rabbit, chicken, and duck
el gazpacho	a cold soup made of raw, blended vegetables
el pan	bread
el pimiento	pepper
el huevo	egg
el ajo	garlic
la panceta	bacon
el aceite de oliva	olive oil
vegetariana / vegetariano	vegetarian
la ensalada	salad
el tomate	tomato
la lechuga	lettuce
la zanahoria	carrot
la aceituna	olive
la tortilla de patatas	potato omelet
la croqueta de queso	cheese croquette

frita / frito	fried
al horno	baked
con demasiado aceite	too oily
el estómago	stomach

Summary of the Story in Spanish

Beatriz y Santiago le hacen un recorrido por el piso a su nueva compañera. A Patricia lo que más le gusta es la cocina porque es cocinera profesional. Les cuenta que trabajó durante tres años en un hotel en Barcelona, pero que ahora está desempleada. Beatriz le habla del restaurante donde trabaja y le dice que va a preguntar si necesitan a alguien. Luego, Patricia les pregunta qué les gusta comer para poder cocinarles, y Santiago y Beatriz le cuentan sus gustos.

Exercises

1. ¿Qué parte de la casa le gusta más a Patricia?

   a. La habitación.

   b. El balcón.

   c. La cocina.

2. ¿Por qué Santiago y Beatriz no pasarán hambre?

   a. Porque a ambos les gusta cocinar.

   b. Porque a Patricia le gusta cocinar.

   c. Porque Santiago se ocupa de las compras.

3. ¿Cuál de estos ingredientes no se usa para preparar migas extremeñas?

   a. Tomates.

   b. Pan del día anterior.

   c. Pimientos.

4. ¿Por qué dejó su trabajo Patricia?

   a. Porque había mal ambiente laboral.

   b. Porque le pagaban mal.

   c. Porque le ofrecieron un trabajo mejor.

5. Beatriz no come uno de los siguientes platos. ¿Cuál es?
   a. Croquetas de queso.
   b. Tortilla de patatas.
   c. Sopa de pollo.

Comprehension Questions

1. ¿Quién es Patricia Solano? ¿Qué edad tiene? ¿De dónde viene?
2. ¿Quién cocina mejor, Santiago o Beatriz?
3. ¿Cómo son los compañeros de trabajo de Beatriz? ¿Y sus jefes?
4. ¿Qué lleva la ensalada mediterránea?
5. ¿Por qué Beatriz prefiere la comida al horno?

Summary of the Story in English

Beatriz and Santiago show their new roommate around the apartment. Patricia likes the kitchen the most because she's a professional cook. She tells them that she worked for three years at a hotel in Barcelona - but that now she's unemployed. Beatriz tells her about the restaurant where she works, and she says she's going to ask if they are looking for someone. Then, Patricia asks them what they like to eat so that she can cook for them, and Santiago and Beatriz tell her their tastes.

Did you know...?

Spanish cuisine is very diverse. Although you can find the most popular dishes - such as *croquetas* or *tortillas* - virtually everywhere, every region of the country has its own specialty. *Migas extremeñas* and *gazpacho*, for example, are typical of the South, where Santiago is from. When you think about it, it's not surprising that Andalucía and Extremadura, the hottest regions of the country, came up with cold soups like *gazpacho* or *salmorejo* (a cold cream like *gazpacho*, but with one crucial difference: it includes processed bread, which generates its characteristic orange color).

On the other hand, Patricia is from Barcelona, Catalonia, a coastal region that specializes in fish dishes (and in pastry!). *Paella*, one of Spain's most international dishes, has many variations throughout the country, but probably the best known is in Valencia, where they take great pride in it. Valencia is not in Catalonia - it's, in fact, in the Valencian Community - but it's close, and both regions have a lot in common - including the use of Catalan, which in Valencia takes the form of a particular dialect, Valencian.

So now you know: if you're going to Spain, don't miss the regional dishes!

Chapter 6: La Búsqueda de Trabajo – The Job Hunt

Story in Spanish: Un golpe del destino

Patricia acude a su cuarta entrevista de trabajo en una semana. Es en un restaurante viejo y un poco sucio. El entrevistador es un tipo serio y algo **receloso**. Después de una breve conversación, le pregunta:

- ¿**Hablas otros idiomas**, además del español?

- Sí. Hablo inglés, catalán y un poco de francés – dice Patricia.

- ¿Y **vives cerca de aquí**?

- Vivo en la calle Ríos Rosas, número 56. Está a solo dos estaciones del metro.

- Vale. Yo te llamo.

El entrevistador le devuelve el currículum y Patricia se marcha a su próxima entrevista, que es en un bar muy moderno ubicado en el barrio de Chueca. La entrevistadora es **encantadora** y parece bastante interesada en el perfil de Patricia.

- Aquí dice que has trabajado tres años en el hotel Mediterráneo, que es muy prestigioso... Pero ¿**ese ha sido tu único trabajo?**

- Sí – responde Patricia – . Antes de comenzar a trabajar, estaba estudiando en el Instituto de Cocina de Barcelona.

- Muy bien. – La entrevistadora le devuelve el currículum – . ¿**Sabes preparar cócteles?**

- Nunca lo he hecho, pero ¡puedo intentarlo!

- Vale. Nosotros te llamamos.

La entrevistadora ya no parece tan encantadora.

Frustrada, Patricia se sienta en la terraza de un bar en la Plaza Mayor de Madrid y pide un té helado. Observa a un grupo de turistas que se toma fotos, mientras piensa en que tiene que encontrar un trabajo *urgente*. De lo contrario, tendrá que volver a Barcelona a la casa de sus padres.

En ese momento, llega la camarera con su pedido.

- Aquí tienes: té helado de fresa con arándanos - dice mientras deja el vaso en la mesa - . **¿Buscas trabajo?** - pregunta al ver la carpeta de currículums de Patricia.

- Así es - responde Patricia, repentinamente feliz - . Soy chef profesional. ¿Necesitáis **personal** en esta cafetería, de casualidad?

- Lo siento, no por el momento - responde la camarera.

- Ah, vale.

- Pero puedes dejarme tu currículum si quieres. Si necesitamos cubrir alguna **vacante** en la cocina, te tendremos en cuenta.

- Vale, muchas gracias - responde Patricia, y le da un currículum a la camarera.

Patricia bebe tranquilamente su té helado mientras mira a los turistas paseando y sacándose fotos en la Plaza Mayor de Madrid. Entonces, alguien le habla.

- ¿Así que eres chef profesional?

Patricia gira el **cuello**. Quien está hablando es una mujer de mediana edad, muy guapa y elegante, que está sentada en una mesa cercana, bebiendo una **caña** de cerveza. Tiene un largo cabello rojo y lleva un bonito vestido blanco y unas grandes gafas de sol.

- Sí - responde Patricia - . He llegado a Madrid hace apenas unos días. En Barcelona, he trabajado durante tres años como jefa de cocina en el hotel Mediterráneo.

- ¿El hotel Mediterráneo? Vaya, ese sitio tiene mucha reputación. He tenido la suerte de hospedarme allí varias veces.

- ¿De verdad? - pregunta Patricia - . Entonces, si ha pedido comida al restaurante del hotel, lo más seguro es que haya probado mis **platos**. Yo misma hice la **carta**.

- Ya veo - dice la mujer - . Sí... Recuerdo una crema catalana verdaderamente exquisita. ¿Tú eres la responsable de eso?

- ¡La misma!

- ¿Y qué me dices de aquellos *calçots* en salsa de romesco?

- También.

- Impresionante - dice la mujer - . Francamente impresionante. ¿Cómo te llamas?

- Patricia Solano.

- Pareces una chica muy simpática, Patricia. Dime, ¿te gusta la televisión?

- ¿La televisión? - pregunta Patricia, desconcertada - . No mucho. Bueno... Nunca he visto mucho la tele.

- Funcionarías bien en cámara. Tienes lo que se dice... *ángel*.

Patricia no sabe qué responder a eso. La conversación se está volviendo algo extraña. La mujer bebe un largo **sorbo** de su caña y luego dice:

- Mi nombre es Isabel Vega Muñoz.

- ¿Isabel Vega Muñoz? - pregunta Patricia, sorprendida - . Lo siento, no te he reconocido por las gafas de sol.

Patricia no puede creer que está ante la mismísima Isabel Vega Muñoz, una famosa presentadora de televisión.

- ¿Has visto alguno de mis programas alguna vez? - pregunta Isabel.

Patricia sabe que Isabel es muy reconocida, aunque *jamás* ha visto uno de sus programas. Sin embargo, cree que no es del todo **cortés** decir eso, así que dice:

- Alguna que otra vez.

- Entonces, seguramente ya sabes que mis programas suelen ser magacines. Hay entrevistas con personalidades, concursos... y una sección de cocina. Pues bien, resulta que estoy buscando a una persona carismática, pero, sobre todo, que sepa cocinar. Necesito que se haga cargo de la sección de cocina de mi nuevo programa, que se **estrenará** la semana que viene.

Patricia no puede creer lo que acaba de oír. ¿Ella, en la tele?

- Pero nunca he estado frente a una cámara.

- Aprenderás - responde Isabel.

– Pero ¿por qué yo? ¿No hay un montón de otras personas con más experiencia en la televisión?

– Creo mucho en el destino, Patricia – le dice Isabel – . Y creo que el destino nos ha ubicado en dos mesas **contiguas** esta tarde por alguna razón. ¿Por qué no lo intentas? Si no te gusta, nadie te obligará a quedarte.

– No lo sé – dice Patricia, nada convencida – . ¿Podemos discutir mis honorarios?

Isabel coge una **servilleta** y extrae un **bolígrafo** de su **refinado** bolso. Apunta algo rápidamente y le pasa el papel a Patricia.

– Esto es lo que ganarías.

– ¡**Ostras**! Es un gran salario. Es más de lo que cobraba en el hotel Mediterráneo.

Patricia lo piensa durante un momento. La verdad es que la ponen un poco nerviosa las cámaras. Pero luego piensa en que podría ser un **desafío** interesante. Además, recuerda que su abuela Rosa es una **espectadora** de los programas de Isabel Vega Muñoz. Patricia se imagina la cara que pondrá cuando la vea en la tele.

– Vale, Isabel. Lo intentaré. Pero... ¿puedo pedirte algo?

– Lo que quieras.

– ¿**Firmarías** un autógrafo para mi abuela Rosa? ¡Ella te adora!

Vocabulary List

Español	Inglés
receloso / recelosa	wary
¿Hablas otros idiomas?	Do you speak other languages?
¿Vives cerca de aquí?	Do you live nearby?
encantador / encantadora	lovely
¿Ese ha sido tu único trabajo?	Was that your only job?

¿Sabes preparar cócteles?	Can you prepare cocktails?
¿Buscas trabajo?	Are you looking for a job?
el personal	staff
la vacante	vacancy
el cuello	neck
la caña	pint (glass where beer is usually served, about half the size of a pint)
el plato	dish
la carta	menu
el ángel	charm (people are said to have "angel" when they have a certain grace in their appearance and/or personality)
el sorbo	sip
cortés	polite
estrenar	to premiere
contiguo / a	adjacent
la servilleta	napkin
el bolígrafo	pen

refinado / a	sophisticated
¡Ostras!	Yikes! (an expression used when someone is surprised or angry. It is used to avoid saying a "bad word")
el desafío	challenge
espectador / espectadora	viewer
firmar	to sign

Summary of the Story in Spanish

Patricia va a sus cuarta y quinta entrevistas de la semana, pero nada parece ir como ella quiere. Frustrada, se sienta en un bar. Allí, comienza a hablar con la presentadora de televisión Isabel Vega Muñoz, quien parece interesada en su experiencia de cocina en un hotel de Barcelona. En poco tiempo, Isabel Muñoz Vega le ofrece a Patricia un trabajo en la sección de cocina de su nuevo programa de televisión. Primero, Patricia duda, pero luego piensa que sería un desafío interesante y decide intentarlo.

Exercises

1. ¿Dónde ha trabajado Patricia antes?
    a. En el hotel Mediterráneo.
    b. En el Instituto de Cocina de Barcelona.
    c. En Ríos Rosas, número 56.

2. ¿Cuáles de estas preguntas le hacen los entrevistadores a Patricia?
    a. ¿Cuántos años tienes?
    b. ¿Hablas otros idiomas?
    c. ¿Llevas mucho tiempo en Madrid?

3. ¿Qué ve Patricia en Plaza Mayor de Madrid?
    a. Turistas tomándose fotos.
    b. Pájaros volando.
    c. Niños corriendo.

4. ¿Quién le pregunta a Patricia sobre sus platos en el hotel Mediterráneo?

    a. El primer entrevistador.

    b. La segunda entrevistadora.

    c. Isabel Vega Muñoz.

5. ¿Por qué Isabel Vega Muñoz quiere contratar a Patricia?

    a. Porque su comida es la más rica que ha probado.

    b. Porque no tiene otras opciones.

    c. Porque cree en el destino.

Comprehension Questions

1. ¿Cómo es el lugar de la primera entrevista?

2. ¿Por qué Patricia debe encontrar trabajo urgente?

3. ¿Cómo es la mujer que le habló a Patricia?

4. ¿Qué piensa Isabel Vega Muñoz de Patricia?

5. ¿Qué le pide Patricia a Isabel?

Summary of the Story in English

Patricia goes to her fourth and fifth interviews this week, but nothing seems to be going her way. Frustrated, she sits down at a bar. There, she starts talking to TV host Isabel Vega Muñoz, who seems interested in her cooking experience at a hotel in Barcelona. Soon, Isabel Vega Muñoz offers Patricia a job in the cooking section of her new TV show. At first, Patricia hesitates, but then she thinks it would be an interesting challenge and decides to give it a try.

Did you know...?

Jobs and job interviews can vary a great deal from country to country. While the Spanish work culture would not be completely unfamiliar to an American, there are some differences worth noting; the main one would probably be the work hours. Spain has one of the most flexible work schedules in the world. Although they tend to start at 9 a.m. and end at 6 p.m., lunch hours are closer to 2 p.m. than to noon (it's not strange to eat something at 11 a.m.). Plus, it's very common to reduce hours in the summer when it's hot and people go on vacation. In many offices, people finish early on Fridays, too, around 3 p.m. And you can still find shops closing for a few hours around lunchtime, for *siesta,* in most towns and small cities.

On the other hand, job interviews are fairly familiar. They usually last about half an hour and consist of a series of open-ended questions about experience and skills. Almost all of them are one-on-one. You'll be okay if you shake hands before and after the interview, and asking questions will be no problem. So, good luck with that!

Chapter 7: Una Emergencia Médica – A Medical Emergency

Story in Spanish: Doctor, ¿qué tengo?

"Los **principios** nunca son fáciles", piensa Damián. Tiene la respiración **entrecortada** y las manos **temblorosas**. Está nervioso, pero eso no es extraño. Es su primer día como médico residente en el Hospital de Santa Bárbara; es, además de un primer día, el final de un largo **viaje**. Y los **finales** nunca son fáciles.

- Este es tu **consultorio** - dice Amparo, la residente de segundo año que lo está introduciendo al hospital - . Aquí recibirás a tus primeros pacientes. ¿Alguna duda?

- No, muchas gracias - dice Damián.

Al escucharlo, Amparo frunce el ceño durante un segundo. **Da la impresión** de no haber entendido bien.

- Disculpa, ¿**de dónde eres**? - pregunta Amparo.

- De Argentina - responde Damián.

- ¡Me imaginaba! - dice Amparo - . Ese acento es **inconfundible**. Así que de Argentina. Madrid está lleno de argentinos, pero me imagino que eso ya lo sabes. ¿Qué haces aquí?

- Cuando terminé la universidad, en Buenos Aires, decidí que quería un **cambio** - contesta Damián - . Medicina es una carrera muy larga. Vi entonces que tenía la posibilidad de aplicar a unas residencias en Madrid, y... Bueno, acá estoy.

- Te encantará la ciudad, ya verás - dice Amparo, mientras se acerca a la puerta - . Disculpa, pero debo irme: hay muchos residentes nuevos a los que orientar. **Avísame** si tienes algún problema, ¡y mucha suerte!

Amparo sale del consultorio y deja la puerta abierta. Damián, **tímidamente**, se sienta detrás del escritorio, con su **bata blanca** abierta, e **inicia** el **ordenador**. Realmente no sabe qué esperar. Es su primer día de **guardia**.

- **Permiso**, doctor - escucha entonces.

Damián **levanta la vista**. Enfrente hay un muchacho muy joven, de no más de veinte años. Se le ve **pálido** y camina **con dificultad**.

- Pasá - dice Damián - . Sentate. ¿Cómo estás?

- Bien - murmura el muchacho.

Entonces el nombre del muchacho aparece en el ordenador: Santiago Martínez.

- Decime, Santiago, ¿por qué viniste? - pregunta Damián. Trata de sonar lo más profesional posible. Es su primer día, pero los pacientes no tienen por qué saberlo.

- Me duele el **estómago** - responde Santiago - , y tengo **náuseas**. Eso es lo principal. Pero también tengo bastante **dolor de cabeza**; creo que hasta siento un poco de **fiebre**. También **sudo** mucho y siento **escalofríos**. Como una **gripe**.

- Suena bastante **molesto** - contesta Damián - . ¿Qué sentís en el estómago?

- No lo siento todo el tiempo - dice Santiago - . Solo viene cada tan...

Santiago calla súbitamente, y su rostro empalidece aún más. Damián puede escuchar cómo el estómago de su paciente hace ruidos extraños.

- ¿Algún otro **síntoma**? - pregunta Damián.

- No creo - responde Santiago - . Doctor, tengo miedo de tener apendicitis.

Damián recuerda sus estudios. Dolores repentinos de estómago, náuseas, fiebre, un paciente joven. Es posible.

- Acostate en la **camilla**, por favor - dice Damián - . Y levantate un poco la **remera**.

Santiago sigue las órdenes del doctor. Damián le **palpa** el lado derecho del abdomen. No hay **inflamación**. Puede **descartar** la apendicitis.

– ¿Cuándo empezaron los dolores? – pregunta Damián, mientras toma distancia y deja que su paciente se vista.

– Ayer por la noche – responde Santiago.

– ¿Qué hiciste ayer? – dice Damián.

– Ayer... – contesta Santiago – . Fui a la universidad, tuve mis clases. Por la tarde estudié en casa, y después vi una serie. Por la noche cené con mis compañeras de piso. En ese momento me sentía bien; y fue una suerte, porque había migas extremeñas. Una de mis compañeras es chef, sabes, y...

– ¿Qué son las migas extremeñas? – interrumpe Damián.

– Es un plato típico de Extremadura, de donde yo vengo – contesta Santiago – . Lleva pan del día anterior, pimientos verdes y rojos, huevos, ajos, chorizo y panceta.

– Suena bastante **pesado** – dice Damián – . ¿Cuántas te comiste?

– No sé... – responde Santiago – . ¿Seis platos?

– ¡Seis platos de pan frito con chorizo! – dice Damián, súbitamente **aliviado**. Su primer **diagnóstico** es mucho más sencillo de lo que esperaba – . No te preocupes, Santiago, vos no tenés apendicitis. ¡Tenés un ataque al hígado!

Vocabulary List

Español	Inglés
el principio	beginning
entrecortada / entrecortado	intermittent
temblorosa / tembloroso	shaky
el viaje	journey
el final	ending
el consultorio	doctor's office

dar la impresión	to look like
¿de dónde eres?	Where are you from?
inconfundible	unmistakable
el cambio	change
avisar	to let know
tímidamente	shyly
la bata blanca	white coat
iniciar	to turn on
el ordenador	computer
de guardia	on call
Permiso	Excuse me
levantar la vista	to look up
pálido / pálida	pale
con dificultad	with difficulty
el estómago	stomach
las náuseas	nausea
el dolor de cabeza	headache

la fiebre	fever
sudar	sweat
los escalofríos	chills
la gripe	flu
molesto / molesta	uncomfortable
el síntoma	symptom
la camilla	stretcher
la remera	t-shirt
palpar	to feel
la inflamación	swelling
descartar	to rule out
pesado / pesada	heavy
aliviado / aliviada	relieved
el diagnóstico	diagnosis

Summary of the Story in Spanish

Damián es un médico de Argentina en su primer día de guardia como residente en un hospital madrileño. Amparo, una residente de segundo año, le muestra el hospital y lo deja en su consultorio. Damián está nervioso y no sabe qué hacer. Entonces, llega su primer paciente: Santiago. Sus síntomas son dolor de estómago, náuseas, dolor de cabeza, sudoración y escalofríos. Tiene miedo de tener apendicitis, pero Damián palpa su costado derecho y descarta ese diagnóstico. Después de que

Santiago le cuenta lo que comió la noche anterior, el médico sabe lo que le pasa: tiene un ataque al hígado.

Exercises

1. ¿Por qué le tiemblan las manos a Damián?
   a. Porque está perdido.
   b. Porque tiene una enfermedad.
   c. Porque está nervioso.

2. ¿Quién es Amparo?
   a. Una paciente.
   b. Una enfermera.
   c. Una médica.

3. ¿Por qué Amparo se imaginaba que Damián era de Argentina?
   a. Por su forma de hablar.
   b. Por su forma de caminar.
   c. Por su color de pelo.

4. ¿Cuál de estos síntomas no tiene Santiago?
   a. Dolor de cabeza.
   b. Desorientación.
   c. Náuseas.

5. ¿De qué tiene miedo Santiago?
   a. De tener apendicitis.
   b. De tener un hueso quebrado.
   c. De tener un ataque al hígado.

Comprehension Questions

1. ¿Hace cuánto trabaja Damián como médico residente en el Hospital de Santa Bárbara?
2. ¿Por qué Damián está en Madrid?
3. ¿Qué hace Damián cuando se queda solo en el consultorio?
4. ¿Qué hace Damián cuando Santiago le dice que tiene miedo de tener apendicitis?
5. ¿Por qué Damián se siente aliviado al final del cuento?

Summary of the Story in English

Damián is an Argentinean doctor on his first day on call as a resident in a hospital in Madrid. Amparo, a second-year resident, shows him around the hospital and leaves him in his office. Damián is nervous and doesn't know what to do. Then, his first patient arrives: Santiago. His symptoms are stomach ache, nausea, headache, sweating, and chills. He's scared he may have appendicitis, but Damián feels his right side and rules out that diagnosis. After Santiago tells him what he ate the previous night, the doctor knows what's wrong with him: he has indigestion.

Did you know...?

Everyday ailments usually have homemade remedies. It's quite logical: why bother going to the doctor for a headache or a stye in the eye? They are just a hassle, not a full-blown illness. They will pass.

However, these discomforts can be very uncomfortable, and that's when homemade remedies come into play. Some of them are very well-known in Spanish culture. Do you have a mouth ulcer? Well, just put a pinch of salt on it. It will hurt a little the first few times – you may even shed a tear – but then it will help close the wound cleanly. Do you have a stye in your eye? There's a solution for that, too: take a golden ring, like a wedding ring, and rub it between your hands or against some fabric. Then, place it over the infection.

That second remedy may sound strange, but it actually has a scientific explanation: the ring heats up when rubbed, and that heat helps your infected pore to open up. That reduces the swelling and helps the healing process. However, as you may have guessed, there are easier ways to apply heat to your eye. So, if you don't have a golden ring at hand, you can always use a piece of cloth dipped in hot water!

Chapter 8: Historias de la Abuela – Grandma's Stories

Story in Spanish: Una visita especial

El **timbre** suena en el piso de Ríos Rosas 56. Inmediatamente, Patricia se pone de pie.

- ¡Muchachos! ¡Llegó mi abuela Rosa! - dice Patricia, mientras se acerca al **comunicador.**

En ese momento, Santiago y Beatriz salen de sus dormitorios. Se acercan a la cocina, donde **la mesa ya está servida.** Son cerca de las ocho de la noche.

- Pasa - dice Patricia junto al comunicador, y **oprime** el botón que abre la **puerta de la calle** - . El ascensor funcionaba hoy, ¿no es cierto? No quiero que mi abuela cargue sus maletas por los tres pisos de escaleras.

- Hoy por la tarde funcionaba - responde Santiago desde la otra habitación.

Tras un minuto o dos, suena el timbre de la puerta del piso. Patricia abre la puerta rápidamente.

- ¡Abuelita! - dice entonces Patricia, y se lanza a abrazar a una mujer de unos setenta y cinco años.

El abrazo dura poco. Rápidamente, Patricia toma las maletas de su abuela y las carga dentro del piso.

– Pasa, te estábamos esperando para comer – dice Patricia – . Ellos son Santiago y Beatriz, mis compañeros de piso.

– Un placer – dice Rosa, mientras entra a la casa.

– Patricia siempre nos habla de ti – dice Beatriz – . Nos contó que tú le enseñaste a cocinar. Quizás por eso le puso tanto **empeño** a la cena... ¡Hay comida como para un **ejército**!

Beatriz señala la mesa de la cocina: hay cinco platos distintos, cada uno del tamaño de dos o tres **porciones** generosas.

– Qué bueno tenerte de visita – dice Patricia – . Siéntate, debes tener hambre. ¿Cómo estuvo el viaje?

– Oh, estuvo excelente – responde Rosa – . El tren desde Barcelona es muy cómodo. ¡Nunca lo había tomado! Es como viajar en primera clase. Todavía me acuerdo de cuando, para venir hasta Madrid, había que tomarse un bus eterno. Yo me llevaba **aguja** e **hilo** y, cuando llegaba a la estación, ya había **tejido** un **chaleco** para uno de mis **nietos**.

– Eran muy buenos chalecos – contesta Patricia, divertida – . Mi abuela viajaba mucho entre Barcelona y Madrid, cuando era joven, junto a mi abuelo – aclara para Santiago y Beatriz.

– ¿Por qué? – pregunta Santiago, mientras se sirve un par de croquetas.

– Jorge era madrileño – responde Rosa – . Veníamos a ver a su familia. Patricia, ¿has visitado a alguno de tus **parientes** de por aquí? Eduardo estaría encantado de recibirte.

– Todavía no, abuela – dice Patricia – . Ya sé que Eduardo es el **primo** del abuelo, pero ¡no lo conozco! Me **dio vergüenza**.

– Tonterías – contesta Rosa – . Mañana iremos a verlo. Eduardo es encantador.

– Patricia, este arroz negro está increíble – dice entonces Beatriz – . Creo que es el mejor que he comido en mi vida.

– Receta familiar – dice Patricia, sonriendo.

– ¡Pero a ti te sale mejor! – contesta Rosa – . Cuando era niña, ella siempre estaba en la cocina. A algunos niños les atrae la televisión; ella solo quería acercarse al **horno**. Yo la ponía junto a mí, le daba un **cuchillo sin filo** y ella **imitaba** todo lo que hacía.

– Así aprendí todo lo que sé – dice Patricia, **encogiéndose de hombros** – . La escuela de cocina fue solo para conseguir un **título**. En realidad, mis mejores platos fueron siempre los que me enseñó mi abuela Rosa.

– ¿Ustedes pasaban mucho tiempo juntas? – pregunta Santiago.

– Sí, porque mis padres trabajaban hasta tarde – responde Patricia –. Entonces, cuando yo salía de la escuela, iba directamente a casa de la abuela. Allí pasaba la tarde. A veces leíamos juntas, a veces ella jugaba a la canasta con sus amigas. Prácticamente me **crio**. Así que ya saben a quién **echarle la culpa** de todo lo que ustedes tienen que sufrir – bromea Patricia, dirigiéndose a sus compañeros de piso.

– Qué exagerada que eres, Patricia – dice Rosa –. A ti te crio tu madre. Yo solo he hecho lo que he podido para ayudar. Y, de todas formas, no creo que estos chicos tan **majos** lo pasen tan mal contigo, ¿no es cierto?

– Para nada – dice Santiago mientras vuelve a llenar su plato. Es evidente que ya se ha recuperado del ataque al hígado de la semana anterior –. ¡Sobre todo cuando Patricia prepara una escalivada como esta!

Vocabulary List

Español	Inglés
el timbre	doorbell
el comunicador	intercom
la mesa está servida	the food is served
oprimir	to press
la puerta de la calle	front door
el empeño	effort
el ejército	army
la porción	serving

la aguja	needle
el hilo	yarn
tejer	to knit
el chaleco	vest
el nieto / la nieta	grandchild
el / la pariente	relative
el primo / la prima	cousin
dar vergüenza	to be embarrassed
el horno	oven
el cuchillo sin filo	blunt knife
imitar	to imitate
encogerse de hombros	to shrug
el título	degree
criar	to raise
echar la culpa	to blame
majo, maja	nice

Summary of the Story in Spanish

La abuela de Patricia, Rosa, va a visitarla al piso y Patricia le prepara una cena con muchos platos diferentes. Durante la cena, Patricia y su abuela le cuentan a Santiago y Beatriz un poco sobre sus vidas. Así, nos

enteramos de que Rosa viajaba mucho con su esposo entre Barcelona y
Madrid para visitar a la familia de él. Además, cuentan que, de niña,
Patricia solía pasar mucho tiempo con su abuela y ella fue quien le
enseñó a cocinar.

Exercises

1. ¿A qué hora llega la abuela Rosa?
   - a. A las 21.
   - b. A las 20.
   - c. A las 19.
2. ¿Desde dónde viene la abuela Rosa?
   - a. Madrid.
   - b. Badajoz.
   - c. Barcelona.
3. ¿Qué tomaba antes para ir a Madrid?
   - a. Un bus.
   - b. El metro.
   - c. Otro tren.
4. ¿Quién es Eduardo?
   - a. El abuelo de Patricia.
   - b. El primo de Patricia.
   - c. El primo del abuelo de Patricia.
5. ¿Quién jugaba a la canasta por las tardes?
   - a. Patricia.
   - b. Rosa.
   - c. Beatriz.

Comprehension Questions

1. ¿Quién carga las maletas dentro del piso?
2. ¿Cómo es el tren desde Barcelona?
3. ¿Qué solía hacer la abuela Rosa cuando viajaba en bus de
   Barcelona a Madrid?
4. ¿Qué hacían Patricia y Rosa cuando Patricia era niña?
5. ¿Cómo está Santiago del ataque al hígado de la semana anterior?

Summary of the Story in English

Patricia's grandmother, Rosa, visits her at the apartment, and Patricia prepares a dinner with many different dishes. During dinner, Patricia and her grandmother tell Santiago and Beatriz a bit about their lives. Thus, we learn that Rosa used to travel a lot with her husband between Barcelona and Madrid to visit his family. They also say that, as a child, Patricia used to spend a lot of time with her grandmother, and she was the one who taught her how to cook.

Did you know...?

Spain is, together with Japan, one of the countries with the highest life expectancy in the world: about 84 years. However, in both countries, there is a large difference between male and female life expectancy. It seems that, for some reason, women tend to live up to five years longer than men.

In any case, older women, and especially grandmothers, play a very important role in Spanish culture. It's not strange that, being retired, they take care of their grandchildren while their parents are working. That means they are very involved in child-rearing and in other domestic chores in general.

But Spanish grandmothers don't just stay at home; they go out too! And they often stay out late. If you take a stroll around Madrid on a Friday night, even at midnight, don't be surprised to find a good number of old women drinking in bars, chatting, and having fun. After all, why stay at home when you can go out to drink a *caña* with the girls?

Chapter 9: Un Día en el Trabajo – A Day At Work

Story in Spanish: La *cantaora*

Beatriz llega al trabajo. Su jefa, la señora Ordóñez, la saluda con un beso en cada **mejilla**. Beatriz lleva trabajando en el restaurante mucho tiempo y ellas tienen mucha **confianza**.

– Buenas noches, Bea – le dice la señora Ordóñez – . ¿Estás lista?

– Sí, como siempre – responde Beatriz, mientras acomoda su bolso detrás de la barra.

– Es que esta no será una noche como cualquier otra – dice Ordóñez – . Pero... ¿es que aún no lo sabes? Miguel, ¿no se lo has dicho?

Miguel, otro de los camareros del restaurante, esboza una sonrisa a modo de disculpa.

– Lo siento, jefa – dice – . Es que no quería ponerla muy nerviosa.

– ¿De qué estáis hablando? – pregunta Beatriz.

– Esta noche tenemos una **reserva** para la *cantaora* de flamenco Sara Alas – explica Ordóñez.

– **Me estáis vacilando** – dice Beatriz.

– Claro que no – responde Ordóñez – . Y quiero que tú te hagas cargo de su mesa.

– ¿De verdad? – pregunta Beatriz. De repente, siente las manos sudorosas – . ¡Soy una gran admiradora de Sara Alas!

- Por supuesto, ya lo sabemos - responde Miguel - . Cuando te toca poner música, ¡siempre pones a Sara Alas!

- Es que me he criado escuchando su música - explica Beatriz - . Cuando era niña, fui con mis padres a ver un espectáculo suyo en un *tablao* de Málaga. Me quedé fascinada con su voz, tan dulce y a la vez potente. Además, sus **letras** son muy poderosas. Si la tuviera enfrente, le diría que es la mejor *cantaora* de Andalucía.

- Pues estás de suerte, porque acaba de entrar - dice Miguel, señalando a la puerta del restaurante.

Sara Alas entra acompañada de su equipo de trabajo. Beatriz reconoce enseguida a Paco Figueroa, el **guitarrista** que suele acompañarla en sus presentaciones. La señora Ordóñez se dirige hacia ellos y, tras saludarlos cortésmente, los conduce por el restaurante hasta la mesa que les han asignado. Los clientes del restaurante, que a aquella hora todavía no son muchos, giran el cuello para verlos y **cuchichean**.

Beatriz sabe que es su momento de actuar. Sin embargo, está demasiado nerviosa.

- Lo harás bien, Bea - le dice Miguel - . Recuerda que eres una profesional.

Bea **respira hondo** y se dirige hacia la mesa de los recién llegados.

- Buenas noches, señora Salas. Quiero decir, señora Alas - dice Beatriz **con torpeza** - . Es un placer que hayáis escogido nuestro restaurante esta tarde. ¡Quiero decir, esta noche! Os dejo las cartas para que consultéis el menú.

Bea se retira en dirección a la barra. En ese momento, la señora Ordóñez aparece con una botella de vino en la mano.

- Toma, llévales este vino **de cortesía**, por favor - le pide a Beatriz.

Beatriz coge el vino y se dirige nuevamente a la mesa. Comienza a servir en las **copas** de Sara Alas y el resto de su equipo. Cuando lo está haciendo, con las manos **temblorosas**, **vuelca** accidentalmente un **chorro** de vino sobre la **blusa** blanca de Sara.

- ¡Ay! - exclama Beatriz - . ¡Lo lamento tanto!

Está muy avergonzada y no sabe qué decir. Sara Alas la mira fijamente. Y entonces, sonríe.

- Descuida. Es solo una blusa. Dime, ¿este es tu primer día?

- ¡No! - responde Beatriz - . Llevo años trabajando aquí. Es solo que soy una gran admiradora suya, y quiero que usted pase una velada perfecta. Usted es la mejor *cantaora* de Andalucía.

- Muchas gracias por ese cumplido - le dice Sara - . ¿Vendrás a mi espectáculo el próximo fin de semana?

- No he conseguido **entradas**, señora Alas - le explica Beatriz.

Sara saca algo del bolsillo y se lo da en la mano a Beatriz.

- Pues ya las tienes. Ven con amigos.

Beatriz mira lo que le acaba de dar Sara. Son tres entradas para la **primera fila** de su concierto en uno de los *tablaos* más famosos de Madrid.

- ¡Muchas gracias! - dice, Beatriz, contenta.

Sin dudas, será un plan de sábado perfecto junto a Santiago y Patricia, sus compañeros de piso.

- Y ahora, por favor sírveme el vino... *dentro* de la copa - le dice Sara Alas, sin dejar de sonreír.

Vocabulary List

Español	Inglés
la mejilla	cheek
la confianza	trust
la reserva	reservation
el cantaor / la cantaora	flamenco singer
Me estás vacilando	You're kidding me
el tablao	place where flamenco shows are performed
la letra	lyrics

el / la guitarrista	guitar player
cuchichear	to whisper
respirar hondo	to take a deep breath
con torpeza	clumsily
de cortesía	on the house
la copa	glass of wine
tembloroso / temblorosa	shaking
volcar	to spill
el chorro	splash
la blusa	blouse
la entrada	ticket
la primera fila	front-row

Summary of the Story in Spanish

Beatriz llega a trabajar al restaurante y su jefa, la señora Ordóñez, le dice que hoy tienen una clienta muy especial: la *cantaora* de flamenco Sara Alas. Beatriz es una gran admiradora suya, ya que cuando era niña sus padres la llevaron a ver un espectáculo de ella y quedó fascinada. Cuando la atiende, está tan nerviosa que se confunde con su nombre y vuelca un poco de vino. Sin embargo, Sara Alas resulta ser muy simpática y le regala entradas para su próximo concierto en Madrid.

Exercises

1. ¿Qué es lo que no le han dicho a Beatriz?
    a. Que hoy no debe trabajar.
    b. Que hoy tienen una reserva para una cantaora famosa.
    c. Que hoy ella debe cantar.

2. ¿Quién se encarga de atender la mesa de Sara Alas?
    a. Beatriz.
    b. Miguel.
    c. La señora Ordóñez.

3. ¿Cómo son las letras de las canciones de Sara Alas, según Beatriz?
    a. Dulces.
    b. Poderosas.
    c. Tiernas.

4. ¿En qué se equivoca Beatriz primero?
    a. En el momento del día.
    b. En el pedido.
    c. En el apellido de Sara.

5. ¿Qué le regala el restaurante a la cantante?
    a. El vino.
    b. El café.
    c. La comida.

Comprehension Questions

1. ¿Cómo se llevan la señora Ordóñez y Beatriz?
2. ¿Por qué Beatriz es admiradora de Sara Alas?
3. ¿Qué hacen los clientes cuando ven a Sara Alas?
4. ¿Cómo reacciona Sara Alas cuando Beatriz le mancha la blusa?
5. ¿Qué le regala Sara Alas a Beatriz?

Summary of the Story in English

Beatriz arrives to work at the restaurant and her boss, Mrs. Ordóñez, tells her that they will have a very special client today: flamenco singer Sara Alas. Beatriz is a big fan of hers because, since when she was a child, her parents took her to see one of her shows, and she was fascinated.

When she serves her, she's so nervous that she gets confused about her name and spills some wine. However, Sara Alas turns out to be really nice and gives her some tickets for her next show in Madrid.

Did you know...?

Flamenco is a Spanish musical genre that developed mainly in Andalusia, in the south of Spain. This genre is very particular and is usually sung, danced, played with the guitar, castanets, and the *cajón flamenco* (a kind of wooden box used for percussion), and even includes clapping and foot stomping!

Flamenco singing is called *cante* and is usually performed without backing singers. Flamenco singers are called *cantaores* and *cantaoras,* as opposed to the Spanish word for singer, *cantante.* The dance (*baile*) includes movements with all parts of the body: hands, legs, arms, head and even facial expressions! Flamenco dancers are called *bailaores* and *bailaoras,* as opposed to the Spanish words for dancer, *bailarín* and *bailarina.* And the playing of the instruments is called *toque,* and it mainly accompanies the *cante.*

And you can see all this in the *tablaos flamencos,* where flamenco shows take place and that are decorated with Andalusian references. The *tablaos* (the stage platform where people perform) is made of wood because it is the perfect material to stomp on and get the right sound. Whatever you do in Spain, you definitely cannot miss a typical flamenco show at a *tablao,* because you won't get the perfect sound and ambiance anywhere else!

Chapter 10: El Vestido – The Dress

Story in Spanish: El vestido

Beatriz, Patricia y Santiago van de compras. Cada uno tiene un motivo diferente: Beatriz quiere comprarse un vestido para el casamiento de su primo Pedro; Patricia está buscando algo sencillo para **ir de fiesta**; y Santiago quiere conseguir un conjunto deportivo para ir al gimnasio.

Beatriz conduce el coche hasta una calle muy **animada** y llena de gente y tiendas. La primera parada es un gran local de ropa femenina casual. Patricia coge varias **prendas** y luego se mete dentro de uno de los **probadores**. A los pocos minutos, sale para mostrarles el **atuendo** a sus amigos. Lleva una bonita camisa azul y un **pantalón de mezclilla**.

– ¿Qué opináis? – pregunta.

– ¡Me encanta! – dice Beatriz.

– Sí, está muy bonito – coincide Santiago.

– Vale, me lo llevo – dice, y se dirige al **dependiente de la tienda** – . Disculpa, ¿aceptáis tarjeta?

– Claro, aceptamos **tarjeta de débito** y **de crédito**.

Patricia paga y salen todos en busca del siguiente objetivo: la ropa deportiva para Santiago. Bea, que conoce Madrid, los lleva a una enorme **tienda por departamentos**, pero Santi no está acostumbrado a comprar en lugares tan grandes y no sabe para dónde ir, se siente un poco aturdido.

– No te preocupes, Santi – le dice Patricia – . Vamos a preguntarle a alguien que trabaje aquí. Oye, disculpa, ¿podrías decirme dónde encuentro la ropa deportiva para hombres?

- Sí, claro - responde un joven que lleva una camiseta con el logo de la tienda - . La indumentaria masculina está en el cuarto piso. Podéis subir por estas **escaleras mecánicas**. Una vez arriba, id hacia vuestra izquierda. Allí está todo lo necesario para hacer deporte.

Los tres amigos suben hasta el cuarto piso y encuentran la ropa deportiva. Santiago selecciona dos camisetas, unos **pantalones cortos** y tres **pares de calcetines**. Después, van al departamento de **calzado** para elegir zapatillas de correr. Santiago se prueba todo y, satisfecho, se dirige hacia la zona de cajas, donde paga **en efectivo**.

La última parada es una tienda de ropa muy elegante que hay **calle arriba**. Beatriz está buscando un vestido formal, pero nada la convence demasiado: uno es muy largo, otro es muy corto, otro es demasiado brillante...

Finalmente, encuentra el vestido perfecto. Es **suelto**, justo por encima de las rodillas, con la **espalda descubierta** y de colores alegres: ideal para una boda en la playa. Además, le queda perfecto, casi como si se lo hubieran **hecho a medida**. Cuando sale del probador, Santiago **aplaude** y Patricia lanza un **silbido halagador**. No hay dudas de que ese es el vestido que tiene que llevarse.

Sin embargo, hay un problema.

- Es demasiado **caro** - dice Beatriz, al ver la **etiqueta** con el **precio** - . Jamás podría pagarlo.

Decepcionada, vuelve al probador y se lo quita. Cuando sale, una dependienta le pregunta cómo le fue.

- Me quedó perfecto, pero está **fuera de mi presupuesto** - le responde Beatriz, muy triste.

- ¿Incluso con el **descuento**? - pregunta la dependienta.

- ¿Tiene un descuento? ¡No sabía! - dice Beatriz, un poco más **animada**.

- Todas las prendas de la tienda tienen un descuento del cincuenta por ciento por el **fin de temporada**.

- ¡¿Cincuenta por ciento?! - exclaman los tres amigos al unísono.

- Entonces sí, ¡me lo llevo! - dice Beatriz, **exultante**.

Vocabulary List

Español	Inglés
ir de fiesta	to go partying
animada / animado	lively
la prenda	item of clothing
el probador	fitting room
el atuendo	outfit
el pantalón de mezclilla	jeans
el dependiente / la dependienta de la tienda	store clerk
la tarjeta de crédito / débito	credit / debit card
la tienda por departamentos	department store
la escalera mecánica	escalator
el pantalón corto	pair of shorts
el par de calcetines	pair of socks
el calzado	footwear
en efectivo	in cash
calle arriba	up the street

suelto / suelta	loose
la espalda descubierta	open back
hecho / hecha a medida	tailored-made
aplaudir	to clap
el silbido halagador	flattering whistle
caro / cara	expensive
la etiqueta	tag
el precio	price
fuera de presupuesto	out of the budget
el descuento	discount
animada / animado	cheerful
el fin de temporada	end of the season
exultante	overjoyed

Summary of the Story in Spanish

Beatriz, Patricia y Santiago van de compras porque los tres necesitan algo de ropa. Empiezan por Patricia, que se compra una camisa y un pantalón de mezclilla en un local de ropa femenina casual. Luego, van a una tienda por departamentos, donde Santiago compra ropa deportiva. Por último, van a una tienda muy elegante para que Beatriz se compre un vestido. Hay uno que le gusta mucho y le queda muy bien, pero es demasiado caro. Por suerte, una dependienta le dice que todas las prendas tienen un descuento del 50%, así que Beatriz se lo lleva.

Exercises

1. ¿Por qué Beatriz quiere comprarse un vestido?
   a. Para ir de fiesta.
   b. Para la boda de su primo Pedro.
   c. Porque le gusta vestirse elegante.

2. ¿Qué opinan Santiago y Beatriz de lo que se prueba Patricia?
   a. A ambos les gusta.
   b. A Beatriz le encanta, pero a Santiago no.
   c. A ninguno le gusta.

3. ¿Qué se compra Santiago en la tienda por departamentos?
   a. Pantalones largos, calcetines y zapatillas deportivas.
   b. Zapatillas deportivas, camisetas, pantalones cortos y calcetines.
   c. Camisetas, ropa interior y zapatos.

4. ¿Cómo paga Santiago su compra?
   a. En efectivo.
   b. Con tarjeta de crédito.
   c. Con tarjeta de débito.

5. ¿Por qué se decepciona Beatriz después de probarse el vestido?
   a. Porque es muy brillante.
   b. Porque tiene la espalda descubierta.
   c. Porque es demasiado caro.

Comprehension Questions

1. ¿Qué quiere comprar Patricia?
2. ¿Cómo es la calle en la que los amigos van de compras?
3. ¿Por qué está aturdido Santiago en la tienda por departamentos?
4. ¿Qué indicaciones les da el dependiente?
5. ¿Cómo es el vestido que compra Beatriz?

Summary of the Story in English

Beatriz, Patricia, and Santiago go shopping because all three need some clothes. They start with Patricia, who buys a shirt and a pair of jeans at a casual women's clothing store. Next, they go to a department store, where Santiago buys sportswear. Finally, they go to an elegant clothing store for Beatriz to get a dress. There's one that she likes very much, and it looks great on her, but it's too expensive. Luckily, a store clerk tells her that all the items have a 50% discount, so Beatriz takes it.

Did you know...?

You can find clothing stores of different styles and prices around Madrid. There are streets full of shops and stores, such as Gran Vía, Fuencarral, Preciados, and Serrano. Some of them, such as Serrano street, have more prestigious and luxurious brands. There are also markets selling vintage clothing and accessories, such as El Rastro, which opens on Sundays.

In Madrid, most stores are open from 10 a.m. until 9 or 10 p.m. and do not close at lunchtime, so you can easily find a time to go during the day, even if you've planned visits to museums or other activities.

And if you're from a non-EU country, you should note that you can be excluded from paying tax on your purchases over 90 EUR in almost all stores. Ask the store clerk for the tax-free form, fill it out, and get it validated at Customs within 90 days of the purchase price. The electronic VAT refund procedure (DIVA) is a simple and speedy way to get your refund.

Chapter 11: El Gran Festival – The Great Festival

Story in Spanish: Una pequeña broma

Patricia **aparca** el coche y **apaga** el motor, pero no quita la llave. Sabe que la parada será corta.

– Santiago, ¿podrías decirle a tu amigo que baje? – dice Patricia. Todavía tiene sueño. Es temprano en la mañana: aún no ha **amanecido**. Pero, si quieren llegar a Haro a tiempo para la Batalla del Vino, tienen que salir realmente **temprano**.

– De acuerdo – contesta Santiago, desde el **asiento del acompañante**, y toma el móvil.

– ¿No vas a tocarle el timbre? Como quieras, supongo – dice Patricia – . Oye, ¿cómo se llamaba este **chaval**? Ya me he olvidado. Es de Colombia, ¿no es cierto?

– Julio – contesta Santiago – . Sí, es de Colombia. Vino a Madrid a estudiar, es **compañero** mío en la universidad. – Entonces Santiago **levanta** la voz – . ¡Mira! Ahí está.

Un muchacho de unos veinte años les **hace señas** desde la puerta de un edificio. Lleva un **pantalón** elegante, de buena tela, una **camisa** blanca fresca y liviana, y **zapatos** de cuero. Se acomoda rápidamente en el **asiento trasero** del coche.

– ¡Buenos días! – dice Julio – . ¿Cómo están? Santi, gracias por invitarme a esto. Tú eres Patricia, ¿no es cierto?

Julio habla rápido. Tiene una actitud entusiasta y **amigable**, muy **contagiosa**.

- Soy Patricia, sí. Oye, ¿piensas ir así vestido?

- Sí, claro - responde Julio - . A una **cata de vinos** hay que ir elegante, ¿no? ¿Hay algún problema?

- Yo no iría a la fiesta así, pero bueno, es tu **elección** - dice Patricia, indiferente. Ella está vestida con una vieja camiseta de algodón y un short deportivo; Santiago lleva prácticamente la misma ropa. Ambos están usando zapatillas viejas.

En ese momento, Patricia nota que, desde el asiento del acompañante, Santiago le está haciendo señas. Son bastante discretas, pero la indicación es clara: no digas nada más. Patricia entiende que Santiago está haciendo una de sus bromas, y decide, un poco **a regañadientes, hacerle caso** a su amigo.

El viaje en coche es rápido y tranquilo. A esa hora, la **autopista** está desierta, por lo que hacen el recorrido en una fracción del tiempo. Llegan a Haro apenas pasadas las ocho de la mañana. Sin embargo, el pueblo, aunque muy decorado, está prácticamente vacío.

- Creí que veníamos a una fiesta   - dice Julio, ligeramente **desconcertado**.

- Es que la fiesta es en los **riscos**   - responde Patricia - . Para no ensuciar el pueblo.

- ¿Ensuciar? Qué ordenados - contesta Julio, y Santiago deja escapar una risa - . ¿Qué ocurre? - continúa.

- Ya verás - dice Santiago.

A los pocos minutos, el coche llega al escenario de la **batalla** del vino. La imagen es **impactante**. Cientos de personas se arrojan vino con **jarras, escudillas** y **pistolas de agua**. Todos tienen la ropa teñida de violeta; muchos llevan pañuelos rojos. Hay **música en vivo, altavoces** a todo volumen, y mucho, mucho vino, que se derrama por los cuerpos, por la calle y por la tierra, formando un **barro** pegajoso y festivo.

- Creí que llegaríamos antes de que empezara - dice Patricia, un poco decepcionada - . Tendríamos que haber salido antes.

- ¡Vamos, Patricia! Todavía quedan un par de horas de fiesta   - contesta Santiago, mientras abre la puerta del coche y sale a caminar **rumbo** a la fiesta. Casi al instante, recibe un **baldazo** de vino en la espalda. Su camiseta blanca se tiñe de rojo al instante.

Sin embargo, Patricia no sale del coche. Espera la reacción de Julio, quien sigue sorprendido en el asiento de atrás. A ella no le gustan las bromas pesadas, y no está del todo satisfecha con haber sido **cómplice**.

– Qué más da – dice Julio finalmente, recuperando su entusiasmo inicial – . Lo único que importa es no arruinar estos zapatos – agrega, mientras se **desata** los **cordones** – . Eso sí sería un problema. ¿Vamos, Patricia? ¡Antes de que se acabe el vino!

Vocabulary List

Español	Inglés
aparcar	to park
apagar	to turn off
amanecer	to dawn
temprano	early
el asiento del acompañante	passenger's seat
el chaval / la chavala	kid
el compañero / la compañera	classmate
levantar	to raise
hacer señas	beckon
el pantalón	trousers
la camisa	shirt
los zapatos	shoes

el asiento trasero	rear seat
amigable	friendly
contagiosa / contagioso	contagious
la cata de vinos	wine tasting
la elección	choice
a regañadientes	reluctantly
hacer caso	to listen
la autopista	highway
desconcertado / desconcertada	puzzled
el risco	cliff
la batalla	battle
impactante	shocking
la jarra	jug
la escudilla	bowl
la pistola de agua	water gun
la música en vivo	live music
los altavoces	speakers

el barro	mud
rumbo	towards
el baldazo	bucket
la cómplice / el cómplice	accomplice
desatar	untie
los cordones	laces

Summary of the Story in Spanish

Patricia y Santiago pasan a buscar a Julio para ir a una fiesta en un pueblo. Julio es un compañero de Santiago de la universidad. El muchacho aparece vestido muy elegante, porque cree que van a una cata de vino. Por su parte, Patricia y Santiago llevan ropa vieja. Al llegar al pueblo, Julio se sorprende de que no haya nadie, y Santiago le dice que es porque la fiesta es en los riscos. Cuando llegan, se encuentran con una guerra de vino. Santiago le había hecho una broma a Julio, pero él no se ofende: se quita los zapatos y se suma a la batalla.

Exercises

1. ¿Por qué Patricia no quita la llave?
    a. Porque es muy temprano por la mañana.
    b. Porque cree que Julio va a tardar mucho.
    c. Porque sabe que la parada va a durar poco.

2. Señala la prenda de vestir que no lleva Julio:
    a. Una camisa.
    b. Un jersey.
    c. Unos pantalones.

3. ¿Cómo hay que ir vestido a una cata de vinos según Julio?
    a. Elegante.
    b. De cualquier forma.
    c. Casual.

4. ¿Cuál de las siguientes afirmaciones es verdadera?
   a. Patricia le hace caso a Santiago a pesar de que no quiere.
   b. Patricia no le hace caso a Santiago.
   c. Patricia está contenta de hacerle caso a Santiago.
5. Patricia no está satisfecha con...
   a. que la fiesta sea en los riscos.
   b. haber sido cómplice de Santiago.
   c. la ropa que lleva puesta.

Comprehension Questions

1. ¿Por qué los amigos salen tan temprano?
2. ¿De dónde se conocen Santiago y Julio?
3. ¿Qué lleva puesto Patricia?
4. ¿Por qué la fiesta es en los riscos?
5. ¿Por qué Patricia no baja del coche?

Summary of the Story in English

Patricia and Santiago pick up Julio to go to a party in a small town. Julio is Santiago's classmate from college. The kid shows up dressed very elegantly because he thinks he's going to a wine tasting. For their part, Patricia and Santiago are wearing old clothes. When they arrive in town, Julio is surprised that no one is there, but Santiago tells him that the party is in the cliffs. When they get there, they find a wine war. Santiago had played a joke on Julio, but he's not offended: he takes his shoes off, and joins the battle.

Did you know...?

Spain has many famous festivals and celebrations. The most famous ones are probably the Sanfermines in Pamplona, and the Semana Santa (Easter) in Sevilla, which is closely followed by the Feria de Abril.

You've probably seen pictures or even a video of the former. San Fermín begins in the morning, in the hot summer of Navarre, when the *encierro* takes place: six fighting bulls – called *toros de lidia* – are set to run from their corral to the bullring, where the bullfight will take place later that day. Ahead of them, hundreds of men, mostly dressed in white, run, trying not to get horned. Many of them carry a rolled-up newspaper in their hand: it's used to show how close they have run to the bull.

Bullfighting is highly controversial, even in Spain, and you can imagine why. Luckily, not all festivals include bullfights. Semana Santa, in Seville, consists mostly of dozens of processions happening at the same time. Each of them is organized by a *hermandad*, a brotherhood whose members carry huge - *huge* - sculptures of Christ, the Virgin Mary, or the saints on their backs. Singers and music bands are also involved. Meanwhile, locals and tourists fill the streets and the balconies and sing, pray and yell compliments to the images.

Chapter 12: El Futuro es Ahora – The Future Is Now

Story in Spanish: El distrito ecológico

Sandra Gutiérrez **está al frente de** una gran **audiencia**. Es la primera vez que representa al **estudio de arquitectos** de su familia. Y es un proyecto importante, así que está bastante nerviosa.

– Muchas gracias a todos por venir hoy – dice Sandra – . Como ya sabéis, os voy a presentar el **proyecto urbanístico** en el que hemos trabajado: el diseño y la construcción del **distrito residencial** EcoMálaga.

Sandra enciende el proyector. Sus manos están algo temblorosas. Echa un rápido **vistazo** al **público**. Allí hay mucha gente: **vecinos** de Santa Julia, **periodistas, empresarios** y **concejales del pueblo.** Todos quieren saber de qué **se trata** el nuevo proyecto del estudio de arquitectos Gutiérrez, S. A.

En la primera fila del auditorio está sentado su hermano, Pedro, que le **sonríe** y **levanta el pulgar**, dándole ánimos. De pronto, Sandra se siente algo más tranquila.

– Bien, como podéis ver en el gráfico, Santa Julia es un pueblo cuya **población** crece año a año. Eso se debe a que mucha gente viene a trabajar al **polígono industrial** que hay cerca, que es el más importante de Málaga y uno de los más importantes de Andalucía. Pues bien, desde Gutiérrez S. A. hemos proyectado un nuevo distrito residencial que **cubrirá** esa **demanda demográfica.** – Alguien **levanta la mano** – . ¿Sí?

– ¿Será un **vecindario** de casas bajas o de **edificios**?

- Serán un total de diez edificios bajos, de hasta tres **plantas**. Se respetará el **código urbanístico** de la provincia. Habrá de dos a cinco **unidades** por edificio.

- Pero ¿qué pasará con los animales? - pregunta una mujer del público - . En los alrededores del pueblo hay **flamencos, garzas y zorros**. También **buitres** y **águilas**. ¿Qué va a ocurrir con todos ellos cuando traigáis vuestras **máquinas**?

- No vamos a construir en ninguna zona con presencia de **fauna autóctona** - dice Sandra - . Además, nuestras políticas de construcción son **ecológicas**. Ninguna casa impactará con el **medio ambiente**. Instalaremos un **panel solar** en el techo de cada uno de los diez edificios, para **reducir** la **demanda energética**. ¡De alguna forma hay que **aprovechar** los 300 días de sol que tenemos al año!

La audiencia sonríe. Como buenos malagueños, disfrutan cada vez que alguien habla bien de su región. Sandra se siente más relajada. Para ella es importante ganarse la **simpatía** de los vecinos y las **autoridades locales**. Después de todo, son ellos los que van a habitar el **complejo**.

En ese momento, un hombre mayor, ubicado en el fondo de la sala, se pone de pie. Rápidamente uno de los **asistentes** le acerca un micrófono, para que todos los asistentes escuchen su pregunta.

- Solo tengo una duda - dice el hombre - . ¿Cómo hay que hacer para conseguir un piso allí? Porque mi hijo está buscando un lugar un poco más grande, ahora que es papá...

- ¡En un momento, le daré la información! - responde Sandra, satisfecha.

Vocabulary List

Español	Inglés
estar al frente de	to be in front of
la audiencia / el público	audience
el estudio de arquitectos	architecture firm
el proyecto urbanístico	urban project
el distrito residencial	residential district
el vistazo	quick look
el vecino / la vecina	resident
el periodista / la periodista	journalist
el empresario / la empresaria	businessperson
el concejal del pueblo / la concejala del pueblo	town councilor
tratarse de	to be about
sonreír	to smile
levantar el pulgar	to raise a thumb
la población	population
el polígono industrial	industrial estate

cubrir	to cover
la demanda demográfica	demographic demand
levantar la mano	to raise a hand
el vecindario	neighborhood
el edificio	building
el código urbanístico	urban planning code
la unidad	unit
el flamenco	flamingo
la garza	heron
el zorro	fox
el buitre	vulture
el águila	eagle
la máquina	machine
la fauna autóctona	native fauna
ecológica / ecológico	environmentally friendly
el medio ambiente	environment
el panel solar	solar panel

reducir	to reduce
la demanda energética	energy demand
aprovechar	to take advantage
la simpatía	affection
las autoridades locales	local authorities
el complejo	complex
el asistente / la asistente	assistant, attendee

Summary of the Story in Spanish

Sandra Gutiérrez está presentando un proyecto urbanístico del estudio de arquitectura de su familia frente a vecinos, periodistas, empresarios y concejales del pueblo. Está nerviosa, pero su hermano, Pedro, le da ánimos. Sandra cuenta las especificaciones del proyecto, habla del crecimiento poblacional del pueblo y menciona el polígono industrial cercano. Luego, responde preguntas de los asistentes acerca de la altura de los edificios y el impacto ambiental. La última pregunta la hace un señor mayor, que quiere saber cómo conseguir un piso en la nueva urbanización, lo que alegra a Sandra.

Exercises

1. ¿Qué es lo que está presentando Sandra?
    a. Una gran audiencia.
    b. Un estudio de arquitectos familiar.
    c. Un proyecto urbanístico.

2. ¿Quiénes de estas personas no estaban entre los asistentes?
    a. Políticos locales.
    b. Organizaciones ambientalistas.
    c. Habitantes de la zona.

3. ¿Dónde está su hermano Pedro?

    a. De pie en la primera fila del auditorio.

    b. Sentado en la primera fila del auditorio.

    c. Sentado en la última fila del auditorio.

4. ¿Qué animales no son mencionados por la mujer del público?

    a. Los peces.

    b. Las aves.

    c. Los mamíferos.

5. ¿Qué medidas se tomarán para no impactar en el medio ambiente?

    a. Se instalarán paneles solares en los techos.

    b. Se instalarán molinos eólicos.

    c. Se construirá una reserva para trasladar la fauna autóctona.

Comprehension Questions

1. ¿Cuántas veces representó Sandra al estudio de arquitectos de su familia?

2. ¿Qué implica el proyecto que está presentando Sandra?

3. ¿Por qué la población de Santa Julia crece año a año?

4. ¿Cómo piensan aprovechar los 300 días de sol al año que tiene la zona?

5. ¿Por qué el señor que hace la última pregunta está interesado en conseguir un piso allí?

Summary of the Story in English

Sandra Gutiérrez is presenting a project of her family's architecture firm in front of neighbors, journalists, businessmen, and town councilors. She's nervous, but her brother, Pedro, encourages her. Sandra explains the specifics of the project, talks about the town's population growth, and she mentions the nearby industrial estate. She then answers the public's questions about the height of the buildings and the environmental impact. The last question is asked by an old man who wants to know how to get a unit in the new urbanization, which makes Sandra happy.

Did you know...?

In general, EU countries have strong regulations against pollution, waste, and energy consumption. Within that group, Spain leads the way: it's the European leader in wildlife and biodiversity conservation. The country has 16 national parks, more than a hundred natural parks, almost three hundred natural reserves, and even more natural monuments. If you add them all up, you'll find that around 36% of the country is protected land.

You read that right! A third of Spanish soil is, in one way or another, a reserve. That makes Spain the most biodiverse country in Europe: it is home to 85% of the EU's plant species and 50% of its animal species. And you too can visit these places! From the seaside beauty of Cabo de Creus on the Costa Brava to the martian exuberance of Bardenas Reales, in Castile and Aragon, Spain is full of the spectacle of nature!

Appendix I: Translation & Answer Sheet

Translations

Chapter 1

Story: The confusion

Santiago Martínez gets to Badajoz airport at eight in the morning. He's with his parents, his younger sister, and his best friend, Luis. They're a little short on time, so they walk quickly and get to the counter to drop off Santiago's luggage. Then, they approach gate fourteen, where the flight is leaving from.

"Well, son, have a nice trip!" says Mr. Martínez and gives him a warm hug. "Study hard... but have fun too. Make good friends."

"But don't change me for another friend!" says Luis, smiling, and hands him a folded piece of paper. "Here's a map of Madrid. I've marked on it the most emblematic places in the city. I'll miss you. I'll visit you as soon as I can."

"I'll be waiting for you all in Madrid," Santiago replies. "Beatriz, my new roommate, has sent me some pictures of the apartment. It's really big. There's a guest room, so you can come and visit me whenever you like." Santiago turns around to say goodbye to his mother... who was in tears! "Mom, don't cry!"

"I'm sorry, honey," says Mrs. Martínez. Her make-up has smudged. "It's just that you've grown so fast... I can't believe you're leaving to study in the big city."

Santiago hugs his mother and then his younger sister.

"Bye!" says Santiago. He looks at his family one last time, with a smile on his face, and hands his ticket to the airline employee.

The flight is surprisingly short, just 45 minutes. Santiago has barely read a few pages of his book (one about dinosaurs that Luis gave him), when the captain announces over the loudspeakers:

"Ladies and gentlemen, we'll be landing at Madrid-Barajas international airport in ten minutes. The temperature outside is 20 degrees Celsius, with clear skies. Thank you for flying with us."

Barajas is... *huge*. A little dazed, dragging his heavy suitcase and a large backpack on his back, Santiago makes his way through people rushing to catch their flight.

A bit later, he finds a glass door that leads outside. When he steps outside, he sees a line of white taxis waiting and hops into one.

"Good morning," Santiago says. "I need to go to Rosas street, number 56."

"Okay," the taxi driver replies and starts driving. "Are you from far away?"

"From Montijo, a little town near Badajoz," Santiago explains.

"You're very young. You look like you're my daughter's age. I guess you've come to study."

"Yes. I've come to study Paleontology at the Universidad Central de Madrid."

"Paleonto... what?"

"It's the science that studies fossils."

"So, you'll discover dinosaurs?" asks the taxi driver.

"Well, I hope so!"

"That's interesting. My daughter will also start studying at the Universidad Central de Madrid this year. She will study Librarianship. Almost as exciting as discovering dinosaurs."

"Librarianship was my second choice," answers Santiago. "I love reading!"

"You'd get along well," answers the taxi driver.

The man continues driving through the streets of Madrid, and Santiago looks out the window. It's ten in the morning, and the city is in full of swing. The streets are full of people. Everyone is walking hurriedly as if they were late for somewhere. The architecture of the buildings is beautiful.

Then, Santiago realizes that something's wrong. He's been in the taxi for half an hour. According to his calculations, the trip from the airport to his new house is much shorter. Besides, he's going through the city center, and it wasn't supposed to be necessary.

The taxi driver stops the car in front of a huge building. That place looks nothing like the one he saw in the picture Beatriz, his future roommate, sent him.

"Well, here we are," says the taxi driver.

"Are you sure this is it?" asks Santiago, nervous. The last thing he wants is to get lost in one of the largest cities in Europe when he's just arrived!

"Yes, Rosas street, number 56."

Santiago pays and gets out of the taxi, which drives away up the street. He raises his head and contemplates the building, which must be about 20 stories high. He's definitely not in the right place. Then, he decides to pull out his mobile phone and call Beatriz.

"Hey, Beatriz! It's Santiago Martínez."

"Oh, my new roommate!" says Beatriz, in a good mood. "I'm waiting for you. Is everything okay? I thought you would get here earlier."

"Yes... Well, not really. I think I told the taxi driver the wrong address."

"Where are you?"

"In Rosas street, number 56."

On the other side of the phone, Beatriz lets out a laugh:

"You're on the other side of the city!"

"What?"

"The apartment address is Ríos Rosas street, number 56."

"No way! What do I do now?"

Santiago looks at his luggage. Going around the city carrying a really heavy backpack and a suitcase is not too tempting... but he has no other choice.

"Don't worry, I'll pick you up in my car," Beatriz says, amused. "I'll be there in half an hour."

"Okay. Thank you very much, Beatriz. See you."

Santiago sighs and sits on the sidewalk curb to wait. He's a bit embarrassed, but luckily, Beatriz seems really nice!

Chapter 2

Story: The roommate

Beatriz is a very charismatic girl... and chatty! She's been talking non-stop during the whole car ride. Santiago has learned a lot about her life: she's 30 years old, she works as a waitress at a restaurant, and she was born in Malaga. She's been living in Madrid for 10 years.

"This is the building," says Beatriz, parking the car in front of door number 56. Ríos Rosas is a lovely street with cobblestones and low buildings. It's quiet, although there is a busy avenue just a few meters away.

"It's an old building, isn't it?" asks Santiago, picking up his luggage and looking around his new home. "I'd say from the 1920s."

"I don't know what decade it's from, but yes, it's *very* old," confirms Beatriz. "The elevator is a million years old. Sometimes it doesn't work, so I hope you don't mind climbing three flights of stairs once in a while. Well... almost always."

Santiago looks down at his very heavy luggage. He's tired and hungry, but he just needs to make one last effort. Soon, he will be able to collapse into bed and get some rest.

"I guess it won't be a problem," he finally replies.

Between the two of them, they carry the luggage upstairs. Finally, exhausted, they reach the apartment.

"Well, welcome home!" says Beatriz.

The living room is spacious and bright. There's a large red sofa with lots of cushions on top. In front of it, there is a TV. Between the sofa and the TV, there's an industrial-style coffee table. Against the wall, there's a bookshelf with some books. Everywhere there are many beautiful plants.

A little further, there's a large wooden table with four chairs around it. In the center of the table, there is a huge flower vase. There's also a small balcony with a view of the street.

Everything is clean and tidy.

"This is the living room and dining room," Beatriz explains. "It's my favorite part of the house. On Thursday nights, I gather here with my friends to watch movies. So, if you don't have other plans, you can join us. This week is horror week."

"I'd love to!" answers Santiago.

"Great," says Beatriz. "Well, let's move on. I'm going to show you the bathroom."

"Wait. What about that painting?" Santiago points to the huge realistic painting. It depicts a woman with long, black, curly hair and expressive gray eyes. "It's awesome. Have you bought it, or did it come with the house when you rented it?"

"None of those things. I've painted it myself."

"I can't believe it! Are you a painter?"

"Oh, of course not. It's just a hobby. A silly hobby, really. I'm just an amateur."

"I think you're an excellent artist."

"Thank you," answers Beatriz.

Santiago can see that she's blushing.

"You're welcome!"

Beatriz starts up again. She shows Santiago the bathroom, which has a shower, a sink, and a toilet, and then leads him into the kitchen. The kitchen has a microwave, an oven, a coffee maker, a toaster, a dishwasher, and a fridge. On the other side of the kitchen, there is a small laundry room which has a washing machine and a dryer.

"Well, I think that's it," says Beatriz.

"And my room?" asks Santiago.

"Oh, of course! I'd forgotten it. Come, follow me."

Beatriz leads Santiago down a corridor. There are a few paintings, all very pretty, hanging on the walls. Santiago wonders if those were also painted by Beatriz. Finally, Beatriz opens the last door in the corridor.

"This is your bedroom," says Beatriz.

It's a small room, but it's practical: it has a bed, a desk, and a large closet. The best thing is that it has a window from which you can see a nice park.

"My bedroom is next door. There are two more rooms. One of them will be available for our guests. The other will be for another roommate. I've posted an announcement on an online forum, and many people have written to me.... but I think I already have the right person. She is coming this weekend.

"I'm can't wait to meet her!" answers Santiago.

"We will get along fine for sure," says Beatriz. "One last thing: you should know that I'm *too* tidy.

"Really?" asks Santiago, hoping it won't be a problem. He isn't exactly untidy, but he's definitely not obsessively tidy.

"My suggestion is that we keep the common areas as tidy as possible: the living room, the kitchen, and the bathroom."

"Okay," answers Santiago.

"Of course, you don't have to worry about Lila. I will take care of buying her food and cleaning her litter box."

"Lila?" asks Santiago, puzzled. "Who is Lila?"

At that exact moment, a huge white cat jumps out of a nearby piece of furniture and lands in Santiago's arms.

"Look, she likes you!" says Beatriz.

Chapter 3

Story: How's Family?

Beatriz opens her eyes. Last night she had to work the night shift at the restaurant, so she's very tired. She realizes that her cell phone has been ringing for a while. She looks at her phone screen: it's an unknown number.

"Hello?" she asks, and yawns.

"Hello, is this Beatriz Gutierrez?" says a man's voice from the other side.

"Yes... Who's this?"

"It's Pedro," the man replies.

Beatriz makes an effort to think about who Pedro is. She's still a little sleepy, but she's sure none of her friends are called that.

"I think you're mistaken," Beatriz says, and she's about to hang up the phone.

And just then, the man says:

"Pedro Gutierrez! Your cousin!"

Cousin Pedro! Of course, she hasn't recognized his voice. She hasn't seen him for many years. The two were very close when they were little because they are the same age, but they lost contact when Beatriz moved from Málaga to Madrid.

"Cousin Pedro, how are you?" Beatriz asks. "Is everything okay? Are you still living in Málaga?"

"I'm still living in Málaga, yes, although I'm in Madrid now. I'm here on business. I have a flight back to Málaga this afternoon, but I thought I could visit you before I leave."

"Of course," replies Beatriz. "Do you want to have lunch at my place today?"

"Excellent. At one o'clock?"

"At one o'clock!"

Beatriz hangs up and gets out of bed. Then she goes to Santiago's room. The kid is sitting at his desk while reading a book with a furrowed brow, concentrated.

"Good morning, Santi."

"Hey, Bea! How are you?"

"I'm good. Listen, in a few hours, Pedro is coming for lunch. He's a cousin I haven't seen for years. I thought I could make *ajoblanco malagueño*, a recipe of my grandmother's. Are you in?"

"It sounds delicious... but I can't," Santiago says sadly. "I have to go to college. Classes begin next Monday, so I have to enroll in my subject."

"Of course," Beatriz says. "I'll save you a share."

"I'd love that," Santiago replies.

Shortly after Santiago leaves, the doorbell rings. From the intercom, Beatriz opens the street door for her cousin. A minute later, Pedro appears at the apartment door. He is a tall, well-groomed young man in an elegant black suit. He also carries a briefcase in his hands. He's a businessman. Quite the contrary to Beatriz, who dresses very casually and is covered in tattoos!

"Cousin Pedro!" Beatriz greets him, and they hug briefly. "I haven't seen you since my brother Manolo's wedding. Come in. Lunch is served. I've made *ajoblanco malagueño.*"

"Just like grandma used to make!" Pedro says as he sits down at the table. "You've always been a great cook, cousin."

"I could never match grandma's recipe," Beatriz replies with a smile, sitting down as well. "Well, tell me, Pedro. How are you?"

"Fine, Bea. I'm still working at the architecture firm. I've come to Madrid to meet with some investors."

"And how's everything going in Malaga?

"Very well. I have lots of news. Do you remember María, my girlfriend? Well, we're getting married in June."

"Congratulations!"

"Thank you very much. I hope you can come. We're having a big wedding on the beach."

"Of course. I will be there. And how are your sister Sandra's children?"

"Beautiful and so big!" replies Pedro. "Andrés is going to be seven soon. He talks your ear off. He's at that age when he asks absolutely everything he can think of. 'Mom, why should I eat vegetables?' 'Mom, how much salt is there in the ocean?'" Pedro and Beatriz roar with laughter. "Little Fernanda turned five last month. She has asked Sandra and her father, Miguel, to sign her up for soccer lessons. She loves sports."

"How are your parents?" Beatriz asks. "I haven't seen uncle Antonio and aunt Francisca in a long time."

"They're fine," Peter replies. "Mom's still working at the hospital. Dad is still in charge of the family architecture firm. He's old: he has gray hair! Sandra and I tell him that it's time to retire. That he should rest and travel. That the two of us can take over the firm. But he insists on continuing to work!"

"But your father has always been very jovial," Beatriz says. "Last time I saw him, he looked like a 40-year-old man. Besides, we Gutierrez are very vigorous people."

"That's true," says Pedro. "Well, Beatriz, tell me something about yourself. How are you? Are you still painting those wonderful paintings?"

"Yes, from time to time," replies Beatriz, slightly blushing. "I don't do that for a living, though. I work in a restaurant a few blocks from here. The truth is, I'm doing well. I like my job, I have lots of friends, and I am in love with Madrid!"

"Who isn't?" says Pedro. "You never get bored in Madrid. Theaters, concerts, parks... There's always something to do here. I'd like to visit more often, but I have a lot of work there in Málaga." At that very moment, Pedro's cell phone starts ringing. "Will you excuse me?"

"Of course."

Pedro holds the cell phone to his ear.

"Hello? Yes, that's me. Aha. Of course. That's too bad. And don't you have...? I see. Thank you very much for letting me know." He hangs up. He looks a little worried.

"Is everything all right?" Beatriz asks.

"More or less. My flight back to Málaga has been canceled, and there is no other flight until tomorrow afternoon." Pedro gets up from his chair. "I think I'd better go, Bea. I need to find a hotel for the night."

"A hotel?" Beatriz asks. "None of that, cousin! You can stay here. There's a guest room. You'll be comfortable there."

"But wouldn't it be too much trouble?"

"Of course not. We are family"

Chapter 4

Story: A Morning in Madrid

On Saturday, Santiago decided to go out and explore the city. It's only two days before classes start at university, and he thinks that he won't have much time to walk around afterward.

While having breakfast, he gets a phone call. It's Bea.

"Hey, Santi. I'm already at work; I had to cover the morning shift today. I wanted to tell you that this afternoon, at three o'clock, our new roommate will be arriving, and she's asked me to pick her up at Atocha train station. Would you like to come with me?"

"Of course, Bea," says Santiago. "I'll walk around the city, but I'll be there at three o'clock."

"Great. Have fun!"

At that exact moment, Santiago's phone turns off. Then, he remembers that he forgot to plug it in last night, and now it's out of battery.

"What a problem!" thinks Santiago. "That means I won't be able to check the GPS... and Madrid is huge."

Then, he remembers that, in Montijo, his best friend Luis gave him a map of Madrid before saying goodbye. After looking for it for a while, he finds it in one of the side pockets of his backpack. On the map, Luis has marked some of the most important places in Madrid.

Santiago dresses in light clothes and sunglasses and goes out, ready to start his Madrid adventure.

His first stop is the Museum of Natural Sciences. According to the map, it's pretty close to his house. In fact, it only takes 15 minutes to get there. The museum is beautiful and houses the largest paleontological collection Santiago has ever seen. He's so excited to see the dinosaur fossils that he spends two hours inside.

When he leaves the museum, he heads to El Retiro park, his second stop. According to the map, it's only a few kilometers away... but he doesn't know how to get there!

"Excuse me, madam," he says to a woman walking by. "I'd like to go to El Retiro park. Could you tell me how to get there?"

"Of course, honey. You need to take the bus on line 14."

"Where is the stop?"

"Right there, in front of the pharmacy."

"Ok. And where do I get off?"

"When you see the Cibeles Fountain. It's a short trip of about ten minutes."

"And do you know how much the bus ticket is?"

"One euro and fifty cents," answers the woman.

"Thank you very much, madam!"

Following the woman's directions, Santiago reaches El Retiro smoothly. It's a giant park full of interesting plants and trees. There are also many monuments, such as statues and buildings. There is even a palace made entirely out of glass!

After the stroll, Santiago is exhausted, so he decides to stop at a small restaurant for a bite to eat.

"Good morning, lad," says the waiter. "What can I get you?"

"What do you recommend, sir?"

"The house specialty is *cocido madrileño*. It's a stew with chickpeas, vegetables, meat and cold meats."

"Perfect, I'll order that. And to drink, I'd like a large glass of orange juice, please. I need to recharge my energy to keep on traveling around the city."

After lunch, Santiago checks the map that Luis gave him. One of the nearest tourist sites is the Oriente Palace, so he walks towards it. Luckily, he arrives at the palace gates right on time to join a guided tour. The guide is a young nice woman.

"My name is Carmen, I'll be your tourist guide this afternoon in Oriente Palace," she says. "This is the official residence of the Spanish monarchs, although they don't live here currently. Let's go inside. Follow me."

Santiago enters the palace with a group of tourists, amazed by what he sees. The tour guide turns out to be really good and knows a lot about the palace and everything about Madrid. Santiago learns, for example, that the palace is one of the largest in the world: it has 3,500 rooms and is twice the size of Buckingham palace in London. He also learns that many subterranean tunnels depart from that building and connect it to different parts of the Spanish capital.

"Okay," says the tour guide after a while. "It's going to be half past two. It's time for a break for you to eat something and freshen up. We'll meet at Plaza de la Armería in half an hour.

"Did you say it's half past two?" asks Santiago, astonished.

He's arranged to meet Beatriz to pick up their new roommate! Since he didn't bring his phone and doesn't have a watch, he's completely lost track of time. As all the tourists begin to leave, Santiago approaches Carmen.

"I forgot I have something to do. I need to be at Atocha train station in half an hour. Do you know the quickest way to get there, Carmen?"

"Sure. You need to take line 2 of the metro at Ópera station. It's right in front of a big supermarket. Get off at Sol station and change to line 1 of the metro. Four stops later, you need to get off at Valdecarros station.

And that's it! You will get to Atocha in 20 minutes."

"Ok, Carmen. Thank you!"

Santiago leaves the palace in a hurry, trying to memorize all the instructions that Carmen gave him.

Chapter 5

Story: *Paellas, Migas Extremeñas* and Mediterranean Salads

Patricia Solano, Beatriz and Santiago's new roommate, is twenty-five years old and has come from Barcelona. Beatriz and Santiago have shown her around the apartment.

"It's a very nice apartment, and very well located," says Patricia. "Although the part that I liked the most, undoubtedly, is the kitchen. It's very well equipped!"

"Does that mean that you like cooking?" Santiago asks.

"Are you kidding? I'm a professional cook!" says Patricia.

"Really?" Beatriz asks.

"Yeah. While I live in this house, you won't starve. I love cooking for myself and for others. It's my passion."

"What excellent news!" says Santiago. "I'm pretty bad in the kitchen. Bea, on the other hand, is quite good. The other day she prepared some *ajoblanco malagueño* that was delicious."

"My grandmother's recipe," says Beatriz, smiling.

"I'd love to try it," Patricia says.

"And where do you work, Patri?" asks Santiago.

"For the last three years, I was head chef at an important hotel in Barcelona. I left because the work environment was not good. I'm currently unemployed. If you know of any jobs, I'd appreciate it if you'd let me know."

"Sure," Beatriz says. "At the restaurant where I work there is a good atmosphere. My coworkers are very cool, and my bosses are fair people. I'm going to ask them if they need people."

"Perfect," Patricia says. "Well, then, tell me, what do you like eating? I would like to know your preferences so I know what to cook."

"I like everything," answers Santiago. "I really like fish, for instance. I love *paella*. I also like *gazpacho* and *migas extremeñas*."

"*Migas extremeñas?*" Patricia asks. "I've never made that before. What's in the dish?"

"They are made with bread from the previous day, green and red peppers, egg, garlic, *chorizo*, bacon, and seasonings. Oh! And olive oil. My mother makes the best *migas extremeñas* in all of Badajoz. I'll ask her what her secret recipe is."

"Very well. What about you, Bea? What do you like to eat?" asks Patricia.

"I'm a vegetarian. I love Mediterranean salad with tomato, lettuce, carrot, and olives. I also like potato omelets. And cheese croquettes."

"And do you prefer fried or baked food?"

"Baked," Bea says. "Oily food gives me a stomach ache."

"I like food cooked both ways," says Santiago.

Patricia smiles and asks:

"Is there anything you *don't* like, Santi?"

Santiago thinks for a moment and then, smiling, he answers:

"I don't think so!"

Chapter 6

Story: A Blow of Fate

Patricia goes to her fourth job interview in a week. It's at an old and somewhat dirty restaurant. The interviewer is serious and wary. After a short conversation, he asks her: "Do you speak other languages besides Spanish?"

"Yes. I speak English, Catalan, and a bit of French," says Patricia.

"And do you live nearby?"

"I live on Ríos Rosas street, number 56. It's two subway stations from here."

"Ok. I'll call you back."

The interviewer hands her the résumé back, and Patricia leaves for her next interview at a really trendy bar in the Chueca neighborhood. The interviewer is lovely and seems pretty interested in Patricia's profile.

"It says here that you worked at the Mediterráneo Hotel for three years; it's really prestigious... But, was that your only job?"

"Yes," answers Patricia. "Before I started working, I was studying at the Instituto de Cocina de Barcelona."

"Very good." The interviewer hands her résumé back to her. "Do you know how to prepare cocktails?"

"I've never done it, but I can try!"

"Ok. We'll give you a call."

The interviewer doesn't seem so lovely anymore.

Frustrated, Patricia sits on the terrace of a bar in Plaza Mayor de Madrid and orders an iced tea. She looks at a group of tourists taking pictures while she thinks that she has to find a job *urgently*. Otherwise, she will have to return to her parent's house in Barcelona.

At that moment, the waiter arrives with her order.

"Here it is: strawberry and blueberry iced tea," she says, while leaving the glass on the table. "Are you looking for a job?" she asks upon seeing the folder with Patricia's résumé.

"That's right," answers Patricia, suddenly happy. "I'm a professional chef. Do you happen to need staff in this bar?"

"I'm sorry, not right now," answers the waiter.

"Oh, ok."

"But you can leave your résumé if you want. If we need to fill a vacancy in the kitchen, we'll keep you in mind."

"Ok, thanks a lot," answers Patricia and hands the résumé to the waiter.

Patricia quietly sips her iced tea as she watches tourists walking around and taking pictures of Plaza Mayor de Madrid. Then, someone speaks to her.

"So you're a professional chef?"

Patricia turns around. The person speaking is a very pretty, elegant, middle-aged woman sitting at a nearby table, drinking a pint of beer. She's got long red hair and is wearing a nice white dress and large sunglasses.

"Yes," answers Patricia. "I arrived in Madrid a few days ago. In Barcelona, I've worked for three years as head chef of the Mediterráneo Hotel."

"The Mediterráneo Hotel? Wow, that place has a great reputation. I've been lucky enough to stay there several times."

"Really?" asks Patricia. "Then, if you've ordered food at the hotel restaurant, you must have tried some of my dishes. I made up the menu myself."

"I see," says the woman. "Yes... I remember a really exquisite *crema catalana*. Are you responsible for that?"

"The very one!"

"And what about those *calçots* in *romesco* sauce?"

"Those too."

"Impressive," said the woman. "Honestly, impressive. What's your name?"

"Patricia Solano."

"You seem very nice, Patricia. Tell me, do you like TV?"

"TV?" asks Patricia, astounded. "Not really. Well... I've never watched much TV."

"You'd work well in front of a camera. You have what they call... *charm*."

Patricia didn't know how to respond to that. The conversation was getting a little strange. The woman drinks a long sip of her pint and then says:

"My name is Isabel Vega Muñoz."

"Isabel Vega Muñoz?" asks Patricia, surprised. "I'm sorry, I didn't recognize you with the sunglasses."

Patricia can't believe that she is in front of the real Isabel Vega Muñoz, a famous TV host.

"Have you ever seen one of my shows?" asks Isabel.

Patricia knows that Isabel is very well-known, although she's *never* seen one of her shows. However, she thinks it's not too polite to say that, so she says:

"Once or twice."

"Then, I'm sure you know that my shows are usually magazines. There are interviews with celebrities, contests... and a cooking section. Well, it turns out I'm looking for a charismatic person but, above all, someone who knows how to cook. I need them to take care of the cooking section of my new cooking show, which will premiere next week."

Patricia can't believe what she just heard. Her? On TV?

"But I've never been in front of a camera."

"You'll learn," answers Isabel.

"But, why me? Aren't there many other more experienced people on TV?"

"I do believe in destiny, Patricia," says Isabel. "And I think that destiny has put us at two adjacent tables this afternoon for a reason. Why don't you try it? If you don't like it, nobody will force you to stay."

"I don't know," says Patricia, not at all convinced. "Can we discuss my fees?"

Isabel grabs a napkin and pulls a pen from her sophisticated purse. She writes down something quickly and passes the paper to Patricia.

"This is what you'd earn."

"Wow! That's a great salary. It's more than I was making at the Mediterráneo Hotel."

Patricia thinks about it for a moment. The truth is that she gets a little nervous in front of the camera. But then she thinks it could be an interesting challenge. Besides, she remembers that her grandmother Rosa is a viewer of Isabel Vega Muñoz's shows. Patricia imagines the look on her face when she sees her on TV.

"Ok, Isabel. I'll give it a try. But... Can I ask you something?"

"Anything."

"Would you sign an autograph for my grandmother Rosa? She adores you!"

Chapter 7

Story: Doctor, What Do I Have?

"New beginnings are never easy," thinks Damián. His breathing is intermittent, and his hands are shaking. He's nervous, but that's not unusual. It's his first day as a resident doctor at Santa Barbara Hospital; it's also the end of a long journey. And endings are never easy.

"This is your office," says Amparo, the second-year resident who is showing him around the hospital. "This is where you'll receive your first patients. Any questions?"

"No, thank you very much," says Damián.

Hearing him, Amparo frowns for a second. She doesn't seem to have quite understood him.

"Excuse me, where are you from?" she asks.

"I'm from Argentina," Damián replies.

"I thought so!" exclaims Amparo. "That accent is unmistakable. From Argentina, then. Madrid is full of Argentines, but I imagine you already know it. What are you doing here?"

"When I graduated from college in Buenos Aires, I decided I wanted a change," Damián answers. "Getting a degree in medicine is a very long journey. Then I saw that I had the possibility to apply for a residency in Madrid, and... Well, here I am."

"You'll love the city, you'll see," says Amparo as she approaches the door. "Excuse me, but I have to go: there are many new residents to guide. Let me know if you have any problems, and good luck!"

Amparo leaves the office, leaving the door open. Shyly, Damián sits behind the desk, with his white coat open, and turns on the computer. He really doesn't know what to expect. It's his first day on call.

"Excuse me, doctor," he hears.

Damián looks up. In front of him, there's a very young man, no more than twenty years old. He looks pale and walks with difficulty.

"Come on in," says Damián. "Sit down. How are you?"

"Fine," the young man whispers.

Just then, the man's name appears on the computer: Santiago Martinez.

"Tell me, Santiago, why are you here?" asks Damián. He tries to sound as professional as possible. It's his first day, but his patients don't need to know that.

"My stomach aches," Santiago replies, "and I feel nauseous. That's the main thing. But I also have an ugly headache; I think I even feel a little feverish. I'm also sweating a lot, and I have chills. Like the flu."

"Sounds pretty uncomfortable," says Damián. "What kind of pain do you feel in your stomach?"

"I don't feel it all the time," Santiago says. "It comes and goes..."

Santiago is suddenly silent, and his face becomes even paler. Damián can hear his patient's stomach making strange noises.

"Any other symptoms?" asks Damián.

"I don't think so," replies Santiago. "Doctor, I'm scared I have appendicitis."

Damián remembers his studies. Sudden stomach aches, nausea, fever, a young patient. It's a possibility.

"Lie down on the stretcher, please," Damián says. "And pull up your t-shirt a little."

Santiago follows the doctor's orders. Damián feels the right side of his abdomen. There's no swelling. He can rule out appendicitis.

"When did the aches begin?" asks Damián as he steps away and lets his patient get dressed.

"Last night," Santiago replies.

"What did you do yesterday?" Damián asks.

"Yesterday..." replies Santiago. "I went to college, I had classes. In the afternoon, I studied at home, and then I watched a TV show. In the evening, I had dinner with my roommates. At that time, I felt good; and I was lucky because there were *migas extremeñas* for dinner. One of my roommates is a chef, you know, and ..."

"What are *migas extremeñas*?," interrupts Damián.

"It's a typical dish from Extremadura, where I come from," Santiago replies. "It has bread from the previous day, green and red peppers, eggs, garlic, *chorizo,* and bacon."

"Sounds pretty heavy," says Damián. How much did you eat?"

"I don't know..." Santiago replies. "Six plates?"

"Six plates of fried bread with *chorizo*!" says Damián, suddenly relieved. His first diagnosis is much simpler than he expected. "Don't worry, Santiago, you don't have appendicitis. You have indigestion!"

Chapter 8

Story: A Special Visit

The doorbell rings in the apartment at Ríos Rosas 56. Immediately, Patricia stands up.

"Guys! My grandmother Rosa has arrived!" says Patricia while she gets closer to the intercom.

At that moment, Santiago and Beatriz come out of their bedrooms. They approach the kitchen, where food is served. It's about 8 in the evening.

"Come in," says Patricia by the intercom and presses the button that opens the front door. "The elevator worked today, right? I don't want my grandmother carrying her suitcases up three flights of stairs."

"It worked this afternoon," answers Santiago from the other room.

After a minute or two, the apartment doorbell rings. Patricia opens the door quickly.

"Grandma!" Patricia then says and rushes in to hug a seventy-five-year-old woman.

The hug doesn't last long. Quickly, Patricia grabs her grandmother's suitcases and carries them inside the apartment.

"Come in; we were waiting for you to eat," says Patricia. "These are Santiago and Beatriz, my roommates."

"It's a pleasure," says Rosa while she enters the house.

"Patricia always talks about you," says Beatriz. "She told us that you taught her how to cook. Maybe that's why she put so much effort into dinner... There's enough food for an army!"

Beatriz points to the kitchen table: there are five different dishes, each the size of two or three generous servings.

"What a joy to have you here," says Patricia. "Sit; you must be hungry. How was the trip?"

"Oh, it was excellent," answers Rosa. "The train from Barcelona is really comfortable. I've never taken it before! It's like traveling first class. I still remember when, to come to Madrid, we had to take an endless bus. I would take a needle and thread, and, by the time I got to the station, I had knitted a vest for one of my grandchildren."

"They were really good vests," answers Patricia, amused. "My grandmother traveled a lot between Barcelona and Madrid when she was young, with my grandfather," she clarifies for Santiago and Beatriz.

"Why?" asks Santiago while he serves some *croquetas* on his plate.

"Jorge was from Madrid," answers Rosa. "We'd come to visit his family. Patricia, have you visited any of your relatives around here? Eduardo would be pleased to welcome you.

"Not yet, grandma," says Patricia. "I know that Eduardo is grandpa's cousin, but I don't know him! I am shy.

"Nonsense," answers Rosa. "We will visit him tomorrow. Eduardo is lovely."

"Patricia, this black rice is incredible," Beatriz says then. "I think it's the best I've ever eaten."

"Family recipe," says Patricia, smiling.

"But yours is better!" answers Rosa. "When she was little, she was always in the kitchen. Some kids are drawn to TV; she only wanted to get near the oven. I used to put her next to me, give her a blunt knife, and she would imitate everything I did."

"That's how I learned everything I know," says Patricia, shrugging. "Cooking school was just to get the degree. Actually, my best dishes were always the ones my grandma Rosa taught me."

"Did you spend a lot of time together?" asks Santiago.

"Yes, because my parents worked late," answers Patricia. "Then, when I got out of school, I'd go straight to grandma's house. I'd spend the afternoon there. Sometimes we read together, sometimes she played canasta with her friends. She basically raised me. So now you know who to blame for everything you have to suffer," jokes Patricia, addressing her roommates.

"You exaggerate everything, Patricia," says Rosa. "You were raised by your mother. I just did what I could to help. And, anyway, I don't think these nice kids are having such a bad time with you, right?"

"Not at all," says Santiago while he refills his plate. It's clear he's recovered from last week's indigestion. "Especially when Patricia prepares an *escalivada* like this one!"

Chapter 9

Story: The *Cantaora*

Beatriz gets to work. Her boss, Mrs. Ordóñez, greets her with a kiss on the cheek. Beatriz has been working at the restaurant for a long time, and there's a lot of trust between them.

"Good night, Bea," says Mrs. Ordóñez. "Are you ready?"

"Yes, as always," answers Beatriz as she sets her purse behind the bar.

"It's just that this won't be a night like the others," says Ordóñez. "But... don't you know yet? Miguel, haven't you told her?"

Miguel, another of the restaurant's waiters, flashes an apologetic smile.

"I'm sorry, boss," he says. "I just didn't mean to make her nervous."

"What are you talking about?" asks Beatriz.

"Tonight, we have a reservation for flamenco *cantaora* Sara Alas," explains Ordóñez.

"You're kidding me," says Beatriz.

"Of course not," answers Ordóñez. "And I want you to handle her table."

"Really?" asks Beatriz. Suddenly, she feels her hands sweating. "I'm a big Sara Alas fan!"

"Of course we know," answers Miguel. "Whenever you put on some music, it's always Sara Alas!"

"I just grew up listening to her music," explains Beatriz. "When I was a child, I went to see one of her shows at a *tablao* in Malaga with my parents. I was fascinated by her voice, so sweet and so strong. Besides, her lyrics are really powerful. If I had her in front of me, I'd tell her that she's the best *cantaora* in Andalusia.

"Well, then it's your lucky day; she just walked in," says Miguel, pointing to the restaurant door.

Sara Alas comes in with her work team. Beatriz immediately recognizes Paco Figueroa, the guitar player who usually accompanies her in her presentations. Mrs. Ordóñez walks towards them and, after greeting them cordially, leads them through the restaurant to the table they've been assigned. The restaurant customers, who aren't many at that hour, turn their heads to look at them and whisper.

Beatriz knows it's her moment to act. However, she's too nervous.

"You'll do great, Bea," says Miguel. "Remember, you're a professional."

Bea takes a deep breath and walks over to the newcomers' table.

"Good evening, Mrs. Salas. I mean, Mrs. Alas," says Beatriz clumsily. "It's our pleasure that you've chosen our restaurant this evening. I mean, tonight! I'll leave the menu for you to check.

Bea leaves in the direction of the bar. At that moment, Mrs. Ordóñez appears with a bottle of wine in her hand.

"Here, take this wine on the house, please," she asks Beatriz.

Beatriz takes the wine and goes to the table. She starts pouring it into the glasses of Sara Alas and the rest of her team. As she does so, with shaking hands, she accidentally spills a splash of wine on Sara's white blouse.

"Oh!" exclaims Beatriz. "I'm really sorry!"

She's very embarrassed and doesn't know what to say. Sara Alas stares at her. And then, she smiles.

"Don't worry. It's just a blouse. Tell me, is this your first day?"

"No!" answers Beatriz. "I've been working here for years. It's just that I'm a great fan of yours, and I want you to have a perfect evening. You are the best *cantaora* of Andalusia."

"Thank you very much for the compliment," says Sara. "Will you come to my show next weekend?"

"I couldn't get tickets, Mrs. Alas," explains Beatriz.

Sara takes something out of her pocket and hands it to Beatriz.

"Well, now you do. Come with friends."

Beatriz looks at what Sara just gave her. They're three front-row tickets for her concert in one of the most famous *tablaos* in Madrid.

"Thank you very much!" says Beatriz, happy.

Without a doubt, it will be the perfect Saturday plan with Santiago and Patricia, her roommates.

"And now, please pour the wine... *inside* the glass," says Sara Alas, still smiling.

Chapter 10

Story: The Dress

Beatriz, Patricia, and Santiago go shopping. Each one has a different reason: Beatriz wants to buy a dress for her cousin Pedro's wedding; Patricia is looking for something simple to go out partying, and Santiago wants to get a sports outfit to go to the gym.

Beatriz drives the car to a very lively street full of people and stores. The first stop is a large casual women's clothing store. Patricia picks up several items of clothing and goes into one of the fitting rooms. A few minutes later, she comes out to show the outfit to her friends. She's wearing a pretty blue shirt and jeans.

"What do you think?" she asks.

"I love it!" says Beatriz.

"Yes, it's very nice," Santiago agrees.

"Okay, I'll take it," she says and turns to the store clerk. "Excuse me, can I pay by card?"

"Of course, we accept debit and credit cards."

Patricia pays, and they all head out in search of the next goal: sportswear for Santiago. Bea, who knows Madrid, takes them to a huge department store, but Santi is not used to shopping in such large places, and he doesn't know which way to go; he feels a bit dazed.

"Don't worry, Santi," Patricia says. "Let's ask someone who works here. Hey, excuse me, could you tell me where I can find men's sportswear?"

"Yes, of course," replies a young man wearing a t-shirt with the store's logo. "The men's clothing is on the fourth floor. You can go up these escalators. Once you get there, go to the left. There's everything you need for sports."

The three friends go up to the fourth floor and find the sportswear. Santiago chooses two t-shirts, a pair of shorts, and three pairs of socks. Then, they go to the footwear department to choose running shoes. Santiago tries them all on and, satisfied, heads to the checkout area, where he pays in cash.

The last stop is a very elegant clothing store up the street. Beatriz is looking for a formal dress, but nothing pleases her: one dress is too long, the other is too short, a third is too shiny...

Finally, she finds the perfect dress. It's loose-fitting, just above the knees, with an open back and bright colors: perfect for a wedding on the beach. Plus, it fits her perfectly, almost as if it had been tailor-made. When she leaves the fitting room, Santiago claps, and Patricia lets out a flattering whistle. There's no doubt that's the dress she has to buy.

However, there's a problem.

"It's too expensive," Beatriz says as she looks at the price tag. "I could never afford it."

Disappointed, she goes back to the fitting room and takes it off. On her way out, a store clerk asks her how it went.

"It was perfect for me, but it's way out of my budget," Beatriz replies, sad.

"Even with the discount?" asks the clerk.

"Is there a discount? I didn't know that!" says Beatriz, a little more cheerful.

"All items have an end-of-season discount of fifty percent."

"Fifty percent?!" the three friends exclaim in unison.

"Then yes, I'll take it!" says Beatriz, exultant.

Chapter 11

Story: A Little Joke

Patricia parks the car and turns off the engine, but she doesn't remove the key. She knows it will be a short stop.

"Santiago, could you tell your friend to get out?" she says. She's still sleepy. It is early in the morning: the sun hasn't risen yet. But, if they want to get to Haro in time for the Wine Battle, they have to leave really early.

"Okay," answers Santiago from the passenger's seat, and he grabs his cell phone.

"Aren't you going to ring the bell? Suit yourself, I suppose," Patricia says. "Hey, what's this kid's name again? I've already forgotten. He's from Colombia, isn't he?"

"Julio," says Santiago. "Yes, he's from Colombia. He came to Madrid to study; he is my schoolmate." Then Santiago raises his voice. "Look! There he is."

A guy in his twenties beckons him from the door of a building. He's wearing smart pants made of a nice fabric, a light white shirt, and leather shoes. He quickly sits down in the rear seat of the car.

"Good morning!" greets Julio. "How are you? Santi, thank you for inviting me to this. You're Patricia, right?"

Julio speaks fast. He has an enthusiastic and friendly attitude that's very contagious.

"I'm Patricia, yes. Hey, are you going to go dressed like that?"

"Yes, of course," Julio replies. "You have to dress elegantly for a wine tasting, right? Is there a problem?"

"I wouldn't go to the party dressed like that, but it's your choice," Patricia says, indifferent. She's wearing an old cotton t-shirt and athletic shorts; Santiago is wearing practically the same. They're both wearing old sneakers.

At that moment, Patricia notices that, from the passenger seat, Santiago is trying to tell her something. He's pretty discreet, but the indication is clear: don't say anything else. Patricia understands that Santiago is making one of his jokes, and she decides, a little reluctantly, to listen to his friend.

The drive is quick and quiet. At that time of the day, the highway is deserted, so they make the route in a fraction of the time. They arrive in Haro shortly after eight o'clock in the morning. However, the village, although highly decorated, is practically empty.

"I thought we were coming to a party," says Julio, slightly puzzled.

"It's just that the party is on the cliffs," replies Patricia. "So we don't make a mess in town."

"Make a mess? How tidy," Julio replies, and Santiago lets out a laugh. "What's going on?" Julio asks.

"You'll see," Santiago says.

A few minutes later, the car arrives at the scene of the wine battle. The image is shocking. Hundreds of people are throwing wine at each other with jugs, bowls, and water guns. All their clothes are violet; many are wearing red handkerchiefs. There is live music, loudspeakers, and a lot of wine, which is spilled over bodies, on the street, and on the ground, forming sticky and festive mud.

"I thought we'd get here before it started," Patricia says, a little disappointed. "We should have left sooner."

"Come on, Patricia! We still have a couple of hours of partying left," says Santiago, opening the car door and walking towards the party. Almost instantly, he receives a bucket of wine on his back. His white t-shirt turns red.

However, Patricia doesn't leave the car. She's waiting for Julio's reaction, who is still surprised in the back seat. She doesn't like pranks, and she's not entirely comfortable with having been an accomplice.

"Whatever," Julio finally says, regaining his initial enthusiasm. "The only thing that matters is not ruining these shoes," he adds while untying his laces. "That would be a problem. Shall we, Patricia? Before the wine runs out!"

Chapter 12

Story: The Ecologic District

Sandra Gutierrez is in front of a large audience. It's her first time representing her family's architecture firm. And it's an important project, so she's pretty nervous.

"Thank you all very much for coming today," Sandra says. "As you know, I am going to present the urban planning project we have been working on: the design and construction of the EcoMálaga residential district."

Sandra turns on the projector. Her hands shake a little. She takes a quick look at the audience. There are many people there: the residents of Santa Julia, journalists, business people, and town councilors. Everyone wants to know all about the new project of the architecture firm Gutiérrez, S.A.

His brother, Pedro, is sitting in the front row of the auditorium. He smiles at her, raising his thumb and giving her encouragement. Suddenly, Sandra feels a little calmer.

"Well, as you can see from this graphic, the population of Santa Julia has been growing year after year. This is because many people come to work in the nearby industrial state, which is the most important in Málaga and one of the most important in Andalusia. Well, in Gutiérrez S.A., we have projected a new residential district that will cover that demographic demand." Someone raises their hand. "Yes?"

"Will it be a low-rise neighborhood, or will it have towers?"

"There will be a total of ten low-rise buildings, up to three stories. The urban code of the province will be respected. There will be two to five units per building."

"But what will happen to the animals?" asks a woman in the audience. "There are flamingos, herons, and foxes around the village. There are also vultures and eagles. What will happen to all of them when you bring in the machines?"

"We are not going to build in any areas where native wildlife is present," Sandra says. "Also, our construction policies are environmentally friendly. The house will have no impact on the environment. We will install solar panels on the roof of each of the ten buildings to reduce the energy demand. We have to take advantage of the 300 days of sunshine we have a year!"

The audience smiles. As good locals, they enjoy every time someone speaks well of their region. Sandra feels more relaxed. It's important for her to win the sympathy of neighbors and local authorities. After all, they are the ones who are going to live in the complex.

At that moment, an older man sitting at the back of the room stands up. Quickly, one of the attendees hands him a microphone so that all those present can hear his question.

"I have only one doubt," the man says. "How do you get an apartment there? Because my son is looking for a bigger place, he has a kid now ..."

"I'll give you the information right now!" Sandra replies, satisfied.

Answer Sheets
Chapter 1

Exercises

1. b. están ajustados de tiempo.
2. c. ¡Qué tengas un buen viaje!
3.
    a. amigo
    b. piso / vivienda
    c. taxi
4. c. Edificios bellísimos.
5. a. Calle Ríos Rosas, número 56.

Comprehension Questions

1. Sus padres, su hermana y su mejor amigo, Luis.
2. En un piso con Beatriz.
3. Paleontología.
4. Llama a Beatriz.
5. En coche.

Chapter 2

Exercises

1. b. Inodoro.
2. c. Contra la pared.
3. a. Lavavajillas.
4. b. Pequeña y práctica.
5. a. El gato de Beatriz.

Comprehension Questions

1. Hermosa, con adoquines y edificios bajos y silenciosa.
2. Una mesa de café.
3. Se reúne con sus amigos en la casa a ver películas.
4. Pintar cuadros.
5. No, pero no es un obsesivo del orden.

Chapter 3

Exercises

1. b. Casual.
2. c. La novia de Pedro.
3. a. La abuela.
4. c. Tiene que inscribirse a las asignaturas.
5. a. En lo de su prima Beatriz.

Comprehension Questions

1. Porque la noche anterior ha tenido que trabajar en el turno nocturno.
2. Porque tienen la misma edad.
3. Desde la boda de Manolo, el hermano de Beatriz.
4. Fernanda tiene cinco. Andrés tiene seis.
5. Los teatros, conciertos, parques. Que siempre hay cosas para hacer.

Chapter 4

Exercises

1. a. En el bolsillo lateral de la mochila.
2. c. 15 minutos.
3. a. Un palacio.
4. b. Triplica el tamaño del palacio de Buckingham.
5. a. No lleva el móvil.

Comprehension Questions

1. Olvidó enchufarlo a la corriente y se quedó sin batería.
2. A una mujer que pasa por allí.

3. Cocido madrileño y un zumo de naranja.
4. En la estación de trenes de Atocha.
5. Debe tomar 2 líneas de metro y tardará unos 20 minutos.

Chapter 5

Exercises

1. c. La cocina.
2. b. Porque a Patricia le gusta cocinar.
3. a. Tomates.
4. a. Porque había mal ambiente laboral.
5. c. Sopa de pollo.

Comprehension Questions

1. Es la nueva compañera de piso de Beatriz y Santiago, tiene veinticinco años y viene de Barcelona.
2. Beatriz.
3. Sus compañeros de trabajo son muy guays. Sus jefes son personas justas.
4. La ensalada mediterránea lleva tomate, lechuga, zanahoria y aceitunas.
5. Porque la comida con demasiado aceite le provoca dolor de estómago.

Chapter 6

Exercises

1. a. En el hotel Mediterráneo.
2. b. ¿Hablas otros idiomas?
3. a. Turistas tomándose fotos.
4. c. Isabel Vega Muñoz.
5. c. Porque cree en el destino.

Comprehension Questions

1. Un restaurante viejo y un poco sucio.
2. Porque si no tendrá que volver a Barcelona a la casa de sus padres.
3. Es una mujer de mediana edad, muy guapa y elegante.

4. Que parece simpática, que funcionaría bien en cámara y que tiene ángel.

5. Un autógrafo para su abuela Rosa.

Chapter 7

Exercises

1. c. Porque está nervioso.
2. c. Una médica.
3. a. Por su forma de hablar.
4. b. Desorientación.
5. a. De tener apendicitis.

Comprehension Questions

1. Es su primer día.
2. Porque, cuando terminó la universidad, decidió que quería un cambio y vio que tenía la posibilidad de aplicar a una residencia en Madrid.
3. Se sienta detrás del escritorio e inicia el ordenador.
4. Le pide que se acueste en la camilla y que se levante la remera. Luego, le palpa el lado derecho del abdomen.
5. Porque su primer diagnóstico es mucho más sencillo de lo que esperaba.

Chapter 8

Exercises

1. b. A las 20.
2. c. Barcelona.
3. a. Un bus.
4. c. El primo del abuelo de Patricia.
5. b. Rosa

Comprehension Questions

1. Patricia.
2. Cómodo.
3. Tejer chalecos para sus nietos.

4. Rosa la ponía junto a ella y le daba un cuchillo sin filo y Patricia imitaba todo lo que hacía.
5. Recuperado.

Chapter 9

Exercises

1. b. Que hoy tienen una reserva para una cantaora famosa.
2. a. Beatriz.
3. b. Poderosas.
4. c. En el apellido de Sara.
5. a. El vino.

Comprehension Questions

1. Tienen mucha confianza.
2. Porque fue a un espectáculo suyo cuando era pequeña y quedó fascinada con su voz y sus canciones.
3. Giran el cuello para verla y cuchichean.
4. Sonríe y le pregunta si es su primer día.
5. Tres entradas para la primera fila de su concierto.

Chapter 10

Exercises

1. b. Para la boda de su primo Pedro.
2. a. A ambos les gusta.
3. b. Zapatillas deportivas, camisetas, pantalones cortos y calcetines.
4. a. En efectivo.
5. c. Porque es demasiado caro.

Comprehension Questions

1. Patricia quiere algo sencillo para ir de fiesta.
2. Es una calle muy animada y llena de gente y tiendas.
3. Porque no está acostumbrado a comprar en lugares tan grandes y no sabe para dónde ir.
4. Les dice que la indumentaria masculina está en el cuarto piso. Que suban por las escaleras mecánicas y vayan a la izquierda.

5. El vestido que compra Beatriz es suelto, justo por encima de las rodillas, con la espalda descubierta y de colores alegres.

Chapter 11

Exercises

1. c. Porque sabe que la parada va a durar poco.
2. b. Un jersey.
3. a. Elegante.

4. a. Patricia le hace caso a Santiago a pesar de que no quiere.
5. b. Haber sido cómplice de Santiago.

Comprehension Questions

1. Para llegar a Haro a tiempo para la Batalla del Vino.
2. Santiago y Julio son compañeros de la universidad.
3. Una vieja camiseta de algodón, un short deportivo y unas zapatillas viejas.
4. Para no ensuciar el pueblo.
5. Porque espera la reacción de Julio.

Chapter 12

Exercises

1. c. Un proyecto urbanístico.
2. b. Organizaciones ambientalistas.
3. b. Sentado en la primera fila del auditorio.
4. a. Los peces.
5. a. Se instalarán paneles solares en los techos.

Comprehension Questions

1. Esta es la primera.
2. El diseño y la construcción del distrito residencial EcoMálaga.
3. Porque mucha gente va a trabajar al polígono industrial que hay cerca.
4. Con los paneles solares que se van a instalar en el techo de cada uno de los diez edificios, para reducir la demanda energética.

5. Porque su hijo está buscando un lugar un poco más grande porque ha sido papá.

Appendix II: Vocabulary Reference

Here you will find all the vocabulary lists we've seen so far throughout the book, given in alphabetical order. In addition, we'll include the type of word, the pronunciation, the definition, and the page number where you can find the word.

¡Ostras!
    (interjection) [ˈo̞s̪t̪ɾäs] Yikes!
    Expression used when someone is surprised or angry.

¡Que tengas un buen viaje!
    (phrase) [ke̞ ˈt̪e̞ŋgäs bue̞n ˈbiäxe̞] Have a nice trip!

¿Buscas trabajo?
    (phrase) [ˈbuskäs t̪ɾäˈbäxo̞]

¿De dónde eres?
    (phrase) [d̪e̞ ˈd̪o̞nd̪e̞ ˈe̞ɾe̞s]

¿Ese ha sido tu único trabajo?
    (phrase) [ˈe̞se̞ ä ˈsid̪o̞ t̪u ˈuniko̞ t̪ɾäˈbäxo̞] Was that your

agradecer
(verb) [äɡɾäde̩ˈseɾ] to appreciate
To show gratitude or give thanks............................... 185

águila
(noun) [ˈäɡ̊ilä] eagle 232

aguja
(noun) [äˈɡuxä] needle 207

ajoblanco malagueño
(noun) [äxo̩ˈblänko̩ mälä ˈɡeɲo̩] ajoblanco malagueño
A popular Spanish cold soup made of bread, almonds
and garlic. 170

ajos
(noun) [ˈäxo̩] garlic 185

ajustado/a de tiempo
(phrase) [äxusˈtädo̩ de̩ ˈtie̩mpo̩] short on time
Used to express that one doesn't have much time left to
do something. 153

al frente de
(adverb) [äl ˈfre̩nte̩ de̩] in charge of
To lead, to be in command of. 171

al horno
(adjective) [äl ˈoɾno̩] baked
Cooked in the oven. 185

aliviado/a
(adjective) [äliˈβiädo̩] relieved 201

almohadón
(noun) [älmo̩äˈdo̩n] cushion 162

almorzar
(verb) [älmo̩ɾˈθäɾ] to have lunch To eat a meal at noon......... 170

alrededor
(adverb) [älre̩de̩ˈdo̩ɾ] around..................................... 162

273

---

camarero/a

(noun) [kämäˈreɾo] waiter/waitress

Someone's whose job is to serve at tables in a restaurant. ... 161

cambio

(noun) [ˈkämbio] change 199

camilla

(noun) [käˈmiʎä] stretcher.. 200

camisa

(noun) [käˈmisä] shirt 224

caña

(noun) [ˈkäɲä] pint

Glass where beer is usually served, about half the size
of a pint. 192

canoso/a

(adjective) [käˈnoso] with gray hair

Of someone, that they have a lot of gray hair...................... 171

cantaor/cantaora

(noun) [käntäˈoɾ] flamenco singer

Only flamenco singers are called cantaores and cantaoras.
Singers of other genres are called cantantes. 212

caro/a

(adjective) [ˈkäɾo] expensive 219

carta

(noun) [ˈkäɾtä] menú

List of all the dishes and beverages offered in a
restaurant, usually listed with their price. 192

casual

(adjective) [käˈsuäl] casually.. 170

cata de vinos

(noun) [ˈkätä de̞ ˈbinos] wine tasting 225

ceño fruncido

(noun) [ˈseɲo̞ fɾunˈsido] furrowed brow

A facial expression used to indicate displeasure or disapproval. 170

centro de la ciudad

(noun) ['sentɾo̞ de̞ lä 'siudäd] city center 155

chaleco

(noun) [tʃä'le̞ko̞] vest 207

charlatán/charlatana

(adjective) [tʃäɾlä'tän] chatty

Someone who speaks a lot. 161

chaval/chavala

(noun) [tʃä'βäl kid

Colloquial term used in Spain to call a kid or young person. 224

chorro

(noun) ['tʃo̞ɾo̞] splash

Chorro actually means a stream of a liquid. However, in Spanish it's usually used to exaggerate or to talk about a constant stream of something, not necessarily a liquid. 213

cielo despejado

(noun) [si'e̞lo̞ de̞s̱pe̞'xädo̞] clear sky 154

coche

(verb) ['ko̞tʃe̞] car

It's used both for an independent vehicle and for a train car. For the first meaning, other countries use carro or auto. 155

cocina

(noun) [ko̞'sinä] kitchen 162

cocinero/a

(noun) [ko̞si'ne̞ɾo̞] cook

A person whose job is cooking and preparing food. 184

código urbanístico

(noun) ['ko̞digo̞ uɾbä̃'nistiko̞] urban planning code 232

confianza

(noun) [koɲˈfiänθä] trust 212

consultorio

(noun) [koɲsulˈtoɾio] doctor's office 199

contagioso/a

(adjective) [koɲtäˈxioso] contagious 225

contiguo/a

(adjective) [koɲˈtiguo] adjacent 194

contra la pared

(adverb) [ˈkoɲträ lä päˈɾed] against the wall 162

copa

(noun) [ˈkopä] glass of wine

Glass to drink from with a stem and base. In Spanish,
copa is the name for the glassware in which we drink
wine, champagne and even some cocktails. 213

cordón

(noun) [koɾˈdoɲ] lace

String made of fiber or thin threads used to fasten shoes. .. 226

cordón de la acera

(noun) [koɾˈdoɲ deˌlä äˈseɾä] sidewalk curb 156

cortés

(adjective) [koɾˈtes] polite

Showing consideration for others and observance of
accepted social usage. 193

criar

(verb) [kɾiˈäɾ] to raise 208

croqueta de queso

(noun) [kroˌketä deˌ ˈkeso] cheese croquette 185

cuadro

(noun) [ˈkuädɾo] painting 162

cuarto de baño

(noun) [ˈkuäɾtoˌ deˌ ˈbäɲoˌ]

demanda energética

(noun) [deˌ mändä̈ eɲeɾˈxetikä] energy demand

It is in charge of distributing energy in a building or complex. 232

To connect an electrical appliance to an electrical outlet.... 177

encima
(adverb) [eɲˈsimä] on top...... 162

encogiéndose de hombros
(verb) [eŋkoˈxeɾse̞ de̞ ˈo̞mbɾo̞s] to shrug
Gesture used to express disinterest, ignorance or to
downplay something...... 207

enérgico
(adjective) [e̞ˈneɾxiko̞] vigorous
That has energy, energetic...... 171

enfrente
(adverb) [eɲˈfɾe̞nte̞] in front...... 162

Enhorabuena
(interjection) [e̞no̞ɾäˈbue̞ɲä] Congratulations!
An interjection used to congratulate someone...... 171

enorme
(adjective) [e̞ˈno̞ɾme̞] very big...... 171

ensalada
(noun) [e̞nsäˈlädä] salad...... 185

entrada
(noun) [eɲˈtɾädä] ticket...... 214

entre
(adverb) [ˈe̞ntɾe̞] between...... 162

entrecortado/a
(adjective) [e̞ntɾe̞ko̞ɾˈtädo̞] intermittent...... 199

equipado/a
(adjective) [e̞kiˈpädo̞] equipped...... 184

equipaje
(noun) [e̞kiˈpäxe̞] luggage
Personal belongings taken on a trip...... 153

escalera mecánica
(noun) [e̞skäˈleɾä me̞ˈkänikä] escalator...... 219

estudio de arquitectos

(noun) [es̺'tudio de̞ ä̱rki'tekto̞s̺] architecture firm 231

etiqueta

(noun) [e̞ti'ke̞tä] tag 219

exultante

(adjective) [e̞ksul'tänte̞] overjoyed 219

fauna autóctona

(noun) ['fäunä'äu'to̞kto̞nä] native fauna 232

fiebre

(noun) ['fie̞bre̞] fever 200

fila

(noun) ['filä] row

A series of people or other things in line waiting for
their turn. 154

fin de temporada

(noun) [fin de̞ te̞mpo̞'rädä] end of the season 219

finales

(noun) [fi'näl] ending 199

firmar

(verb) ['firmä] to sign 194

flamencos

(noun) [flä'me̞nko̞] flamingo

Besides the bird, flamenco is a style of music from the
South of Spain. 232

florero

(noun) [flo̞'re̞ro̞] flower vase 162

frito/a

(adjective) ['frito̞] fried

Cooked in hot oil or fat. 185

fuera de presupuesto

(phrase) ['fue̞rä de̞ pre̞s̺u'pue̞s̺to̞] out of the budget 219

energy to lead it to an electrical energy converter

pantalla del teléfono

(noun) [pän'täʎä deɫ te̞'lefo̞no̞] phone's screen

pantalón

(noun) [päntä'lo̞n] trousers

pantalón corto

(noun) [päntä'lo̞n 'ko̞ɾto̞] pair of shorts

pantalón de mezclilla

(noun) [päntä'lo̞n de̞ me̞θ'kliʎä] jeans

In Spain people call "denim" mezclilla.

par de calcetines

(noun) [päɾ de̞ kälse̞'tine̞s] pair of socks

parada

(noun) [pä'ɾädä] stop

The act of stopping, and also the place where
someone or something (like a bus) usually stops.

pariente

(noun) [pä'ɾie̞nte̞] relative

parlante

(noun) [päɾ'läte̞] speakers

pasaje

(noun) [pä'säxe̞] ticket

A document that shows that you have paid a fare to
board a means of transport.

pasar hambre

(verb) [pä'säɾ 'ämbɾe̞] to starve

To suffer from lack of food, used literally but mostly
metaphorically.

pasatiempo

(noun) [päsä'tiempo̞] hobby

pasear

(verb) [päse̞'äɾ] to walk around

Here's another book by Lingo Publishing that you might like

Free Bonuses from Cecilia Melero

Hi Spanish Learners!

My name is Cecilia Melero, and first off, I want to THANK YOU for reading my book.

Now you have a chance to join my exclusive Spanish language learning email list so you can get the ebooks below for free as well as the potential to get more Spanish books for free! Simply click the link below to join.

P.S. Remember that it's 100% free to join the list.

Access your free bonuses here:
https://livetolearn.lpages.co/spanish-short-stories-paperback/

Made in the USA
Middletown, DE
17 October 2023

40959834R00175